Aesthetics in India

Transitions and Transformations

Aesthetics in India

Transitions and Transformations

Edited by

V.S. Sreenath
Anandita Pan
Punnya Rajendran

Orient BlackSwan

AESTHETICS IN INDIA: TRANSITIONS AND TRANSFORMATIONS

ORIENT BLACKSWAN PRIVATE LIMITED

Registered Office
3-6-752 Himayatnagar, Hyderabad 500 029, Telangana, India
e-mail: centraloffice@orientblackswan.com

Other Offices
Bengaluru, Chennai, Guwahati, Hyderabad, Kolkata,
Mumbai, New Delhi, Noida, Patna

First published by Orient Blackswan Private Limited 2023

ISBN 978-93-5442-402-1

041570

Typeset in
Crimson 11/13 pt *by*
Shine Graphics, Delhi 110 094

Printed at
Avantika Printers Private Limited, New Delhi 110 020

Published by
Orient Blackswan Private Limited
3-6-752, Himayatnagar, Hyderabad 500 029, Telangana, India
e-mail: info@orientblackswan.com

Contents

Section Three

The Scattered Present of Aesthetics

Acknowledgements

Sheldon Pollock, "The Social Aesthetic and Sanskrit Literary Theory", *Journal of Indian Philosophy* 29, 197–229 (2001). Reprinted by permission from *Springer Nature*. Copyright © 1969, Kluwer Academic Publishers, 1969.

Yigal Bronner, "What is New and what is Navya: Sanskrit Poetics on the Eve of Colonialism", *Journal of Indian Philosophy* 30, 441–462 (2002). Reprinted by permission from Springer Nature. Copyright © Kluwer Academic Publishers, 2002.

V.S. Sreenath, "What To Do with the Past?: Sanskrit Literary Criticism in Postcolonial Space", *Journal of Indian Philosophy* 49, 129–144 (2021). Reprinted with permission from Springer Nature. Copyright © 2021.

K. Satchidanandan, "The Critical Scene: Towards an Alternative Aesthetics," *Indian Literature*, vol. 35, no. 6, (152), pp. 7–10, Nov–Dec, 1992. Reproduced with permission of The Sahitya Akademi.

Partha Chatterjee, "Critique of Popular Culture," *Public Culture*, vol. 20, no. 2, pp. 321–344. Copyright 2008, Duke University Press. All rights reserved. Republished by permission of the copyright holder, and the Publisher. "http://www.dukeupress.edu" www.dukeupress.edu

Introduction

Aesthetics can be broadly defined as a reflexive and systematic preoccupation with the ontology and epistemology of art. During the classical period, in most parts of the world, aesthetics was an inward-facing field of inquiry concerned to no extent with the socio-economic reality of everyday life. The exponents of the classical form of aesthetics spoke—or, so it appeared—in the ahistorical voice of timeless truths and universal values. Ironically, art has always flourished in all societies as a direct product of the very socio-economic reality that aesthetics long ignored. While classical aesthetics remained mostly aloof from the socio-political concerns in art, the classical art, which was the sole form of art aesthetics considered worthy of theoretical engagement, represented life in an ornamental fashion. This selectiveness perhaps explains the seemingly organic schism that separates classical art from folk art—arguably, folk art is life itself whereas classical art is a second-order vehicle which represented life in a highly stylised and metaphysical manner.

In the Indian context, this state of affairs began to change in the seventeenth and eighteenth centuries, the cusp and height respectively of the point of contact with colonial powers. During this period, realistic representations of human lives start slowly replacing the highly stylised representations of the world found in classical texts—a rupture in the Indian context that mirrors to no small degree the corresponding rupture in the West effected by the birth of the novel which sought to replace the emperors and epic heroes of yore with rogues and prostitutes and tradesmen, and empires with poorhouses and chattels. Aesthetics was naturally prised out of its comfort zone of abstraction, ideation and preoccupation with form, and now dealt with issues that art represented, such as poverty (as opposed to karmic cycles of poverty and prosperity) and human rights (as opposed to a spiritual interpretation of death and devastation).

Such subject matter and ideas refused to play a transcendental function in art as easily. An abundance of books and literature emerged in the wake of nationalism and the zest for representing the nation, for representing social evils, poverty, corruption, mobility, and the newfound notions of liberation. Caste, class, and gender were finally acknowledged as aesthetic coordinates. Social realism also heralded the death of codified practices in art. Beauty began to slowly assume the grimness of truths rooted in historical materialism instead of spirituality.

Such a radical transformation not only formed new directions for aesthetics as it always existed (realism begins to be theorised with all seriousness after the initial shock of its apparent lack of style/beauty), but also formed newer possibilities of reconceptualising aesthetics in relation to—and at times, in contrast to and as a contortion of—how it was always conceptualised in the old world order. In many ways, it is thus impossible today to talk about aesthetics without oscillating between a sense of the old and the new, the traditional and the possible. This is what spurred our interest in putting together this volume of essays which can provide a road map for the reader to understand this productive oscillation, to ponder over the many theoretical and ethical impasses, and to be inspired by the range of possibilities that now appear in front of us.

The primary thrust of this volume being of a speculative kind—that is, an attempt to push into what aesthetics *can be* (rather than what it is or has been) in relation to the major upheavals through which it has been put by modernity—the essays featured in this book have not been designed with the comprehensive zeal towards a representation that captures the comparatist spirit of contemporary academic scholarship. This volume does not throw its net across time and space to capture the idea of 'Indian' by means of a diversity of subjects: for example, to explore aesthetics as a category across a range of cultural milieus from Western, Central, North-eastern parts of the country, or across a range of time-periods and linguistic communities. Rather, this volume seeks to present to the reader a sample of essays that provide a glimpse as well as inspiration in terms of what we can do with the idea of aesthetics today, how we may deploy the dissipation of classical aesthetics into a reconstituted toolkit of potentially critical terms (anger, shock, beauty, form, praxis, affect, etc.) in the humanities.

We hope that the hybrid configuration of essays in this volume points the reader towards a new future for aesthetics in which many of its culturally sacred concepts (such as *rasa*) as well as its theoretically sacred concepts (such as affect) are dislocated from their original sacrality and made commonplace by means of their continuous use and playful misuse in English studies. In other words, we hope to signal by means of this volume that today aesthetics can be treated less as a body of knowledge and more as an approach or a method in the humanities in a manner that is somehow both ahistorical and comparatist at the same time. In this book, therefore, we posit that critical use rather than a hermeneutics of suspicion can be the way forward in negotiating the relationship between aesthetics and English Studies in India.

* * *

In the Sanskritic context, classical aesthetics first brings to mind *nāṭya* (dramatic representation on stage) and *kāvya* (poetry and literary prose)—two terms which were almost synonymous with the idea of aesthetics in the ancient subcontinent. Although there were attempts to systematically study other forms of art like painting, sculpture and so on, the amount of work dedicated to them was virtually meagre, compared to the large corpus of work dealing with *nāṭya* and *kāvya*. So, the idea of aesthetics in the classical world order was synonymous with drama and literary art, thereby forming two primary streams of knowledge, *nāṭyaśāstra* and *kāvyaśāstra*. It is interesting to note that although *nāṭyaśāstra* and *kāvyaśāstra* were considered systematic and scientific studies of drama and literature, they were often unscientific and ahistorical when it came to formulating the theories about the origin of *kāvya* and *nāṭya*. For example, according to Bharata (the mythical sage who composed the treatise on dramaturgy titled *Nāṭyaśāstra*) *nāṭya* was invented by Brahmā. Bharata says that gods, faced by the depravity of the *tretāyuga* (*grāmya-dharma* or indecorous lifestyle), requested Brahmā to create a new Veda so that people of all castes could watch and learn the righteous way of life. Thus, at the behest of the gods, Brahmā created *nāṭya* as a tool of didacticism (I.6). According to Brahma's declaration about the function of *nāṭya,* reported by Bharata in *Nāṭyaśāstra, nāṭya* aims to instruct the spectators of all time about everything in the world (*lokopadeśajananam nāṭyametat bhaviṣyati*; I.86). The parallel between this approach and the moral and instructional concerns we find in Plato and Aristotle (the lacuna of mere mimesis and the therapeutic excess of catharsis for poetry and drama respectively) is self-evident.

The same is the case with the origin of *kāvya* (poetry and literary prose). Soon after listening to the story of Rāma (who is considered to be the worthiest man who ever lived) from the celestial sage Nārada, Vālmīki chances upon a hunter shooting down a mating pair of birds—an act of high cruelty according to his standards and purportedly, universal standards. Overcome with pity, Vālmīki curses the hunter: 'Since, Niṣāda, you killed one of this pair of krauñcas, distracted at the height of passion, you shall not live for very long' (I.1.14). Hearing his own words, Vālmīki gets surprised. He realises that it is a linguistic composition considerably different from the ordinary form of speech. More than a mere representation of grief or the mimetic copy of a thing or an Idea, the *śloka* is an autochthonous emergence of grief (in the Heideggerian sense) in an unprecedented, authentic and superior form.

He thinks 'Stricken with grief for this bird, what is this I have uttered?' (I.2.15). The primary reason for Vālmīki's astonishment is that the style of his utterance is drastically different from the ordinary form of speech that he is familiar with. It became a cause of wonder or *atiśaya* for him.

This conception that literature was a special mode of expression, distinctly different from the ordinary form of speech by the presence of deviant expression (*vakratā*), is championed by almost all the literary theoreticians in the Sanskrit cosmopolis, irrespective of their spatio-temporal locations. Sanskrit *kāvyaśāstra* always held a formalist view of literature (to borrow a modern adjective that offers some equivalence here). That is to say, *kāvyaśāstra* believed that it is the presence of certain special linguistic features such as poetic suggestion (*dhvani*), figures of speech (*alaṅkāra*), figurative deviation (*vakrokti*), etc., that attribute literariness to a work of art and set it apart from other uses of language in an essential manner. Therefore, throughout its history of almost a millennium, Sanskrit *kāvyaśāstra* was exclusively preoccupied with the task of identifying and analysing the formal devices generating literariness in a work of art. Considering *kāvya* as a 'specialised' mode of language marked by the 'ingenious' use of certain distinctive linguistic devices, *kāvyaśāstra* always made it a point to delimit *kāvya* from other uses of language such as *śāstra*, the *Veda*s, and of course, workaday language. A poem that resembles the style and texture of ordinary speech was unthinkable for *kāvyaśāstra*. The same was the case with *nāṭyaśāstra* which aimed to represent life in a stylised rather than realistic manner on stage. It is also significant to note that the experience of *rasa* or aesthetic emotion, be it in drama or poetry, was always considered a positive experience leading the spectator or reader ultimately to bliss. Abhinavagupta (11 CE) in his commentary on Ānandavardhana's *Dhvanyāloka* says that the ontology of aesthetic relish is '*alaukika*' or supernormal (1.18 L). Viśvanātha (14 CE) in his *Sāhityadarpaṇa* even went to the extent of terming it *brahmasvadasahodara* or the kin of spiritual meditative bliss (40).

By the mid-twentieth century, as noted earlier, a new notion about literariness started taking deep root in India around the same time as the literary world made a slow transition from Sanskrit to English and the vernacular languages, and during this period, the highly stylised representation of life (endorsed by the *nāṭyaśāstra* and *kāvyaśāstra* traditions) gave way to the realistic representation of life. This revolutionary break from the conventional notion of literature was primarily facilitated by the introduction of Western literature in the syllabi of schools and universities in India. Following the birth of the novel, aesthetics moved on to ordinary everyday speech and everyday emotions, into broader polyglossic concerns about language, and the memory of classical literariness served as a theoretical foothold to examine the latter. Needless to say, this moment cannot be explained through a simplistic theory of influence or a neat passage from the irrelevant past to a new contemporary, for it was a period when our literary history was rife with an obsession with the past, glorification and defence, criticism and introspection.

The past protruded into the present and vice versa in a variety of comparatist, nationalist, and spiritual interventions by writers and literary critics.

Relatedly, another component of aesthetics that underwent a drastic change was the idea of aesthetic emotion. 'Aesthetic emotions' or *rasa,* as Sanskrit literary theoreticians point out, is always distinguished from the experience of emotions in real life. Conventional aesthetic notions, at least the ones that set the standards for literature in India, insisted that aesthetic emotions should always be pleasurable in effect, even while depicting negative emotions such as grief or disgust. In other words, disgust as *rasa* is harmonious (hence, pleasurable) on the stage when it adheres to theoretical dictates and thus, by extension, will be pleasurable to the spectators. The sheer absence of the genre of tragedy in Sanskrit literary tradition attests to the fact that literature was always seen as a pleasurable activity.

Classical aesthetic notions always insisted that even emotions that are considered otherwise unpleasant should be presented in such a manner that they do not run roughshod over the sensibilities of the spectators or the readers. It is this classical notion about the expected emotional impact of art upon the readers/spectators which came under fire during the colonial and postcolonial period, especially with the emergence of literary works from the margins including women's writing and Dalit writing that took unprecedented liberties with the possibility of expressing shock, rage, and anger in art. This does not mean that the old order of stylised emotions in art was now fully replaced by a new mode of writing. Rather, new writings chose to engage differently with certain classical emotions, perhaps to make them 'un-classical' in their depictions of a world in which nobility, villainy, grief and guilt looked and behaved differently and towards different and more democratic political ends.

In this regard, the case of mainstream cinema in India is significant, for popular movies continued to resort to stylised depictions in order to appeal to the emotional desire for predictability and control. This newfound aesthetics of the box office has, of course, been theorised to no small extent by scholars in India and we may identify aspects of that scholarship that bear weight on our more general discussion about aesthetics. For example, the early sentimental films that converted the experience of poverty and moral outrage into a sublime emotion on the screen continue to be '*alaukika*' or supernormal albeit not in the sense indicated previously in the ancient texts of poetics and dramaturgy. It is 'supernormal' both in terms of the emotions felt by the audience as well as in terms of the internal composition of melodramatic scenes and dialogue. Ironically, we find the 'supernormal' here within the interstices of avowedly 'realist' cinema—not very far in directorial ambition from that of King Lear teetering at the edge of a cliff.

The clearest example of this modern disjunction of aesthetics can be found in the most fundamental affective grammar of popular cinema featuring superstars in which a very codified stylisation and grandeur returns to the screen from an older era: in particular, fixed body language for characters based on their status in the plot—the hero of an action movie, for example, will never trip and fall comically whereas the comic sidekick will never interrupt the climactic speech of the hero. The comic sidekick being slapped will elicit laughter from the audience while the hero being slapped serves as a poignant moment of insult, violence or dramatic confrontation.

In India, aesthetics was also employed as a nationalist tool to decolonise the highly anglicised terrain of contemporary criticism. Influenced by the Orientalist approach to ancient epistemologies, many critics in modern India considered Sanskrit *kāvyaśāstra* as an effective critical framework to replace western literary theory. They argued that Sanskrit poetics can effectively evaluate the literary merits of any contemporary literary work. This tendency in the first instance came out of a strong desire to decolonise 'western critical sensibilities'. Although these critics aimed to decolonise themselves from the clutches of western critical concepts, their attempt to vindicate the efficacy of Indian poetics remained mostly dependent on their western counterparts. To substantiate their claim that ancient Indian literary theories are as modern and sophisticated as any other modern critical theory, they compared Sanskrit *kāvyaśāstra* theories with their western counterparts and brought out the points of convergence shared by the two.

While it is important to record how the idea of aesthetics was originally understood and practised at various historical junctures, an obsession with this process will only impede new courses of development in this field. What we need is an interventionist historiography of ideas which will critically examine these theoretical positions from different vantage points and will prevent them from becoming static categories or being treated as completed episodes in history. Each new reading of a knowledge system dislodges it from our canonical conceptions about it and leads us to the production of new knowledge about/from such texts.

There is, without doubt, a need to reconsider the term 'aesthetics' in conjunction with all the possibilities and theoretical traditions that have hitherto been identified with it from ancient to modern times. There is also a need to explore the myriad manifestations of the term 'aesthetics' in current research in English Studies—for this discipline has a far more interestingly complicated relationship with 'aesthetics' than philosophy or Sanskrit studies. Based on this body of scholarship, we also begin to understand that English Studies does not and cannot offer aesthetics in contradistinction to critique which has a long legacy of use now. Aesthetics—unlike what it used to be earlier—is an extension of critique, a balancing and a fulfilling of the possibilities of critique.

* * *

Keeping in mind all of the above, the essays in this book are divided into three sections. The first section, titled 'The Cultural Turn Within Classical Aesthetics,' brings together four essays which exemplify the radical re-tellings of classical treatises on art and aesthetics by Indologists with a leaning towards historicism, by post-structuralist interventions, and in general, by a contemporary desire to approach classical texts while at the same time being liberated from the need to bracket such a study from the concerns of the world today. The common attempt made in these essays is to not shy away from finding common ground between the past and the present in terms of sociocultural practices and to resist elevating the aesthetics of the past as a world outside of the rational purview of the present.

An obsession with the processes by which classical knowledge systems were originally understood and practised has led to the sequestering of Sanskrit aesthetics for all intents and purposes—

except when it is pulled up ever so frequently to facilitate a socio-historical examination of the caste system, for example, or to facilitate neo-Orientalist celebrations of uniqueness, or to demonstrate the possibilities of computational linguistics. For English Studies, however, what is the need of the hour would be an interventionist historiography of ideas that will critically examine theoretical positions and ideas from different vantage points so as to prevent them from becoming static categories.

'The Social Aesthetic and Sanskrit Literary Theory' by Sheldon Pollock is an excellent example (and one of the earliest) of how theoretical grounds are laid to shift the direction of classical Indian aesthetics from a solipsistic interest in the ontological features of art towards an exploration of its underlying social and moral imagination. The aforementioned basic assumption regarding the ontological uniqueness of literariness in language and expression results in a mode of literary analysis (exemplified in the writings of Anandavardhana, for example) which cannot integrate the social determinism of Sanskrit aesthetics. Offering a contrastive analysis of the literary criticism of Bhoja, Pollock asks for a historical recuperation of the social in Sanskrit literary criticism. Thus, for Pollock, the painstaking commentaries written by Sanskrit aestheticians about the four-line compact evocations of *vastudhvani* poetry try to integrate its semantic and formal organicity with morality and beauty and meaning—but without noting that the most foundational aspect of its semantics lies in certain social knowledge about the characters involved such as the wandering mendicants, the conniving lovers, the jealous partners, and clever consorts, along with the social semantics of other life forms that populate the drama such as lions and dogs. The significance of the manner of appearance of, say, a flower, in the poem—indicative of a wide range of social implications such as romantic love, respect for the king or a deity or a guru, a mystical sign from the heavens, a secret signalling between illicit lovers—can be determined not merely by an analysis of linguistic units and formal structures but also with a wider knowledge of implicit social codes of conduct. The paper provides us with a useful prototype of how the philosophical depth of a treatise on aesthetics and the corresponding social configurations can and should illuminate each other in analysis.

Yigal Bronner's 'What is New and what is Navya: Sanskrit Poetics on the Eve of Colonialism' is a rejoinder to the orientalist conception that during the medieval period, Sanskrit poetics produced nothing new and it was a period of mere reproduction of the old critical paradigm. According to Bronner, the literary theoreticians in the medieval phase attempted to constitute a new relationship with their past. Instead of inventing any radically new critical concept like *dhvani* or *vakrokti*, they directed their energy mainly to critically examine the views of their predecessors and to answer the old questions in new ways. To mark their departure from their predecessors in terms of their mode of operation and views, these new poeticians identified themselves as *navya* or 'new', in contrast to their predecessors who they called *prācīna*. Bronner's essay makes a powerful intervention in the orientalist historiography by debunking the myth that the medieval period in the history of Sanskrit poetics was a chasm of intellectual slumber. Placing the essay with the general context of this volume also allows us to consider the efforts of medieval Sanskrit aestheticians alongside a longer and markedly 'modern' tradition within aesthetics of rewriting the past out of a sense of dissatisfaction with tradition and history. 'Tamil Sangam Poetry: The Plebian in the Classical Tradition' by Mini Chandran situates the aesthetics of Tamil Sangam poetry within the larger context of rhetorical traditions across the world, with an emphasis on the uniqueness of the myriad images, metaphors, and other literary figures of speech employed in the texts. Highlighting the linguistic possibilities of subversion underlying the evocation of images in Sangam poetry, Chandran maps the role played by aesthetics in both representing as well as contravening the sociocultural limits of a milieu. The presence of the common man and the agrarian landscape in *akam* poetry and the panegyrics of *puram* poetry are dissected by the author at the level of unusual and particularly insightful imagery, leading us to a possible survey of social personas who correspond to a fascinating range of self-expressions found in Sangam poetry—such as the startling analogy of a raincloud on a hill to the layer of fat on a chunk of meat, which the author surmises rightly to be a natural aesthetic extension for women whose days oscillate between agricultural tasks outside and cooking inside. The aesthetics of Sangam poetry is thus identified at the intersection between ecological and social hierarchies as well as illuminative of the possible subjectivities that might have inspired the evocation of such a wide-ranging and yet specific collection of metaphors, tropes, and other literary figures of speech. The introduction of a historicist zeal to the analysis of classical poetics is, without doubt, one of the first signs of a truly becoming-contemporary of aesthetics.

In Sreenath's essay, 'What To Do with the Past?: Sanskrit Literary Criticism in Postcolonial Space', the author notes the resolute obsession of Sanskrit *kāvyaśāstra* throughout its history of almost a millennium and a half with the task of unravelling the ontology of *kāvya*; he points out how the unanimous agreement among literary theoreticians in Sanskrit that *kāvya* was a special mode of expression characterised by the presence of certain unique linguistic elements changed towards the turn of the twentieth century when, all of a sudden, *kāvya* finds itself forced to engage with everyday speech rather than the notion of literariness. Following the severing of its natural ties with literature, Sanskrit aesthetics faces a crisis of use and contemporaneity. It cannot die on account of its sheer scope and depth but at the same time, it struggles to find a location in the present that is not a niche. Does Sanskrit poetics have any relevance in the field of criticism or is it merely a museum piece with no pragmatic value? The author tackles this question of uncertainty by placing key Sanskrit concepts about language (such as *dhvani*) alongside poststructuralist theories of languages (such as 'play') and prompting us to erase the genetic and pragmatic differences between these two schools of thought—not to find common ground or to erase distinctions but to allow an easier intermingling of ideas across the aisle, a necessary risk in the face of a prolonged disciplinary impasse.

* * *

The second section of the book is titled 'Beyond Classicism: Contemporary Aesthetics as Method'. The essays featured in this section display the contemporary flexibility of aesthetics as it moves beyond the study of aesthetics as an object or as a body of knowledge, and towards deciphering a methodological use-value for aesthetics today. Each of the four authors in this section have interpreted the scope of the term 'aesthetics' in fascinatingly diverse ways. The range of use of the term in each of these four essays bears testimony to the potential use of aesthetics today and also offers us a glimpse into the exact nature of the relationship between aesthetics and modern academic approaches in the humanities.

Partha Chatterjee's essay about Indian visual culture raises critical questions about how the idea of aesthetic value and artistic freedom is inscribed within dominant theories of the popular sphere. He describes the manner in which objects and images that may traditionally be considered banal or devoid of aesthetic finesse (his examples are wedding collages, calendar art, select lithographs, and primarily, contemporary Durga puja pandals) move back and forth between the world of art and the world of kitsch, resisting our desire to theoretically pinpoint the exact nature of their aesthetic value. His exploration of the shapes, forms, materials and practices that keep evolving and declining around the culture of Durga puja pandals in West Bengal also indicates that pre-existing theories about art (autonomy, freedom, composition, etc.) may be inadequate to understand the fluid nature of the popular sphere. The author makes a methodological recommendation in this regard: immersing oneself in the practices of popular culture and allowing a critique to emerge from each of them (based on contingencies of doing, making, selling art at the home and in the marketplace, during festivals, etc.) rather than matching what is found in the field with essential conceptual structures which are larger than and predetermine individual case studies of the actual practice of popular art in India. The example provided by the author of Durga puja pandals identifies specific modern disciplinary practices that dictate the production of pandals and their changing contemporary aesthetics which transcend even religious identity at times. It is a compelling methodological suggestion which re-engages with traditional notions of art and aesthetics exactly at those points where they dissolve into the modern in a reluctant push-and-pull of mass culture.

'On *Mumbai Police* and *Drishyam*: Reading Desire into Two New Wave Crime Thrillers in Malayalam' by Jenson Joseph is yet another example of the contemporary revival and incisive use of aesthetics as method—in this case, within the specific disciplinary possibilities of media studies. Outlining the emergent aesthetics of what can be referred to as New Generation communities of film enthusiasts in Kerala, it proceeds to explore the aesthetics of desire and subjectivity in two recent films in Malayalam as symptomatic of a larger flow of desire in popular culture shaped by the interaction between film and the Internet—in particular, the proliferation of memes and other online content celebrating/epitomising cinephilia in Kerala. The paper identifies the spectre of 'subjective perfection' that seems to pervade the so-called New Generation Malayalam cinema in general and *Mumbai Police* in particular, as well as the self-conscious reverberations of cinephilia one finds in Internet cultures (the resurgence of film as snippets in contemporary popular media) in general and *Drishyam* in particular. Departing methodologically from an analysis of film which is poised towards an exposition of the cultural process, Joseph integrates his formal analysis of both films and the cultural analysis of Internet cultures into a critical language of desire and aesthetics in New Generation cinema. Of great import to the contemporary life of aesthetics as method, we find in the paper a close textual analysis of the movies which is then abstracted into a theory of desire and into speculations about the aesthetics of cinema/Internet as a form of mediation that is in flux as we speak.

'Of Pain and Other Tragic Emotions: A Study of Divinity in the Folktales from Kaṟisial Kādu' by Swathi Sudhakaran and Milind Brahme reorients aesthetics in terms of narrative or textual emotions (referring to emotions found encoded within the structure of a story as well as the reader's or listener's emotional transactions with the story) in order to locate folktales and the concept of divinity in the background of a resolutely non-Sanskritic and non-classical semiotics. The methodological insights offered in the essay include close analysis of affective moments in the tales which range from the strange to the truly bizarre—such as the depiction of God being fearful, the winding up of seemingly parabolic plots without moral instruction or dramatic resolution, characters who do not undergo change or signify anything stable, and of course, the elevation of pain into a truly chaotic and de-signifying experience in a world without cause, effect, or justice. The contrast that we may draw here with the moral preoccupations of classical poetics and aesthetics begs the start of a much longer and multi-faceted discussion of folk aesthetics. Alongside pain, terror is yet another emotion that emerges from the paper. Contrasted with the individual pain of the tragic flaw and collapse of the classic hero, the essay allows us to think of pain and terror in these folktales as communitarian and intersubjective experiences of the non-Hindu margins, of an immanent aesthetics (rather than an institutionalised one) in South India—the details of which remain to be sketched in the light of the contemporary with ever growing clarity.

E.V. Ramakrishnan's article, 'From Dialectics to Dialects: A Reading O.V. Vijayan's Legends of Khasak' uses the wealth of criticism and popular/academic responses to Vijayan's iconic Malayalam modernist masterpiece of the sixties in order to compose a timely reminder of the true nature of an aesthetic inquiry which exceeds academic and political considerations about meaning, plot, and representation. The author criticises the manner in which mainstream responses to the novel have subsumed aesthetics to questions of rationality and existentialism which disregard the symbiosis between local community, local ecology and identity in the novel. At the same time, he also tries to re-establish aesthetics as an attempt to highlight, ironically, the most indescribable and fleeting of affective mechanisms in the novel. This aspect of the novel is identified by the author by means of an analysis of both the English translation of the novel as well its theatre adaptations. He highlights the problems of semiotic equivalence in both cases and as the title of his essay indicates, he advocates the move from an obsession with dialectics to an immanent appreciation of the ethno-ecological dialects underlying the plot which allows us to see that the aesthetics of the novel is a window into the aesthetics of a community's world-view in Khazak. The modern reader should not strive to 'understand', the text but to realise his/her own deliberate marginality in that 'strange' text.

* * *

The third section titled 'The Scattered Present of Aesthetics' contains four essays which offer sprawling surveys of the different intellectual shades of the term 'aesthetics' as it has been used in the distant and near past, the major breaks and ruptures in this history, and how these antecedents intersect in the manner of its use in the present. The four essays adopt four different vantage points and survey the field with interestingly diverse intentions when it comes to the definition and scope of aesthetics.

K. Satchidanandan's paper 'Indian Literary Criticism Today: The Challenges and Responses' offers an exhaustive survey of both the long history and the wide contemporary in India when it comes to writings about literature, both philosophical musings and critical interventions. Placing the question of Indian literary criticism in the background of a modern society in flux (that is with the birth of 'literature' in the modern sense, different classes and castes cannot maintain their social positions and intellectual isolation as easily as in the older eras in order to write homogenous and uninterrupted treatises about art), Satchidanandan's stance is interestingly one of dissociating the category 'Indian' into a series of varying interactions with the world and documentation of these cross-cultural references. Starting from a static inward-facing phase in the classical period, he proceeds to dismantle the 'Indian' into an essence that is more than the sum of a string of dynamic influences from all over the world. The first of these influences being from Britain, Satchidanandan proceeds to talk about the influx of ideas from the Western European nations in the form of Marxism, deconstruction and psychoanalytic theory, followed by the socialist interventions from the Latin American nations, all of which culminate in the rise of a homegrown rebellion in the form of subaltern studies which itself borrows from a range of methodological tools and approaches. The most illustrative example documented by Satchidanandan is perhaps the case of recuperating the aesthetics of the poetic and philosophical writings of Sree Narayana Guru in a past-present continuum as done by Udaya Kumar in *Writing the First Person: Literature, History, and Autobiography in Modern Kerala*. Via subaltern studies, one returns to the question of philosophical aesthetics as a modulation and expression of the writer's social reformist attitude and the images in his poetry, forming an excellent example of the contemporary relevance of aesthetics as methodology in a way that straddles the old and the new, the ancient and the contemporary.

Invested in proposing a contemporary theory of labour as performance, Soumyabrata Choudhury's essay titled 'Labour, Service, Performance: Towards a Global Shudrafication of Aesthetics and Politics' is an entertaining and anecdotal essay which is useful to any scholar who wishes to think about aesthetics as a future-past continuum of ideas from which one can freely and critically borrow in service of a larger theorisation about the contemporary. From Manusmriti's description of the *shudra* as 'serving without resentment', the author abstracts the concept of a *commanded ontology*—a perverse *rasa* that is rigorously codified in the modern world for the sake of capital. He uses this as the starting point for a critical discussion of various forms of services in the world of late capitalism such as the services offered by the air hostess and other front-desk services in the global hospitality industry. The essay also expands in the latter half to redefine a series of critical moments in the recent past (such as the impact of COVID-19 on theatre performances, the protests staged in the wake of the killing of George Floyd in the U.S., as well as the surge of student activism in India) in an incisive language of post-structuralist philosophical aesthetics. Interestingly, Choudhury transforms the very idea of a survey by bringing into the ambit of his essay a wide and unexpected range of historical moments, objects, and relations that are united by him through one aesthetic framework. The methodological ambition of this essay also points towards a model that can be emulated and developed further in the humanities in a bid to weld critique with the legacy and tools of an aesthetic inquiry that exceeds the artwork but understands its affects.

Anandita Pan's essay 'Caste and/in Literary Imagination: A Critique of Brahmanical Aestheticism' surveys the specific response within India to the classical idea of aesthetics as a result of the rise of subaltern and Dalit studies. Posing a twin challenge to both universalist notions of art as the repository of beauty and formal harmony and to the specific Sanskritic tradition of extolling the ontological supremacy of art, the writings of a range of thinkers (such as Om Prakash Valmiki, Sharankumar Limbale and Gopal Guru, among many others) in India are described by the author as a moment of rupture in the larger history of aesthetics and aesthetic theory. The movement saw the rise of Dalit life-writing, poetic images that re-territorialise the abject, a disregard of the need for catharsis in art, and the deliberate use of art as a bare communicational device to pass on stories of injustice instead of creating configurations of the sublime—a critique of standards in myriad, unrelenting ways. In particular, Pan's essay highlights three important developments in the multifaceted drama of this modern, emotional, political, and rebellious history of a counter-aesthetics in India—the development of a theory of Dalit *chetna* which marks the literary movement's attempt to redefine the use of the Indian in service of aesthetics, the debates surrounding the value of experimental realism which sought to construct a new relationship between realism and modernism as it emerged in the West and what its ethical/aesthetic counterpart can be in India, and finally, the pervasive intellectual concern that marked Dalit aesthetics and literary criticism regarding the role of language in marking agency and assertion.

In the essay 'Aesthetics and Methodology in English Studies: A Fragmented History', Punnya Rajendran signals at the heterogenous and semi-complete engagements with the idea of aesthetics that have marked and continue to mark the history of English studies as an academic discipline. The essay also attempts to disambiguate the relationship between aesthetics and affect theory and to keep track of English Studies's engagement with philosophy and critique. Into this nebulous history of aesthetics, she also introduces the need for a balancing act between questions about the ontology of the artwork as well as its social function in the light of art movements that are formed around war zones and communities subjected to forced migration, the institutional history of art (which begins in the modern age) as opposed to the timeless social life of art as communitarian practice. The author directs this heterogenous survey towards a demand for the dissociation of the term 'Indian aesthetics' while at the same time placing great emphasis on both 'Indian' and 'aesthetics' separately and in conversation with each other. The central inspiration for the call for revival of method in the essay comes from Spivak's use of the *apoman* in conjunction with Coetzee's 'disgrace' to make an argument about the emotional values underlying the Indian school system, and Rajendran highlights the urgent need for such free and 'undisciplined' cross-associations of emotions and affects in understanding the contemporary.

* * *

Whether or not in conjunction with or wrestling with the longer legacy of aesthetics as a field of study, or threaded with a political and philosophical preoccupation with the idea of affect, there can be no doubt that 'aesthetics' as a functional keyword in the humanities stands at a crossroads today. Defining aesthetics in any definitive modern sense is farthest from the aim of this volume. In fact, the purpose of this collection of essays is to emphasise that we are no longer in need of definitions. Under aesthetics, it becomes possible to experiment with method. Every attempt to engage with the question of aesthetics becomes a part of its definition. Aesthetics is not concerned exclusively with the documentation of literary forms. Rather, objects of study should yield their own reconfigurations of what a contemporary interest in aesthetics can look like. Aesthetics can and must dip into an ancient toolkit but with an irreverent curiosity.

For several decades now, the relationship between text and method has become one of contingency and speculation ever since the influx of cross-disciplinary inquiries, despite the fact that this 'crisis' inaugurated an enriching period of self-reflexivity and extra-disciplinary ethos (an indiscipline, to evoke a tired wordplay) that refused to look away from uncertainties within disciplines. What is truly exhilarating about the possibilities of 'aesthetics' as a keyword is the fact that it promotes precisely this free play of ideas and concepts and contingent methods that is the hallmark of the discipline, tracing back and forth all the while between the poles of the old and the new, the classical and the contemporary, the sublime and the banal.

Section One

The Cultural Turn Within Classical Aesthetics

1

The Social Aesthetic and Sanskrit Literary Theory

Sheldon Pollock

Scholarship on Sanskrit literary theory, like Sanskrit scholarship more generally, tends to cleave to the intellectual agenda set by the tradition itself. There are good reasons for this conformism, of a historical anthropological sort: if we are to make sense of Sanskrit culture we need to know in the first instance what the Sanskrit tradition itself thought worth knowing. Thus, if Indology has been indifferent to the social-and-moral imagination of Sanskrit literary texts—throughout this essay I will take the social and the moral as forming a unified sphere of knowledge in premodern India—it is in part because the shastric tradition has not thematized it in any pronounced way. To be sure, poets as early as Aśvaghoṣa, literary theorists starting with Bhāmaha, commentators from Aruṇagiri on may describe the purposes of literary discourse as the formation of moral persons—*vyutpatti* or education in the largest sense—but they provide little in the way of strong argument or analysis to ground their claim.[1] In terms of sheer column inches, the topic is certainly the least discussed of any in *sāhityaśāstra*.

We might highlight this point by contrasting the understanding of *vyutpatti* in medieval India with another highly consequential intellectual value of antiquity, *paideia*. Both were ideally based on a tripartite knowledge: a *vidyātraya* of *vyākaraṇa*, *mīmāṃsā*, and *nyāya* in the first case, a *trivium* of *grammatica*, *rhetorica*, and *dialectica* in the second. It is the middle term here that marks a large difference in these otherwise strikingly similar (and in fact almost contemporaneous) systematisations:[2] Indian literati were trained in the science of discourse analysis (*vākyaśāstra*, as mīmāṃsā is often called), European literati in the arts of persuasion, especially forensic persuasion. Mīmāṃsā, developed to enhance the understanding of the Vedas, teaches the conditions of meaning to philosophers of language; *rhetorica*, which emerged largely out of the Sophist movement and its complex democratic politics, means to shape behaviour on the part of people acting in the world. The one conceives of literature as verbal icon, the other as exhortation. And it was the analysis of literature as a specific kind of language use that truly came to engage the interests of the Sanskrit readers (the ones we know most about, commentators and literary theorists), or better put, the orientation that produced the most influential kinds of reading. Beyond that, such readers were concerned at the theoretical level with literary experience not as a form of social knowledge but as a form of abstraction from, even transcendence of, the social by way of aesthetic self-transcendence. According to Sanskrit literary theory—or, at least, according to usual interpretation of this theory—one does not ultimately *learn* anything specific to the reading of Sanskrit literature from the reading of Sanskrit literature. True knowledge as such belongs, axiomatically, to the domain of *śāstra*, social and moral knowledge in particular to the domain of *dharmaśāstra*.

It may not be entirely accurate, however, to say that medieval readers understood Sanskrit literature according to the model just described, and it is almost certainly not a trans-historical predisposition of Indian culture to understand it that way. On the contrary, it seems to me something of a new emphasis, even a new mentality produced in large part by the remarkable achievements of literary theory in Kashmir between 850–1050. In the case of the commentarial tradition, the precise impact of this transformation is a matter of some conjecture, since (and here is a fact not often registered) we have no scholia on Sanskrit literary texts before this period.[3] But the history of *sāhityaśāstra* certainly corroborates this assessment of the influence of the Kashmiri transformation. This was a complex shift, consisting in a range of new conceptual moves, but two of them were especially crucial. For one thing, this was the first time that *mīmāṃsā* was directly appropriated by literary theory, signalling a far more intense concern than previously with *kāvya* as a linguistic system.[4] For another, whereas the relationship between *kāvya* and religious values had often been a close one, literature for the first time came to be seen as a model or even kind of religious experience. Emblematic of this conceptual move is the redefinition of aestheticized emotion, *rasa*. In the same way that literary theory itself now became less prescriptive of the writing process and more descriptive of the reading process, the notion of *rasa* was radically displaced from text to reader. What had long been the defining question, how the literary artifact embodies human affect, was transformed into a question of reception, how the reader actually experiences this aestheticized emotion. The answer was found to lie in a close analogy with religious experience.[5]

The preoccupations of Kashmiri theorists with language philosophy and theology, which have colored our understanding of the entire tradition, have preoccupied much of the most serious contemporary scholarship on Sanskrit literary theory, again for very good reasons. Kashmiri theory was, after all, highly influential, and thoughtful students of Sanskrit—and Daniel Ingalls was pre-eminent among them—know that careful reading of the literature of others presupposes careful listening to others' theory. This is all the more true when this theory was some of the most sophisticated in antiquity and hardly equaled in modernity. The concentration on language philosophy and religion, however, was also reinforced by certain proclivities in the modern West, especially a pervasive indifference in Indology itself to the social in Sanskrit literary discourse. The reasons themselves for this indifference are complicated, but they include the character of the critical trends that dominated western literary theory and philology during the formative period of Sanskrit literary studies (formalism and its progeny, and linguistics), the subservience of Sanskrit in the western academy (as handmaiden to religious studies), the intellectual politics of Sanskritists themselves (predominantly conservative). One manifestation of such tendencies that many readers will recall is Ingalls' critique, largely justified if entirely subjective, of D.D. Kosambi's mechanical, Plenkhanovian denunciation of the literary text he himself had so brilliantly and devotedly edited.[6]

I want to ask here whether we can historically recuperate the social in Sanskrit literary theory and find ways to understand its significance as something other than a feature merely inside the text (a mere narrative addition, say, such as could be stripped from the pure textuality of the literary work), or merely outside (as the ideology of an exploitative class, for example). It is striking to observe, as I hope readers will agree we can observe, how fundamentally the social grounds Sanskrit literary theory, and yet at the same time how this grounding is often occluded in the theory itself. The treatment of two central problematics of *Sāhityaśāstra, dhvani* (aesthetic suggestion) and *rasa* or more particularly *rasābhāsa* (the invalid shadow of aestheticized emotion), illustrates this well: if *rasābhāsa* foregrounds sociality for theory, *dhvani* seems to hide it. I examine these in the first two parts of this paper, and in the third, I address a specific body of literary theory, Bhoja's early eleventh century masterpiece, the *Śṛṅgāraprakāśa* (*Light on Passion, ŚP*). Here the social occupies a place in the conceptual scheme of Sanskrit literary culture very different from what we might be led to believe from most scholarly accounts of *Sāhityaśāstra*, and from the Kashmiri focal points, linguistic and theological, upon which they are based. If I disagree on occasion with Daniel Ingalls in my understanding of some of these issues, it is disagreement made possible only by the strong and serious arguments he himself provided in his magisterial scholarly oeuvre. And that Bhoja's work is at last becoming available to us in a definitive edition is partly due to his long and distinguished work as editor of the Harvard Oriental Series.

Social Suggestion

At the beginning of his *Dhvanyāloka* (*Light on Aesthetic Suggestion,* DĀ) Ānandavardhana makes a claim for scientific innovation that, viewed from a purely intellectual-historical perspective, is perhaps without precedent in India. He declares he intends to analyze a feature of literary speech that all sensitive readers grasp but that no one before him, because of its subtlety and complexity, has yet been able to theorize. Ānanda's analysis of *dhvani* or aesthetic suggestion is remarkable both for the overall design of his argument and the subtlety of his exposition, and has rightly absorbed the attention of all who have studied his great work. But more pertinent for the present inquiry than what Ānanda is concerned to theorise is what he is unconcerned to theorize. And this is an unconcern shared by all later writers, who in literary-critical texts over ten centuries following Ānanda pondered his problems and the poems he adduced in illustration. If we reflect on what they omit from the sweep of their conceptualisation, what they fail to analyze that is patently required in order to understand *dhvani*, we begin to see at once how central social discourse is to the constitution of the theory of suggestion, yet how consistently it escapes the language-philosophical inquiry promoted by Ānanda and his followers.

We may begin with the first example of dhvani that Ānanda offers:

> You're free to go wandering, holy man.
> The little dog was killed today
> by the fierce lion making its lair
> in the thicket on the banks of the Godā river.
> (*bhama dhammia*, etc.)[7]

Ānanda prefaces this illustration with a general account, well-known to every student of Sanskrit literature, of how literary texts signify. In addition to the explicit meaning of a literary discourse, he tells us, there is a second signification that "comes to be understood" (*pratīyamāna*), one "thrown forth" (*ākṣipta*) by the explicit meaning when one senses one cannot "rest content" with it, and which one 'gets' immediately when one's mind is looking for the truth.[8] Three text features can be projected in this process of literary implication: a figure of sense (*arthālaṅkāra*), an aesthetic emotional state (*rasa*), and, as in the above verse, some bare narrative matter (*vastumātra*). Ānanda's first five examples are of this third category, not only because implication is most easily demonstrated in *vastudhvani*, but also because it is no doubt this form that first suggested the phenomenon that Ānanda elaborated into a unified theory of literariness. *Vastudhvani* contains various subspecies, usually characterized in terms of the commands or prohibitions they communicate (given the traditional Sanskrit understanding of sentence meaning, which Bhoja, discussed below, p. 218 explains for us). The first, in which the explicit meaning is a command whereas the meaning one "comes to understand" is actually a prohibition, is illustrated in the poem "You're free to go wandering, holy man."

Ānanda is explicitly concerned only with the "bare narrative matter" implied, and not with the question of who understands the prohibition that comes to be understood. And indeed, whose mind is "looking for the truth"? Is it the mendicant, someone else in the poem listening on, the reader? The next four examples complete his typology and provide us with the answer (I give them in the fine translation of Ingalls):

(2) Mother-in-law sleeps here, I there:
look, traveler, while it is light.
For at night when you cannot see
you must not fall into my bed

Here, an explicit prohibition implies a command (an invitation), which, like the express meaning, is directed to and meant to be understood by the addressee, the traveler (and misunderstood by the mother-in-law listening on);[9]

(3) Go, and let the sighs and tears
be mine; nor let them rise
from you as well, tortured,
being without her, by your hateful courtesy.

Here, the point of the explicit command is not to tell the male addressee either to leave or to stay, but just to reproach him; this implied meaning, like the express statement, is directed to the addressee.

(4) Turn back, I beg you. You are making trouble
for other ladies stealing to their lovers.
The moonlight of your countenance destroys
their covering darkness, wretched woman.

Here again, the point of the explicit prohibition is not to tell the female addressee either to go or not to go, but just to pay her a compliment; this implied meaning, again like the express statement, is understood by the addressee.

(5) Who wouldn't be angry to see
his dear wife with her lower lip bitten?
You scorned my warning to smell
the bee-holding lotus. Now you must suffer.

This last example differs from the previous four, according to Ānanda's explicit statement, in that the literal meaning and the implication are directed to two different people.[10] In the first verse, we must therefore assume, Ānanda believes it is the mendicant who is meant to understand the implied prohibition, as well as the express command.

It is easy enough to see, in the second example, what the implied command to the traveller is, and why it has to be conveyed by way of an express prohibition (which only the mother-in-law takes at face value). But what precisely is the prohibition to the mendicant, why should it be conveyed by implication, and who in fact is speaking? One might assume, in view of example two, that the prohibition is "You're not free to go wandering," but why is he not free? The presence of the lion presumably is meant to cancel out what the absence of the dog makes possible, but the lion has its lair at the riverside, no obvious place for a mendicant to be told to go wander. Yet it is there, evidently, that the prohibition is directed, since the only thing mentioned in the poem that can negate the explicit permission is the lion. Example two, again, would lead us to suppose that the prohibition is conveyed by implication because a third party is listening whom the speaker may be trying to deceive, but that seems not to be the case here, and there appears to be no deception. And from the information in the four bare lines of the poem itself, we have no clear idea who is speaking—beyond the fact that he or she is aware of the mendicant's earlier troubles with "the" dog—and it is the identity of the speaker that would seem to be key to answering the other questions and to making sense of the verse.

Moreover, why would someone speak this way, and not just issue a prohibition plainly and directly: "Stay away from the river"? One can hardly imagine the speaker to be another mendicant, for example, for he would simply have said, "You can go wandering wherever you want but don't go near the river, there's a lion there." To assert that this is poetry and poetry is precisely a use of language that differs from plain and direct statement—*vakratā* or indirection is actually a category familiar from the earliest Sanskrit systematic thought on literariness—would only be to restate the problem of meaning production, not analyze it. What we want to know is what we need to know to unravel the problem of indirection satisfactorily. To put this in Sanskrit terms: underlying all implication is some contradiction (*bādha*) in the denotation, a contradiction that itself derives from a specific intention (*prayojana*), and it is this intention we cannot begin to make sense of without more information. From the fact that the speaker only expresses the prohibition implicitly we might infer some reluctance to evince interest, or a desire to evince a lack of interest, in the mendicant's keeping away from the riverside. But who wants to stop him without saying so openly, and to avoid indicating too keen a desire—or again, to conceal all desire—in doing so? Someone who has something to hide, perhaps, about something in the thicket at the riverside. But that is as far as the rational common reader can go, with the mere four-line poem at hand—and remember that the mere quatrain is not a fragment of some larger work but constitutes in itself a complete and self-sufficient piece of literature.

Ānanda comments no further on his first example of *dhvani*, and the analytical system he proceeds to construct does nothing to help in understanding the verse. Evidently, unless the poem is embedded in a more complete context, a richer language, so to speak, that supplements the sign system in use, there can be no access to the implication let alone its significance, that is, the *dhvani*.[11] Such a language or context can only be the socio-literary tradition itself; in the case of *bhama dhammia*, the social conventions traditionalized in Prakrit poetry. The commentators on Ānanda will, of course, contextualize the poem, albeit without explaining why it is necessary, let alone reasoning through the process of contextualization. And that this is indeed a matter in need of rationalization becomes evident when we observe the social complexities, and sometimes confusions, of the interpretations themselves.

Here, for example, is what Abhinavagupta, Ānanda's only extant commentator, has to say about the verse: "These are the words of a certain woman spoken in order to save a trysting place ... from the intrusions of a mendicant.... His walking in that place is a natural activity that has been inhibited by fear of a dog." Abhinava's interpretation seems strikingly underdetermined; indeed, his translators believe it even misses the point of the verse. Nothing in the poem itself tells us the speaker is a woman, that the thicket is a place of rendezvous, and that the point of the verse is to keep the mendicant away, and the commentator does nothing to justify or even conceptualize his understanding. Moreover, as Ingalls et al. rightly point out, if the dog had frightened the mendicant from the place of rendezvous, what is the point of her inventing a lion to terrify him further? It would certainly be astonishing if the celebrated commentator failed to grasp, or did not care to show he wholly grasped, the point of the first illustration of the central matter of the book he is setting out to explain.[12] Evidently the "richer language" called for above is necessary not only for outsider readers such as ourselves.

Abhinava's contemporary, Bhoja, who is the next commentator in chronological order, is too terse to allow us to see his full understanding of the verse, but at least he explains the difference between the implied and the suggested meanings: "In this poem, whereas the statement of command, 'You are free to wander' is explicit, a prohibition is understood: 'There is a lion in that thicket, and since you are afraid even of a dog, don't go there.' The prohibition implicit in the express command suggests [another] meaning, i.e., about [the speaker's] rendezvous with someone in a thicket at the river," a suggestion that, obviously, only the reader understands.[13] In the generation after Bhoja, Mahimabhaṭṭa offers a fuller explanation. Mahima's principal objective throughout his *Vyaktiviveka* is to prove that the logical procedures of inference are entirely adequate to explain the phenomenon of suggestion (or at least implication), and that therefore no new category, such as "dhvani," need be invented. Our interest here is in his understanding of the verse itself (rather than in how he understands the logical process of understanding), and he shows just how complicated this is:

> A certain woman, hungry for the sweet pleasure of undisturbed lovemaking, has made a rendezvous with some lucky fellow in a deserted forest spot alive with bees attracted by the sweet-smelling flowers. There is an ascetic who wanders there to pick the flowers, and she perceives his coming to her spot as an impediment to her plans. Being clever, she acts like a simple girl in mentioning to him only the absence of any reason to fear through the death of the dog—though of course she knows full well that lions are vicious creatures—in hopes of giving him some good news. And thus by means of a command she brings about a prohibition of his wandering.[14]

The same problems as in Abhinava's interpretation confront us in Mahima, and it will not be until Hemacandra (ca. 1175) in his subcommentary on his own *Kāvyānuśāsana* that things seem to get fully sorted out:

> A certain loose woman is always leaving her house, under the pretext of fetching water from the river, in order to meet her lover in a thicket on the bank of the Godāvarī river. She regards a mendicant as an obstacle in

> that he destroys the thicket by gathering flowers [for his worship]. And though she is a clever woman she speaks here like an ingenue: "The dog" that used to harass you whenever you entered our compound was careless and, to our good fortune, was "killed" or slaughtered today by "the," i.e., well-known, "fierce," i.e., taking no pity on the dog, "lion," i.e., invincible.... The lion will not bother you here [in the village], since it is "making its lair" or constantly staying in a thicket on the banks of the Godāvarī. You may therefore continue to wander without worry.[15]

We are now told that it is the mendicant's wandering, not at the river (so Abhinava and Mahima) but at the woman's house in the town that had been interrupted by the dog, and it is there that he is being invited to continue.[16] That would make no sense in the case of the riverside, however, where he is implicitly prohibited from going. Hemacandra, accordingly (as both Mahima and Abhinava) adds that mendicants gather flowers for their religious observances at riversides and even end up stripping bare the dense camouflage offered by thickets on riverbanks. It still remains unclear, however, why a village dog would be killed at the river side; some commentators suggest the point of the adjective "fierce" is to indicate that the lion has entered the town, but that of course would stand in hopeless contradiction with the express command as understood by Hemacandra.[17]

Moreover, unlike example two, where the explicit is cancelled by the implicit ("Don't get into my bed at night" → "Get into my bed at night"), here a command is not negated ("You're free to go wandering" →/ "You're prohibited from going wandering"), but only restricted or otherwise prohibited: The mendicant is free to go in one place, but not in another; he can continue to beg, but must not go to the river. The problem of the absence of co-referentiality (*vyadhikaraṇatva*) of the command (to beg at the house) and the prohibition (to stay away from the river) was intimated by Mammaṭa when restating Mahima's logical argument, but only fully answered by Kamalākara in the seventeenth century.[18]

What should be clear from this example is that the linguistic theory of suggestion it is adduced to illustrate (like Mahima's inferential logic meant to challenge that theory) does nothing to help us grasp what we really need to grasp in order to understand this verse. We should note at once, too, that the absence of its semantic core is no peculiarity of this verse, but is actually fundamental to *vastudhvani* poetry (and in a more general way, to much Sanskrit poetry); similar complexity attaches to the other examples. At first glance, the fifth example seems to have no point at all—that of course is precisely the reason we seek something more. We know this is a poem (though Sanskrit theory is uninterested in how we know), and poets do not write poetry that ends in pure banality. But how do we come to understand what more is in play here? What else is implied and suggested and to whom? Again, the commentators only supply the putative context and are unconcerned with explaining how it is known, but, again, nothing about it is self-evident. According to Abhinava, "The literal sense is directed to an adulterous wife. The suggested (*vyaṅgya*) sense, on the other hand, is directed to her husband, and informs him that she is not guilty of offense."[19] Bhoja similarly identifies both the implication and the suggestion: "The literal sense is the girlfriend's reproach, which is meant to carry the implication (*pratyāyayan*) to the husband, so as to allay his jealousy, that his wife's lip was wounded by a bee and not by her paramour, and it suggests (*dhvanati*) the friend's cleverness at hiding indiscretions."[20] Once more, we find interpretation underdetermined by the poem itself—obviously, none of this essential information can be gotten except from a social subtext altogether unthematized by the commentators. Even then the meaning of the verse is not self-evident, but rather depends on what element is emphasized. Ānanda's exposition so far has led us to assume that the implied meaning is the meaning truly intended ("Do not go to the riverside"; "Come to my bed") emerging out of the duplicitous express meaning ("You're free to go wandering"; "You must not fall into my bed"). Here, accordingly, we might assume that the literal sense is intended rather for the husband ("It is just a bee-sting"), and the implicit sense ("It is really a lover's bite"), if not for some third person in the vicinity, or simply the reader, then for the wife herself, who is thereby being admonished by her friend with reference to the effort required to keep her affair secret. This will be reversed if it is the suffering that is stressed. Here the wife becomes the addressee of the explicit statement, "You will have to suffer your husband's jealous anger because of his misinterpretation of your act," even though the wife knows it is not a misinterpretation, and the husband becomes the addressee of the implication that it would be a misinterpretation. But here again, whatever the truth (if there is a singular truth) of the meaning of this or any of the other verses—and much Sanskrit and Prakrit poetry are indefinitely interpretable—it is clear that far more than a theory of implication and suggestion is necessary to explain implication and suggestion. Later theoreticians do try to supplement Ānanda's system with a theory of speech pragmatics; Mammaṭa offers the first full systematization: "Aesthetic suggestion is a semantic function (*arthasya vyāpāraḥ*) that produces in sensitive readers the idea of something different [from the direct sense], by means of [nine different factors of pragmatic] specificity (*vaiśiṣṭya*): that of the speaker, the addressee, the tone of voice, the syntagm of the sentence, the expressed sense, the presence of a third person, the context, the time, or the place."[21] Yet it remains uncertain whether Mammaṭa's system does more than organize the knowledge presupposed to exist, while failing to explain how the knowledge comes about in the first place. Consider his first example:

> It's a very heavy water jug I'm carrying,
> my friend, and I've come back quickly.
> I've got to rest a second since I'm weak
> and sweating and sighing from exhaustion. (*KP* 3.13, p.73)

Now, it is perfectly true that what makes it possible for the sensitive reader to understand that this verse is about "concealing stolen lovemaking," as Mammaṭa puts it, is the "specificity of the speaker." But the only thing that allows us to specify this specificity is the reader's participation in and acceptance of a particular universe of social meaning as made available in the texts of a literary culture.

It is precisely the embededness of these poems in a set of particular conventions and rules of literary communication, their particularity and localization, that constitutes their meaning, but in a way that Ānanda, Mammaṭa, and the rest seem unable to observe. Although they show uncommon acuity in revealing the mechanisms by which implication and suggestion arise, nowhere do they tell us how we come to know what we need to know in order to understand them. What is necessary for us to know is not available through any pure theory of language, such as is envisioned in the analysis of semantic powers (*vṛtti*) that Ānanda offers, and the whole analytical tradition that follows him.[22] What is needed, instead, is an account of the social particular. In other words, the semantics of Sanskrit literary theory requires supplementation not only by a general linguistic pragmatics but by a specific social pragmatics, which can explain to us what thickets on riverbanks signify (beyond the fact of their being thickets on riverbanks), what people do there, why privacy in thickets should be desirable; how adultery is regarded in this world, how it is hidden, who does so and why.

Except by acquiring and theorizing this social-literary competence, we cannot know that riverbanks in Prakrit poetry, especially densely overgrown riverbanks, are places where lovers go, that is to say, unmarried couples who have no other place to be alone together. But couples who are not married cannot, in Prakrit poetry, licitly be together (though of course, they are always together in Prakrit poetry). An so calling attention to one's desire to preserve the privacy of the rendezvous spot—by use of a direct prohibition ("Don't go there!")—is tantamount to revealing the illicit liaison itself. The very linguistic form causes us to ask who would make such a statement, and it is only from familiarity with the larger social text that we can know it is the woman in the illicit relationship. The gender relations that constitute the social world of Prakrit poetry demand that it is always the woman, never the man, who organizes adultery. Only when we know such social-literary facts does the real suggestion behind the poems become available: the very formulation of the statements—meaning without saying, communicating by not communicating—suggests that the women speakers are sophisticated and clever, and ardent to preserve, in the one case, a place of lovemaking, and in the other, a girlfriend's marriage (or rather, her affair). And in a way, once we know all this, our own reading becomes a satisfying exercise in the revelation of our own sophistication, since not only can we understand the meaning of the clever women's meaning, but we understand something that the holy man and the cuckolded husband necessarily cannot, since the whole point is artfully to allay their suspicions, in the first case about the place of rendezvous while keeping him away, and in the second, about his faithless wife.

More important than supplying the conditions for aesthetic suggestion to succeed, however, the social text of the Prakrit world is presupposed and thereby reproduced as a stable text. When both readerly expectation and theoretical concern are focused on the linguistic mechanisms of meaning, and the complexities that allow different meanings to occur, the social conditions of aesthetic suggestion escape observation let alone interrogation. The conditions for understanding this literature are the permanence, predictability, the common-sense of the social world, and by the very writing and reading of this and all other poetry—and this seems to be a crucial social effect—these conditions are made all the more permanent, predictable, and commonsensical. It is the very taken-for-grantedness of this world, for its part, that renders it invisible to readers like ¯ Ananda; the sphere of social (or literary) convention was one they inhabited too deeply to see. Language is only the mechanism of such poetry, yet it has monopolized theoretical reflection. The poetry is about the people and their world, and is intelligible only through that world. Yet it is a world occluded to theory because it is too far inside consciousness to be rendered an object of consciousness. In a word, literary suggestion is social, and sequesters the social from critical inspection.

False Feelings

On its face, the problem of rasa, aesthetic emotion, and its complement, *rasābhāsa*, the semblance of such emotion, would hardly seem to impinge on the problem of the social aesthetic. As conventionally understood, *rasa* refers to the reader's emotive response to literature, and especially to the uniqueness of this response, the fact that we take pleasure in sad stories, for example, but not in real sadness. It is accordingly often treated as a philosophical question.[23] *Rasa*—and here is the common understanding—is a produced when certain "stable" or primary emotions (*sthāyibhāva*) of ours are fully developed by stimulation from a suitable object (*ālambanavibhāva*) under appropriate external conditions (*uddīpanavibhāva*), and nuanced by more evanescent feelings (*vyabhicāribhāva*) that are themselves made manifest by physical reactions (*anubhāva*). All this activates our own latent dispositions (*vāsanās*, *saṃskāras*) to respond sympathetically. *Rasābhāsa*, for its part, is usually understood to refer to a "counterfeit" form of readerly response that results from some deficiency in the causal set, as when the object of the primary emotion is an unsuitable one. This negative analysis of *rasābhāsa*, as an inauthentic, deficient aesthetic experience, is widespread; it is implicit in the following remarks of Ingalls and his collaborators:

> The concept of *rasābhāsa* is highly restrictive of literature. If we are to limit *rasa*, the sole aim of literature, to only such subjects as conform to propriety and even to the *śāstras*, as Udbhaṭa would have it, not a little of Sanskrit literature and surely the greater part of Western literature will be judged to be of little worth. Abhinava seems to have been the first Indian critic to face this problem and find an answer: the *ābhāsatva*, the impropriety, of such experiences is something we realize only later; during the actual experience we are absorbed.... Interesting are [Abhinava's] remarks on *rasābhāsa*, false or improper rasa.... If one guides one's criticism strictly by the words of Bharata ... such false love should lead to comedy. In fact, says Abhinava, it may lead to comedy only at a time long after our experience. When we hear Rāvaṇa's passionate words in the *Rāvaṇakāvya* [now lost] there is no occasion for relishing comedy.... This qualification opens up to favorable evaluation much that would have been rejected or reprehended by older standards.[24]

This assessment of *rasābhāsa*—as an audience response that is somehow inauthentic—seems to me misleading. For one thing, far from solving an old problem, Abhinava and the school to which he belonged may be said to have created a new one. For another, the category *rasābhāsa* is not the cause of unfavorable literary evaluation, but rather is constitutive of the moral concern at the core of Sanskrit literature and literary theory, if one with its own long and complicated history. Understood in accordance with the dominant tradition that preceded Abhinava, *rasābhāsa*, like *rasa* in general, had originally far less to do with psychology and axiology than with the sociology of the Sanskrit aesthetic.

To sustain the first part of this argument, it is necessary briefly to recapitulate the history of thinking about *rasa* and to grasp the true magnitude of the Kashmiri transformation of the concept.[25] Like the "taste" that *rasa* metaphorically references, which may be regarded as a property of the food, of the taster, or of the act of tasting, *rasa* can theoretically be regarded in three dimensions: as a dimension of a textual object, as a competence of a reader-subject, and as a transaction between the two. It is a process that exists as a totality even while its moments can be analytically disaggregated, and it is this analytical disaggregation—or rather the different emphases that such disaggregation permits—that marks and makes the history of Indian thinking on the subject. Thus, one issue that fundamentally concerned theorists (it is well known, since it is widely discussed in *alaṅkāraśāstra* itself) pertains to the location of *rasa*: Is aesthetic emotion to be considered, in the first instance, as a text-immanent phenomenon, relating primarily to the narrative itself, or as a reception phenomenon, relating primarily to the audience? In Sanskrit terms, who "has *rasa*," the character or the reader?[26] The "old view," ascribed by Abhinava to Lollaṭa and others, unequivocally accepted, and no doubt only knew, the first alternative: "*Rasa* is nothing more than what in its initial stage is a stable emotion after this has combined with the transitory feelings and so on to become fully developed; and it is located in the character and there alone." This was more or less the position of Ānandavardhana himself in the mid-ninth century; he seems to know nothing of the doctrine of readerly rasa. It is certainly the position of Bhoja, Sanskrit's greatest synthesizer of literariness (a contemporary of Abhinava, as noted, and ignorant of his work). Indeed, it is widespread misunderstanding about the analytical primacy of the literary text in Bhoja's account of *rasa* that has produced such confusion about the sense of his doctrine of "Passion."[27]

This long-standing conception of *rasa* was first challenged in the theological aesthetics of Kashmiri writers of the late tenth and early eleventh centuries. Viewing literary and religious experience as paradigmatically related, they redirected the analysis of *rasa* toward the consciousness of the experiencer. For Bhaṭṭa Tauta, for example, the focal point became the commonalities of reader, writer, and character; for Abhinava, the processes of response itself; for Bhaṭṭa Nāyaka, the language operations underlying this response and the specificity of its epistemological status. One move in this transformation that encapsulates it entirely is Abhinava's recoding of Bharata's foundational *rasasūtra*: *rasaniṣpatti* is made to refer, no longer to the production of *rasa* in the text, but to the production of *tadviṣayarasanā*, the tasting of the object of *rasa*.[28]

It was only when *rasa* and its semblance-forms became a matter of the reader's reading rather than the character's character, that the idea of *rasābhāsa* became a problem to be solved.[29] The psychological and axiological difficulties that bothered Abhinava—when precisely do we realize that our aesthetic experience is only a semblance, a shadow of the real thing, and what precisely are we feeling before we come to that realization?—arise only when *rasābhāsa* is held to be in essence a reception event. He offers an interesting solution: "The *ābhāsatva*, the impropriety, of [our] experiences is something we realize only later; during the actual experience we are absorbed," whereby, accordingly, the aesthetic experience of *rasābhāsa* itself becomes a semblance, a *carvaṇābhāsa*, specious aesthetic relishing.[30] But this, I believe, is a solution to a problem of his own making.

In the episteme Abhinava so successfully overthrew, what is at issue is the genuineness or semblance, or better, validity or invalidity of a character's affective state as such, qualifications that we shall see are eminently social (and not philosophical, as when Aristotle terms feelings false when they are irrational and groundless).[31] Here, the idea of *rasābhāsa* can in no way be construed as "restrictive" or evaluative of literature, as if *rasābhāsa* signified a shortcoming, "only *rasābhāsa*."[32] For Bhoja, it is in fact a species of *rasa*:

> *Rasa* is of three sorts: developed (*prakṛṣṭa*); remaining in the form of a feeling (*bhāvarūpa*); and a semblance (*ābhāsa*). A "developed" *rasa* is that which the leading character, the one who occupies the chief role in the narrative, comes to feel in reference to a commensurate object. That which "remains in the form of a feeling" is what a supporting character comes to have, and which is not fully developed. That which the antagonist comes to have, or is ascribed to an animal, is a semblance of *rasa*.[33]

Like *guṇa*, *bhāva*, and *rasa* itself, *rasābhāsa* is an *alaṅkāra*, a general factor of literary beauty, according to Bhoja's terminology. Its presence in combination with these other components (*saṃsṛṣṭi*) is a necessary feature of *rasāviyoga*, the indispensable presence of *rasa* in a work of art. In all this, as so often elsewhere in his work, Bhoja seems to me to express a general consensus of the entire earlier tradition.[34]

Accordingly, *rasābhāsa* represents, not deviation or deficiency needing some new theory of response, but a necessary dimension of complex narratives, those that explore the complexity of the sentiments of persons acting in the world, and what it is that makes some valid (according to some social scale) and some invalid. But the presence of *rasābhāsa* as such does not enfeeble literature, as if, since "the sole aim of literature" is *rasa*, when "real *rasa*" is not present, the true aim of literature is not attained.[35] How, after all, could one have a *Rāmāyaṇa* without Rāvaṇa? What is most important for our concerns here, it is through the process of the reader's gaining an awareness of this aesthetic, by grasping how and why certain sentiments as presented in literature are counterfeit and false while others are genuine and true, that its social force is generated. The issue is not the invalidity of our emotional response to a narrative, but rather what in narrative is taken to constitute invalid emotion.

Obviously the entire question of *rasābhāsa* becomes intelligible only against the background of a broader normative discourse on what constitute true and false emotions. This discourse finds expression in a variety of ways from the earliest periods of systematic reflection to the latest. In the *Nāṭyaśāstra* itself, for example, although the term *rasābhāsa* is not used, the social boundaries of aesthetic sentiment are clearly delineated. As is well known, characters are categorized according to a social-moral typology (the two concepts, again, forming an indissoluble whole) as "high, middle, and low" (*uttama, madhyama, adhama*), and *rasa* is achieved only when these types are properly aligned. In the case of *śṛṅgāra*, the erotic sentiment, for example, the characters must be a heterosexual couple, young, and socially-morally "high" (*strīpuruṣahetuka, uttamayuvaprakṛti*).[36]

The normative discourse first is clearly articulated where the term *rasābhāsa* itself is first used, in the work of the early ninth-century thinker, Udbhaṭa. But there is no question that he meant to reprehend certain texts let alone reject them from the domain of the literary. He is instead interested in the problem of an ethical aesthetic. For him, *rasa* seems to have been a form of moral consciousness, a peculiar one that, unlike other such forms, has a dimension of physicality. There is no reason to believe he would have disagreed with the verse his commentator cites: "*Rasa* is that specific kind of consciousness of the moral order (*caturvarga*)—what should and should not be done—that can be 'tasted' (*āsvādya*)." For its part, *rasābhāsa*, for which Udbhaṭa also uses, as part of an older typology, the term "the vehement trope" (*ūrjasvin*), is "composition of emotions or rasas where the action violates social norms (*anaucityapravṛtta-*) because of desire, anger, and so on."[37] As his commentator Indurāja remarks: "In the literary form known as 'the vehement,' rasas and *bhāvas* are represented as immoral (*anaucityena*) because [here the actions underlying the rasas and *bhāvas*] are caused by passion, hatred, and delusion. That is in fact why it is called 'the vehement' form (*ūrjasvin*): vehemence, that is, physical force (*bala*), exists in it given that the use of force is prompted by one's miscognition of reality [that invariably underlies action motivated by passion, etc.]."[38] The example supplied by Udbhaṭa is a verse describing Śiva's impetuous (*haṭhena*) and immoral (*apāsya satpatham*) sexual impulses toward the virgin Pārvatī—a verse from his own (lost) *Kumārasaṃbhava*.

A more explicit dimension of this social discourse, already glimpsed in some of the remarks cited above, came to be articulated through the concept of *aucitya*, propriety, in the last centuries of the first millennium, leading to a synthetic statement in Kṣemendra's mid-eleventh century *Aucityavicāracarcā* (Inquiry into the Analysis of Propriety).[39] *Aucitya*, which according to Kṣemendra's definition is a kind of correspondence between a textual signifier and an extra-textual signified (*sadṛśaṃ kila yasya yat*, vs. 7), is a category applicable to every feature of the literary work: from the most minute formal element, the individual lexeme or even sub-lexical preverb and particle, to the largest component of the signification: the time and place of the action, the social status of the hero, and so on. As a state of being in accordance with the *svabhāva* of a person or thing, *aucitya* is clearly related to and extends a wide range of earlier conceptions. But Kṣemendra's importance for us, if not his novelty, lies in his unequivocal affirmation of the constitutive relationship of propriety and aesthetic sentiment: *Aucitya* now has become explicitly the life-force (*jīvita*) of *rasa* itself: how laughable and disruptive of the heroic mood, Kṣemendra says, is martial violence directed toward a suppliant, or, in the case of the piteous mood, compassion toward an enemy.[40]

This perspective on true and false feelings as essential components of a rounded narratives does, however, begin to shift noticeably in later thinkers. Particularly instructive is the discussion in Jagannātha Paṇḍitarāja's mid-seventeenth-century masterpiece, *Rasagaṇgādhara* (The [Five-Faced] Śiva of Aesthetic Emotion, RG). As so often in his work, Jagannātha begins his analysis by exploring a finer point of controversy. There is no uncertainty as to the fact that *rasābhāsa* results from some transgression of the social order measured against a set of moral norms. Jagannātha wants to elucidate this set, however, and thereby the causal mechanism of *rasāabhāsa*,[41] by drawing a distinction between an emotion directed toward an inappropriate object and an emotion inappropriate in itself:

> The property *rasābhāsa* derives from there being an inappropriate object or other cause." [This *kārikā* appears to represent an older position under examination]. The impropriety of an object or other cause is something people understand from social practices (*vyavahārataḥ*). Some critics hold that [*rasābhāsa* arises only when] it is the object cause [or other factor][42] that people regard as unsuitable. Others disagree, on the grounds that, whereas that would cover such cases as desire for the wife of a sage [who is an inappropriate love-object], it would not include desire for more than one lover or desire not shared by both partners in a relationship. In the latter two cases there is no impropriety in the object cause as such [in the first, the cause is the fact of many lovers, all of whom may be appropriate love-objects; in the second, the cause is the attitude but not the social status of one of the partners]. Therefore, the primary emotion itself [in this case the emotion of desire, *ratisthāyibhāva*] has to be characterized by impropriety [for there to be *rasābhāsa*]. And in this way both desire for an inappropriate object, as well as desire for more than one lover or not shared by both partners would be included. "Impropriety" would remain as defined above [i.e., established by social convention]. (RG, p. 118)

It may seem a fine point to distinguish between inappropriate feeling and inappropriate object in the production of invalid sentiment. But it is easy enough to grasp, and the general thrust of Jagannātha's argument becomes clear through his examples, which concern the paramour of a queen, a girl casting her seductive glances at the many suitors at her front door, and a new bride trembling before her husband's embraces. A summary verse that he cites anonymously indicates that adultery, in addition to these three other conditions, all produce *rasābhāsa* in the case of *śṛṅgāra*.

What becomes clear in reading through Jagannātha's account is that aesthetic sentiment has transmogrified into something like aesthetic moralism. Here is how he lays out the social-moral boundaries of the emotions underlying each of the *rasas*:

> Desire for an inappropriate object (a teacher's wife, a goddess, a queen), desire that is not reciprocated, desire on the part of a woman for more than one lover: none of these can produce the erotic *rasa* (*śṛṅgāra*) in its pure or authentic form. A father's grief for a son who is querulous and wicked, or grief on the part of ascetic [who has given up all attachments]; transcendental disenchantment with life (*nirveda*) on the part of an untouchable, who has no right to participate in transcendental Vedic knowledge; martial energy on the part of a low-born man, or anger on the part of a timorous man or directed toward someone like one's father; amazement in response to a mere magic trick; laughter directed at one's father; fear in a hero; disgust felt for the fat or flesh or blood of a sacrificial animal—all these produce the semblance of the *rasas* of (respectively) pity, tranquility, the heroic, cruelty, wonder, the comic, terror, and loathing. (RG, p. 122)[43]

If *rasa* is a way of speaking about the literary promulgation of an ideal-typical social order, *rasābhāsa* seems now to be viewed, not as its necessary complement, something required to complete that ideal type, but as the literary promulgation of an immoral order, against which theory imposed increasingly harsh strictures. Desire for someone beyond one's station (a queen, a teacher's wife), like desire for someone who does not share it, and a woman's desire for more than one lover, violate this order and so are false feelings. So, too, when a father is shown to grieve for a wicked son, or when an untouchable is shown to have gained wisdom. Low-born men do not or cannot show martial energy, any more than cowards can show anger or heroes fear. Laughter and rage toward one's father are as much violations of this order as disgust in the face of sacrificial slaughter. All these are inversions, so to speak, of real eroticism, and pity, and heroism—and real sentiments, moreover, are absolute and unchanging, not situational and adaptive.[44] Clearly, not only is literary theory concerned with the moral discourse that lies at the heart of literature. It seeks to explore, by use of the components of *rasa* analysis, precisely how that moral discourse is violated. In Jagannātha, *rasābhāsa* does indeed verge on becoming an index, not only of a different order of literature, but of an inferior, even reprehensible kind of literature; no longer a category for explaining the dynamics of affect in the complex narratives that mark real life, but a sign of the unwanted intrusion of real life into literature.

This negative evaluation was already there in Abhinavagupta himself, and construes with much broader trends we will find expressed by Bhoja, too. Abhinava's concerns with reader-response notwithstanding, he retained a commitment to precisely the social-moral aesthetics that we find extending from Bharata to Jagannātha:

> Appropriateness of the [*sthāyi*]*bhāvas* is derived from appropriateness of the characters. Characters differ by their having the emotions (*bhāvas*) of the upper, middle, or lower classes and by their having the emotions of gods or humans. A basic emotional drive [*sthāyibhāva*] that is described by following these distinctions and not confusing them will be "appropriate".... If we assign a type of love to characters of the upper class by recourse to what is appropriate to the lower class [*uttamaprakṛti, adhamaprakṛti*], how ridiculous will be the result. Even in India what is appropriate in love differs according to the three classes of men. If the "attainment" (*sampad*) appropriate to one's caste and family (*nijajātikulānurūpa-*) is not present, sexual desire must not be represented (*anupadeśyā*) at all, because it does not lead to the fulfillment of the life-goals.[45]

Here we glimpse what it was that did eventually become "restrictive of literature." This was not *rasābhāsa* itself—which was a necessary component of narrative complexity, and a consequence of it—but some angst in the face of real-life socio-moral problems, and the threat posed by their reproduction in literature.

In addition to the assumption, implicit everywhere, that literature is not supposed to surprise with deviations from the typical, *rasa* and *rasābhāsa* become the principal locus where criticism of the literary work and criticism of life intersect, where literary practice becomes a social practice. If propriety lies at the heart of *rasa, rasa* becomes the heart of a moral economy of literature. It can produce its effects only to the degree that the imaginative discourse represents, and thereby inevitably serves to reproduce, what is appropriate to a given situation, which in turn is intelligible only in terms of a unified vision of the social order. Thus when one learns what literature is, how it works and the canons by which it may be said to represent what is valid or invalid, when one learns to be a good reader, a *rasika* or a *sahṛdaya*, one is learning what is normative in the everyday world. To produce readers of Sanskrit literature is to produce certain kinds of social subjectivities. *Rasābhāsa* and the *anaucitya* that provides its logic are the locus where criticism of literary form and criticism of literary representation—criticism of life—intersect.

Moral Passion

If the social structuring of Sanskrit literary theory was obscured after the linguistic and theological turn of Kashmiri criticism, or remained unthematized precisely because it was so taken for granted,[46] its true significance is still visible in Bhoja's remarkable *Śṛṅgāraprakāṣa*. Bhoja is by no means uninterested in literature as a particular kind of language—the work as a whole is in fact organized around the topics "word," "meaning," and modes of "unity" of the two (ŚP, pp. 6.8–17). But his express concern with the social grounds of literary imagination manifests itself with a clarity not easy to parallel in other *alaṅkāra* texts. This may be attributable, not only to his main objective of providing a summa poetica of the entire antecedent tradition, and making explicit what was often simply assumed, but also to the fact that as king of the Paramāra dominion, Bhoja was especially sensitive to his social role: The writer of the ŚP, Bhoja tells us in his commentary on the first *kārikā* of the work, "is not just anyone but a great king appointed by his elders to protect all that has been inherited, and who in this verse beseeches God that there should be no violation against the established order (*sthita*) and practices of estates and life stages while he is engaged in the composition of this book."[47]

There are three specific themes in Bhoja's treatise centrally concerned with the social aesthetic that I want to concentrate on here: the argument for the unitary meaning of a literary work and the idea of plot revision; the varieties of Passion; and the nature of the hero. In brief, Bhoja's general conception seems to me as follows: Literary texts make moral arguments, and in view of this fact, received plots must be revised in the interests of such arguments. A moral argument is a general discursive phenomenon, however, not specific to literature. What is specific is *rasa*, and Bhoja shows that the moral order is inseparably connected with it: Passion—*śṛṅgāra*, the one *rasa*—is moral force. This is no Platonic-Christian conceptual scheme where the virtues and the passions are at war with each other; passions are virtues. The different kinds of protagonists embody the four main species of this force, and each one's relationship with his antagonist must manifest this.

The validity of such a summary depends, of course, on how carefully Bhoja's idiom, categories, and modes of argument have been understood. Since these are sometimes unusual—and his work is essentially unknown—I have tried to provide as much of the argument as possible in literal translation.

That the literary work has a unitary meaning above and beyond the meanings of the individual verses of which it is composed is something almost never addressed in Sanskrit theory except in the most perfunctory manner. Bhoja's rich account therefore merits close attention. I re-arrange the sections into an order more appropriate for our purposes here, starting with a passage where the literary text as a whole is situated within the overall structure of his exposition:

> So much for what we have called "the necessary presence of *rasa*" (*rasāviyoga*) at the level of the sentence. Now we may consider it at the level of the work (*prabandha*). This, too, manifests itself by the eliminating of faults, the procuring of virtues, and the mixing of elements of beauty, and becomes thereby a source of intellectual delight for intelligent readers. The "eliminating of faults" is the avoidance of impropriety.... (711.13) The "procuring of virtues" is the perfect construction (*susūtratā*) of a composition such as is achieved through adherence to genre rules (*samyaglakṣaṇayoga*) of the different kinds of literary works we will discuss. The "mixing of elements of beauty" is excellence in the arrangement of [the thematic components] of these works, such as the various descriptions of cities, oceans, and the like. (710.19ff.)

It is necessary for Bhoja next to establish the logic that allows us to comprehend the literary work as an individualized formal structure:

> With regard to that [definition of the "procuring of virtues"], a "literary work" is a sequence of words, a succession of sentences, or a series of episodes that has a specific intended meaning (*iṣṭārthavyavacchinna* [cf. Daṇḍin 1.10]). Words whether verbs or nouns are commonly used for many purposes and cannot be more narrowly specified on the strength of their mere form; sentences are no less commonly used for all kinds of activities and have no [inherent] distinction that allows us to differentiate one [use] from another; similarly, episodes—for example, the portions of poems that describe mountains, cities, oceans, and the like—are components of

> every poetic text and contain in themselves no distinctiveness (*vyatireka*). Accordingly, there must be some large meaning (*mahāvākyārtha*) above and beyond that of the individual sentences, which is made available by these [sequences, successions, and series], a definite meaning that can delimit (*avacchedahetu*) a literary text like a courtly poem, which is a totality of many [words], sentences, and episodes. This "meaning above and beyond" [the parts] "specifies"—that is to say, particularizes—the sequence of words, succession of sentences, or series of episodes, which thereby become a literary work: something like *Jānakīharaṇa* (The Abduction of Jānakī) or *Kumārasaṃbhava* (The Birth of the Divine Prince). (712.3ff.)

But the literary work is not just a totality different from other totalities in its words, sentences, and episodes. It also has a unified meaning:

> Now, the larger meaning (*mahāvākyārtha*) generated by these episodes, [in any of the three great genres], whether courtly verse epic, historical prose-poem, or [the mixed form of the drama]; with its various parts standing in a hierarchical relationship (*kṛtānyonyaviśeṣ aṇaviṣeṣyabhāva*); which is known by a name reflecting this larger meaning—*Subhadrāharaṇa* (The Abduction of Subhadrā), for example, or *Jānakīharaṇa*—is called the "penultimate unified meaning of a work of literary art" (*prabandhaikārthībhāvo 'paraḥ*). There is, however, an "ultimate unified meaning beyond the larger meaning" (*paro mahāvākhyaikārtha*). It is a particular kind of insight (*pratibhāviśeṣa*)[48] as to moral right and wrong generated in a person with innate receptivity (*upahitasaṃskāra*) by the act of contemplating the meanings of a literary work—some insight like "act like Rāma, and not like Rāvaṇa" in the case of the *Rāmāyaṇa*. This [moral consciousness] is the sole cause of attaining the four life-goals, and undergirds the cosmos. It may rightly be called the beginningless and endless perfect *śabdabrahma* transformed into the form of verbal meaning.[49] (471.16ff.)

A *prabandha* or literary work results from a connected series of sentences that make an episode, and a connected series of episodes that make a total meaning, and a total meaning that makes a moral argument. Elsewhere this series of equations is collapsed into its simplest form: "The literary work is a sentence totality that causes us to understand what we should and should not do" (*vidhiniṣedhāvagatihetuḥ mahāvākyaṃ prabandhaḥ*, p. 194.6). The fact, however, that literature has a capacity for moral communication—that the ultimate meaning of a literary text resides in a deontic statement—is grounded in a larger theory of sentence meaning. Bhoja elaborates on this definition in an important argument in Chapter Six:

> Every sentence terminates in communicating a command or a prohibition. Even where an optative [imperative, or gerundive] is not expressly used we find that they are contextually supplemental (*vākyaśeṣa*) to every sentence, since every sentence aims toward a command or a prohibition. For example, in the sentence, "Alms are readily given in this region," what is understood is [the command] "Remain here"; . . . in the sentence, "There are sharks in the water," what is understood is "Do not swim here." A "larger meaning,"[50] too, like the *Rāmāyaṇa* also communicates (*vyutpādyate*) in a similar manner: Rāma though dwelling in the forest obeyed his father's command and achieved success, whereas Rāvaṇa, though capable of victory over the whole world, lusted after another man's wife and was destroyed. Therefore, obey your father's order, do not lust after another man's wife, act like Rāma and not Rāvaṇa. (337.7ff.)

Given his view that the literary work has a unified meaning and necessarily communicates an ultimate moral commandment or prohibition, Bhoja is able more convincingly to argue the position, which after Ānanda came to be widely held, that a work as a whole has a unified overall aesthetic impact (*prabandhaviśaye rasāviyoga*). For Bhoja, this comes about especially through the "elimination of faults" by the avoidance of impropriety (*anaucityaparihāra*). One way to achieve this is to revise historical narratives. These constitute one of the five bodies of literary composition (*prabandhaśarīrāṇi*): those derived from the epics (*itihāsāśraya,* e.g., *Kumārasaṃbhava*), those derived from story literature (*kathāśraya,* e.g., the Udayana cycle), those that are pure inventions (*utpādyetivṛttam,* e.g., *Kādambarī*), those that are historical (*anutpādyetivṛtta,* e.g., *Harṣacarita*), and those, finally, whose plots stand in need of emendation (*pratisaṃskāryetivṛtta*). On the last he remarks as follows:

> If one were to compose a literary work on the basis of a story just as it is found to exist in the epics, it could come about that [one character,] though acting properly (*nyāyapravṛtteḥ*), might not only fail to attain the desired result but might attain precisely the result he does not desire; whereas [another character,] though acting improperly, might attain the result [he desires]. In such cases, emendation must be made in such a way that the character acting properly is not denied the result he desires, whereas the

> other not only should fail to attain his desire but should also attain what he does not want. Such is what [the category *pratisaṃskāryetivṛtta*] causes us to understand (*vyutpādayati*) (p. 746.7).

Bhoja offers a range of examples of literary works whose plots have been revised in the interests of removing faults and so producing a unified aesthetic experience: the *Nirdoṣadaśaratha* (Faultless Daśaratha), in which Rāma is exiled by two magical creatures imitating his father Daśaratha and his step-mother Kaikeyī; Bhavabhūti's *Mahāvīracarita* (Story of the Great Hero), in which Vālin is slain by Rāma after provoking Rāma (rather than Sugrīva) to a fight; Bhaṭṭa Nārāyaṇa's *Veṇisaṃhāra* (The Tying of the Braid), in which Duḥśāsana's blood is drunk not by Bhīma but by a demon who had taken possession of him; the *Harivaṃśa* (Lineage of Hari, a *mahākāvya*, and not the appendix to the *Mahābhārata*), in which Māyāvatī is not really the wife of the guru of her lover Pradyumna, but is represented, along with Pradyumna himself, as reincarnations of the god of love and his wife Rati; and, most famously, Kālidāsa's Śākuntala, in which it is because of Śakuntalā's insult to the sage Durvāsa that Duṣyanta is caused to forget about his relationship with her, and not because his love is inconstant.[51]

Bhoja's argument in general will be familiar to readers of Ānandavardhana:

> [A]nother means by which a work as a whole may become suggestive of *rasa* is the abandoning of a state of affairs imposed by historical reality [*itivṛttavaśāyātā sthiti*] if it fails in any way to harmonize with the *rasa*; and the introduction, by invention if need be, of incidental narrative appropriate to that rasa. This is to be carried out as it is done in the works of Kālidāsa and in the *Harivijaya* of Sarvasena and in my own *mahākāvya*, the *Arjunacarita*. A poet when writing a poem must concentrate with all his soul on the *rasa*. If he observes some state of affairs in the historical fact that goes against the *rasa*, he should eliminate it and invent some other story appropriate to the rasa. No purpose is served in a poet's providing merely the historical facts (*itivṛttamātra*). That is a task accomplished by historiography itself (*itihāsād eva*).[52]

What Bhoja and Ānanda both insist upon (and there were dissenters) represents a real and an important historical tendency.[53] Some of the texts Bhoja cites are no longer extant, but there is no reason to doubt that they all did once exist; they are no invention. The broader history of Sanskrit literary culture—we saw precisely this in the history of the idea of *rasābhāsa*—fully testifies to a progress, slow but certain, in the elimination of core varieties of conflict, a gradual retreat to an ever more complete disengagement from the world of life's unpleasant realities, in favor of a single moral vision. In literature if not in life, as Bhoja says, "It must be the good guy, not the bad guy, who wins."[54]

That the social informs the most basic architecture of Bhoja's work is equally evident in what self-avowedly constitutes his single most original contribution. As I read his treatise, Bhoja's important new insight, one informing his entire exposition, is the nature of passion itself. He argues that the forces and principles operative in what *rasaśāstra* had always called *śṛṅgāra*, the erotic or, more simply, passion, are actually found to be present as the animating principle in all affective states (common language usage shows this, he notes: people can be said to "love to quarrel, or "love to joke" p. 662.12). To this higher-order Passion (I signal it thus) Bhoja gives a variety of other names: *abhimāna* (here a highly valorized trait, something like self-confidence and self-esteem, *amour de soi* as distinguished from *amour propre*), *ahaṃkāra* (sense of self), *prema* (love), and *rasa* (in the singular). Passion is what enables people—and again, he appears to mean those people selected for representation in literary texts—to experience the world richly. It represents their capacity for emotional intensity as such, and hence may be taken as the origin of all other affective states, or *rasa*s (plural). Moreover, it is this intensity that leads them to strive to fulfil the most crucial life-needs: "Passion alone is *rasa*, [and] the sole means of fulfilling the four life-goals" (p. 5.16), identical with the kind of moral consciousness (*pratibhā*) that, as we saw above, emerges out of penultimate literary meaning.[55] In its fullest explication, Passion is shown to be understood fundamentally according to a moral typology, one that accordingly structures the interpretation of all features of the literary text.

There are four species of Passion, one relating to each of the four lifegoals, *dharma, artha, kāma,* and *mokṣa*.[56] In each of the four contexts "Passion" is defined as *abhimāna*, the confidence and drive that enable one to proceed toward the acquisition of the value in question.[57] Passion for *dharma*, for example, is illustrated by Duḥśānta's conviction, on seeing Śakuntalā, that she must be a suitable mate in terms of caste, for otherwise his noble heart would not long for her; Passion for *artha*, by Rāvaṇa's words as suitor to Janaka (from *Mahāvīracarita*) explaining the social profit the king would derive in giving him Sītā in marriage.

The entire literary work, for Bhoja, is structured in accordance with these four life-goals. For each one of the four forms of Passion a different variety of dramatic mode (*vṛtti*), costume style (*pravṛtti*), and compositional technique (*rīti*) is to be employed.[58] Most important, a different kind of protagonist (*nāyaka*) incarnates each of the four kinds of Passion. What makes us call a hero a hero is the fact of his possessing "continuity" or "stability" of character (*dhairyam*). "This is a mental attribute (*cittadharma*) that keeps the senses from perturbation. When it is present, despite his many virtues [as for instance his caste (*jāti*), which could be a source of pride, *garva*, p. 1083], arrogance (*utseka*) and the like do not arise at all." Bhoja goes on to define the four kinds of firmness that characterize the different heroes: the dignified (*udātta*) [for *dharma*-Passion], the energetic (*uddhata*) [for *artha*-Passion], the romantic (*lalita*) [for erotic-Passion], and the serene (*praśānta*) [for liberation-Passion]." In the case of the dignified hero, his kind of firmness makes for the absence of arrogance in the event of success; of anguish in the event of grief; of sadness in the event of tragedy; he never violates *dharma* out of passion, he strives for virtuous conduct, abhors vile things, shows forbearance even when he has the power to act, is patient with those who stray in error. The firmness of the energetic hero makes for pride in the event of success, anguish in the event of grief, despondency in the event of failure, the readiness even to oppose dharma because of passion (p. 1108), and so on.[59]

What is important to register here is not simply Bhoja's well-known fascination for formal analytical structures that are elegant in their symmetry but ultimately empty (the normal scholarly response). The point of all this—and Bhoja's full exposition demonstrates this—is that the varieties of Passion that make up literature, and the varieties of heroes that embody them, are all to be understood principally under the rubric of moral agency. That the hero is conceived of as moral agent, indeed nothing but moral agent, finds its most pointed expression when Bhoja discusses the narrative relationship of hero to antihero, a topic on which there had long been some uncertainty in the Sanskrit critical discourse.

One of the double figures of sound and sense (*ubhayālaṃkāra*, p. 728.11) is termed by Bhoja "adherence to the two ways" (*mārgadvayānuvartanam*). This, he explains, "makes reference to a certain literary convention followed by great poets" regarding hero and antihero. Its basis is Daṇḍin's old prescription, which Bhoja goes on to cite:

> The naturally agreeable procedure is when the poet, having first established the protagonist's virtues, has him overcome the antagonist. However, it enhances the hero's achievement if the antagonist he defeats has also been shown to be of high birth, brave, learned and the like, and this brings the reader pleasure.[60]

This contrasts with Bhāmaha's position that the poet should not, in an attempt to elevate his hero, establish the antagonist's high birth, bravery, and learning before he is destroyed. For it is futile to describe and praise a character at the beginning of a work if he is not going to be present throughout the narrative and win in the end. Here is how Bhoja adjudicates the dispute:

> It may be asked, Is the enemy whom the hero is going to destroy a virtuous or a flawed man? What difference does that make? Well, if he is flawed, his flaws are sufficient cause of his destruction. It is no achievement of manly effort to push a man into the water when he is sitting on a riverbank ready to crumble. As [Kauṭilya] says, "Like a log eaten by termites a royal family with undisciplined princes will break apart the moment it is attacked." If, on the other hand, the enemy is virtuous he should not in fact be destroyed.[61] For who would place any stock in acquiring virtues if even a virtuous man is shown to be destroyed? Furthermore, if both the hero and his enemy are equally virtuous, then it would be necessary to specify some hard and fast cause for the victory of the one and the defeat of the other—but [given their equality, ex *hypothesi*] what could that be other than fate? And if success is brought about by fate, then the hero would be engaging in no manly effort, and there would be no difference between such a hero and his antagonist.
>
> The answer to this is, first, that literary texts are meant to provide moral instruction (*vidhiniṣedhavyutpattiphalatvāt prabandhānām*). In the *Rāmāyaṇa* and similar works, by the poet's showing the pre-eminence of a virtuous

> man and the destruction of a flawed man, we are being taught to act like Rāma and not like Rāvaṇa: As Rāma obeyed his father's order and despite being exiled to the forest achieved ultimate victory, whereas Rāvaṇa, though he was capable of conquering the three worlds, was destroyed because he had lusted after another man's wife, so will it turn out for others. Such is the moral instruction of this text, and of other literary works, courtly epics and the like, composed in the same spirit.
>
> As for the other questions—i.e., what pre-eminence could accrue to a hero shown to destroy a flawed enemy who would be brought down as a matter of course; and who would place any stock in acquiring virtues if even a virtuous man is shown to be destroyed?—my answer is as follows: The antagonist's flaws are not described in connection with [the hero's] manly effort, nor his virtues as a grounds for his destruction. Quite the contrary, his flaws are described as the grounds for his destruction, and his virtues in order to magnify the hero's pre-eminence. And the grounds for the antagonist's destruction is his violation of social norms. Thus in the *purāṇas*, we see that antagonists like Hiraṇyakaśipu, who had acquired great power by worshipping the gods, were destroyed because of their cosmic evilness. The pre-eminence they possess owing to their high birth, bravery, learning, becomes in turn a source of pre-eminence for the hero who defeats them. (ŚP 741.5ff.)

This position, which for the first time a literary critic has argued out in any detail, is fundamental to the entire tradition of reading and writing Sanskrit literature, to the very end of its creative history, when Jagannātha returns to the question under the rubric of faults relating to *rasa,* arguing that the greatness of the protagonist must also be established directly, not just indirectly as a consequence of defeating someone great.[62] And the greatness of the hero is not just an aesthetic condition, but a social and a moral one.

* * *

The social thus impinges on Sanskrit literature and literary theory at every possible level. Aesthetic suggestion presupposes and reproduces social knowledge of, and correspondingly assent to, a structure of social action, and without this knowledge suggestion itself often remains all but incomprehensible. The emotional experience coded in the literary text works homologously. As the category of false feelings serves to highlight, aesthetic sentiment becomes intelligible only against a broader discourse on social sentiment. Characters act the way they do, and we may discriminate among their actions, only by a theory of socially valid and invalid emotions. That the ability of Sanskrit thinkers to theorize the social ground was completely constrained in the case of suggestion, partially so in the case of sentiment, seems to have been due, at least to some extent, to the language-philosophical and theological turn of criticism in the last quarter of the first millennium.

By contrast, the work of Bhojarāja, the last great representative of the tradition before this development became normalized, illustrates just how self-consciously literary theory could recapitulate social theory. Literature has totalizable meaning, its meaning is Passion, and Passion for its part is something understood within a conceptual framework that is entirely social-moral: that of the four life-goals, which, as Kenneth Burke might have put it, offer the strategies for action that have direct bearing on matters of human welfare. And Bhoja shows us, too, that only by going through theory, and doing so historically, can we go beyond it, to see that literature in India was conceived of not only as verbal icon or metaphysical experience, but also and eminently—even when denied—as social practice, indeed, equipment for living.[63]

Notes

1. *Saundarananda* 18.63–64 (*kāvyavyājena tattvam*, etc.); *Kāvyālaṅkāra* 1.3 (*dharmārthakāmamokṣeṣu vaicakṣaṇyam*); Aruṇagirinātha's *Prakāśikā* (twelfth century?) on *Kumārasaṃbhava* 8.92 (TSS ed. p. 327: *evaṃ nānāvidhātra prabandhe puruṣārthavyutpattir bhavati*).
2. Although in both cases the three forms of knowledge are ancient, it is only in the medieval period in India that *padavākyapramāṇa* seems to become a disciplinary unit (perhaps first in the Bhavabhūti, early eighth century, see *Uttararāmacarita*, 1 + in most mss.; from then on it is common, from e.g. Mukulabhaṭṭa, *Abhidhāvṛttimātṛkā* vs. 13, to Nīlakaṇṭha, colophon to MBh. 5.46 vulg.). The *trivium*, for its part, is a coinage of Alcuin's in the latter half of the eighth century.
3. The first extant commentarial writing is that of Prakāśavarṣa of Kashmir (fl. 950), who wrote a *Laghuṭīkā* on Bhāravi's *Kirātārjunīya* (still unpublished). He was the teacher of Vallabhadeva, who produced the first widely-circulated commentaries on the courtly poems of Kālidāsa and Māgha (references to earlier scholia are found in inscriptions from the seventh century, e.g., the

ṭīkā by King Durvinīta of the western Gaṅgas on the *citrakāvya* chapter of the *Kirātārjunīya*). Bhoja's ŚP, in the generation after Vallabha, gives evidence throughout of an intense exegetical concern with the literary classics; he also refers to commentators on Bhāravi and Kālidāsa (p. 667.9). The beginning of the second-millennium witnesses the first flowering of commentaries in other traditions, too. Maṇakkuṭavar's commentary on the *Tirukkuṛaḷ*, for example, which dates from the end of the tenth century, is the first known Tamil commentary devoted to a literary work.

4. The best account of the paradigm shift in literary theory in Kashmir and the role of mīmāṃsā is McCrea, 1997, especially Chapter Two. See also the discussion of authorial intentionality, and metaphor/metonymy in Pollock in press.
5. For this argument, see Pollock, 1998.
6. Kosambi, 1957: xlv–lxii ("The analysis must therefore derive from the class divisions of every society in which literature was cultivated," etc., p. lvii); Ingalls, 1963: 49–53 ("[Who] is more unreasonable than one who will not listen to beauty until he knows that it comes from a new economic class that advances the techniques of production?" p. 53).
7. DĀ, p. 52.
8. *vācyārthavimukhātmanām | buddhau tattvārthadarśinyāṃ jhaṭity evāvabhāsate*, DĀ 1.12.
9. Abhinava implicitly believes the mother-in-law to be present, and it is for this reason he understands *maha* as "our [bed]" (not as a royal plural, as taken by Ingalls et al., 1990: 99) (DĀ, p. 71). Mahimabhaṭṭa is explicit about her presence (*śvaśrūsaṃnidhau*, VV, p. 468). This militates against the interpretation of *ṇimajjaï* as "sleeps dead to the world" (found in other commentators), which is meant to allay the traveler's worries of being discovered, and which would hardly be used in the mother-in-law's presence.
10. DĀ, p. 76: *vācyād vibhinnaviṣayatvena vyavasthāpitaḥ*. Abhinava affirms here that in the first four verses, both the literal and implied meanings are supposed to be addressed to the same person (DĀ, p. 76).
11. Observe that Ānanda does not make clear with respect to this verse that the *vastumātra* does not itself constitute the content of the aesthetic *suggestion*. Bhoja seems to be the first to do so; see below.
12. A fact not, perhaps, fully appreciated by Ingalls et al., who only record the error ("One may correct Abhinava's comment.... Abhinava's incorrect interpretation of the verse here leads him to a farfetched hypothesis," 1990: 84; 98).
13. Bhoja adds: "Since this suggested meaning is perceived as something above and beyond the meaning of the sentence, it is the type of suggestion known as echo (*pratiśabdadhvani*) rather than the type known as reverberation (*anunādadhvani*)" (ŚP, pp. 390, 395).

14. VV, pp. 463ff. I understand-*māraṇamātrātrāsa* (for-*māraṇamātratrāsa*).
15. *Kāvyānuśāsana*, p. 47.
16. This is actually connoted, according to Ingalls et al., by the word *bhama*, which they accordingly translate "go your rounds" (1990: 83), though neither Abhinava nor Mahima heard such a connotation.
17. Mahima thinks it entirely "inappropriate" (*anucita*) to have a noble lion, fierce or not, kill a dog ("I have given this a lot of thought and still cannot figure out the poet's intention"), and in despair decides to emend the text (to "fierce bear") (p. 466).
18. KP, pp. 254ff. (note that Mammaṭa silently emends Mahima's interpretation of the verse). The implicit problem of *vyadhikaraṇatva* in Mammaṭa is addressed in the *Kamalākarī*, p. 186.
19. Ingalls et al., 1990: 104. They seem to mistranslate on p. 105: *sahasvety api ca tadviṣayaṃ vyaṅgyam* means: "The sentence 'Now you must suffer'"—i.e., swallow your anger—"contains another implication directed to the husband" (not, "There is also a suggestion that he must suffer"). Abhinava's usage of *vyaṅgya* here is loose, as Bhoja shows in what follows.
20. ŚP, p. 395. Bhoja adds, "This is suggestion of the echo type [rather than the reverberation type] because what is meant as admonition [about bees] for one person [the wife] produces its effect [about her fidelity], contrarily, in the mind of another [the husband]" (*anyopadeśaparatvena pravṛtto 'nyasya cetasi pratiphalitaḥ*).
21. KP, p. 72. The seeds of Mammaṭa's system are found in the work of his teacher, Mukulabhaṭṭa, see *Abhidhāvṛttamātṛkā*, pp. 24 (*kārikā*) and 31–41 (*vṛtti*). I thank Lawrence McCrea for this reference.
22. Or contemporary western theory. A literary application of speech-act theory, for instance, might help make more precise the perspectival shift whereby one sort of speech act is transformed into another. (Thus a constative utterance, a statement of something's being true or false, becomes really a performative of the illocutionary sort, seeking to bring about a new state of affairs—to stop the mendicant from wandering along the Godāvarī river—and not to make a statement about the wild kingdom or any such thing.) But that, I believe, is about as far as such an analysis is going to take us. For a suggestive exposition see Hanks, 1992: 99ff. (on Grice's "conversational implicatures"), who makes the important point that "Literal meaning is defeasible: If you alter the situation of utterance, the literal meaning of the form will change" (p. 108).
23. Indeed, sometimes as a "speculative paradigm for theology," see Gerow, 1994. What follows here is a historical critique, not a philosophical evaluation, of Abhinava's aesthetic. To measure just how sophisticated this is, one need only compare the relatively simplistic solutions to the same problem that the best in contemporary aesthetics has to offer, e.g., Feagin, 1997.

24. Ingalls et al., 1990: 111; 37. For some general remarks on the topic of *rasābhāsa*, see also Krishnamoorthy, 1974 and Bhattacharya, 1935.
25. I can be brief here, since I have set forth my understanding of the problem at length in Pollock, 1998.
26. I ignore here less consequential views that invested the actor with *rasa*, or the poet. The first is quickly dismissed. The second remains in play as a supplementary position, though for some it is the principal, thus Rājaśekhara (see *Kāvyamīmāṃsā*, pp. 45ff., especially p. 46.8: it is the expressions of the poet, not the characters, that have or do not have *rasa*; whatever the *rūpa* of the thing itself, the fact of its having *rasa* or not is dependent on the particular talents of the poet).
27. Abhinava discusses the history of the idea of *rasa* in various places; I cite from DĀ, p. 184. The one time Ānanda actually mentions the locus of *rasa* he identifies it as the character or the narrative voice (p. 318). Ingalls et al. note the difference between him and his commentator (1990: 18–19; especially p. 413: "It is perfectly clear that Ānanda is here using *rasa* in its old sense of a particularly vivid emotion . . . not in the new sense established by Abhinava, of aesthetic delight"), but the implications of this difference are not developed in their work.
28. See in general Pollock, 1998: 117–142; and for Abhinava in particular, NŚ, p. 279.
29. The term is first used in Udbhaṭa (see below), but his own views on *rasa* are hard to work out. He describes *rasavat* as "[a trope] in which the rise of *rasas* is clearly displayed" ("that is, by which *rasa* is manifested, *āvirbhāvaḥ*, in a clear form," says Indurāja, p. 58), suggesting strongly that *rasa* for him is in the hero. Indurāja accordingly comments, on the example quoted, that "Śiva's *śṛṅgāra* is set forth literarily" ([*upa*]*nibaddhaḥ*) (on 4.3–4).
30. NŚ, p. 289; DĀ, pp. 78–79.
31. A remarkable recent account of varieties of analysis (philosophical, moral and so on) of the emotions is de Sousa, 1987.
32. Ingalls et al., 1990: 37.
33. ŚP, p. 665.12ff. For *rasābhāsa* as ornament, see p. 666.3ff. and p. 693.15. The expression of passion on the part of animals becomes a stock example of *rasābhāsa*, despite the fact that the "grief" of a krauñca hen lies at the origin of Sanskrit poetry (or at least is the cause of the real grief in the poet that lies at the origin of poetry, *Rāmāyaṇa* 1.2.9ff.). Yet some later thinkers rejected the view that the causal factors of *rasa*, including primary feelings, do not apply to animals, and accordingly they are said to have *rasa* (so Vidyādhara and Bhīmasena Dīkṣita, cited in Bhattacharya, 1935: 241). Considerably less discussed was the question whether a *mleccha* can be the site of *rasa* (this is denied by Vidyānātha, *Pratāparudrīya*, p. 60).

34. Moreover, thinkers after Abhinava increasingly found his views on *rasābhāsa* problematic. Thus Viśvanātha, while unequivocally accepting the view that *rasa* is located in the reader, rejected the his account of the cognitive status of its semblance form. For Viśvanātha, *rasābhāsa* is simply *rasa* (*Sāhityadarpaṇa* 3.260).
35. Even in its own terms I can make little cultural-historical sense of Abhinava's argument that readers realize a *rasa* to be *ābhāsa* only at the conclusion of the literary event, whereas in the course of it they experience it as *rasa*. In what sense would any traditional Indian experiencing the *Rāmāyaṇa* believe Rāvaṇa's feelings for Sītā to be not an *ābhāsa*, that is, to be in some sense "valid" (as Sanskrit culture understands that phrase) prior to the point of narrative closure? Surely we are aware from the start that it is a counterfeit, ultimately failed affect—real desire (*rati*), no doubt (though again Abhinava calls it *ratyābhāsa*), but false love (*śṛṅgāra*).
36. NŚ prose after 6.45, p. 295. Bhoja brings out the full implication of this in the *Sarasvatīkaṇṭhābharaṇa*: *śṛṅgārabhāsa* will always result in the case of a low character (*hīnapātra*), an animal, the antagonist (*nāyakapratiyogi*), as well as in cases of anthropomorphism (p. 477; see also Krishnamoorthy, 1974: 125–129). Given that Bharata's definition of *rasa* is itself social, the view of some commentators that *rasābhāsa* lies in a failure to accord with the definition of *rasa* is really identical with the view that it lies in a violation of social norms, which therefore does not constitute an opposed position (*pace* Bhattacharya, 1935).
37. *Kāvyālaṅkārasārasaṃgraha* 4.5–6. The sentence "*Rasa* is that specific kind . . ." is cited anonymously by Indurāja ad loc. (it is not known to Tilaka). The four types of literary text, *rasakāvya, bhāvakāvya, rasābhāsakāvya*, and *samhāhitakāvya* (this last is where a break occurs in the continuity of *rasa* because the intensity of the *vāsanā* of the prior *rasa* inhibits any other from manifesting itself, see Indurāja on 4.8) are equated with the older categories (cf. *Alaṅkārarasarvasva* cited in *Pratāparudrīya*, p. 208: *rasabhāvatadābhāsatat praśamananibandhane rasavatpreyaūrjasvisamāhitāni*).
38. I am not altogether certain about the last phrase: *svakalpanāparikalpitatvena*.
39. For a brief historical overview of the category see Raghavan, 1942. He argues that, although the term *aucitya* is first used in literary discourse only in Yaśovarman's early eighth-century play, the *Rāmābhyudaya* (lost), and in literary-critical discourse first in Rudraṭa's (probably early ninth century) *Kāvyālaṅkāra*, the concept is already implicit in the NŚ (pp. 205, 209ff., 198). In the case of the *Aucityavicāracarcā*, too, if its analytical focus is certainly novel, it seems to me to enunciate a great deal that is implicit in earlier thinking.
40. See *Autcityavicāracarcā* vss. 8–10 for the programmatic statement, and, on *rasa* in particular, vss. 3, 4, 5 + prose, vs. 6 + prose. I noted above that both

Ānanda and Abhinava take *rasa* and *autcitya* to be intimately related (and *rasābhāsa* and *anaucitya*); see also DĀ 3.15 and 3.32; so *Vakroktijīvita kārikā* 53 and 54.

41. Jagannātha asks whether the term *rasābhāsa* is a *karmadhāraya* compound ("It is *rasa* and an *ābhāsa*"): "One view holds it cannot be such because once a thing is a mere semblance, it ceases to be what it was, as in *hetvābhāsa* [a mere semblance of a good reason, a non-reason or logical fallacy]. On the second view, the essence of a thing is not lost just because it has some flaws: we can call an old horse a 'pale shadow of a horse' (*aśvābhāsa*) without its thereby ceasing to be a horse' (RG, pp. 118–119). Jagannātha seems to accept the second view.
42. The *-ādi* (in *vibhāvādau*) seems impossible to me, since it is precisely the additional factors, notably the *sthāyibhāva*, that are under examination.
43. Krishnamoorthy (1974: 135) errs in ascribing a similar passage to Govinda Thakur; the passage he cites is actually Vaidyanāth Tatsat's paraphrase of Jagannātha.
44. At one point Jagannātha seems to suggest the opposite when discussing what is suggested in a verse depicting Draupadī's glances at her five new (or soon-to-be) husbands. The *navyās*, he tells us, consider this is a case of *rasābhāsa* because the objects of her desire are multiple, whereas the *prāñcas* restricted the *ābhāsa* of *śṛṅgāra* to a case of multiple lovers to whom the woman is not married (p. 121). Whatever else this observation might mean, Jagannātha apparently saw his social world as discontinuous from that of the past; the scope of "impropriety" has changed. On the distinction between "new" and "old" scholars in the intellectual history of seventeenth-century India, see Pollock, 2001.
45. DĀ 3.10–14 (trans. Ingalls et al., pp. 428, 432); NŚ, p. 305, and especially p. 265: *arthaḥ prayojanaṃ ca prītipurassaraṃ vyutpattimayam* ("The 'meaning' [of poetry] also signifies its purpose, which is moral instruction through a pleasurable experience").
46. As Viśvanātha puts it (p. 5), *caturvargaprāptir hi kāvyato . . . supratītaiva* ("It is perfectly well known that poetry enables us to achieve the four life-goals").
47. ŚP, p. 405.10ff.; see Pollock, 1998: 140.
48. *Pratibhā*, along with *bhāvanā* and *vidhi*, constitute for Bhoja the three types of sentence-meanings (p. 336, defined p. 339).
49. Note that, whereas Bhoja employs the *brahma* metaphor to capture the core of moral insight, Bhaṭṭa Nāyaka likens the experience of *rasa* with that of *brahma* as negating awareness (*parabrahmāsvādasabrahmacāritvam . . . rasāsvādasya* (cited by Abhinava, DĀ, p. 190). So later writers such as Viśvanātha: *vedyāntarasparśaśūnyo brahmāsvādasahodara*□ (["*Rasa*], emptied of

all contact with other objects of cognition, is akin to the taste of the *brahma*") (*Sāhityadarpaṇa* 3.2)

50. I am assuming the reading *mahākāvyaiḥ* is an error for *mahāvākyaiḥ*.
51. ŚP, p. 711. The *Chalitarāma* (lost), *Tāpasavatsarāja*, and *Vikrāntaśūdraka* (lost) are adduced as further revisions of the *Rāmāyaṇa*, *Svapnavāsavadattā*, and legends associated with King Śūdraka. Similar questions are discussed in *Vakroktijīvitā*, pp. 249–251. Kuntaka sees the invention of the new plot rather as enhancing the requirements of *rasa* than removing a moral impropriety; but of course, these are two sides of the same coin.
52. Somewhat different is the translation by Ingalls et al., 1990: 435. 53.
53. A school of thought represented by the king-poet Yaśovarman of the eight-century that insisted on "no departure from the [received] story" (*kathāmārge na cātikramaḥ*) (cited by both Bhoja [p. 711], and Ānanda [3.14, p. 335], but with no indication that they saw a discrepancy).
54. ŚP, p. 728.24: *jigīṣuṇā guṇavataiva bhāvyaṃ na doṣavatā*.
55. Abhinava discusses the relationship of *rasa*s with the purposes of man in NŚ, pp. 275–276
56. A particularly unfortunate lacuna in the text occurs at the beginning of Chapter 13 (p. 840), where these categories are first discussed. To what degree Bhoja is indebted to earlier thinking on this subject is unclear. He surely knew NŚ 18.72ff. (GOS ed.) (*śṛṅgāraḥ kartavyo dharme cārthe ca kāme ca*, etc., even if he nowhere cites the verses, cf. Raghavan, 1963: 455), though Bharata is interested only in the different motivations of love, and Bhoja's understanding of the four types of Passion, as the full array of his illustrations shows, is far more capacious. For an account of the abiding structure of the *trivarga* and *caturvarga* amid the manifold ramifications in traditional Indian thought, along with some of the few coherent reflections on Bhoja's analysis here, see Malamoud, 1982, especially pp. 46ff.
57. *tatra* [sc., *dharme*] *pravartamānasya tadavāptyabhimāno dharmaśṛṅgāraḥ* (p. 1079); [*up*]*āyataḥ pravṛttau tadavāptyabhimāno 'rthaśṛṅgārah*. (p. 1106); *tadanukūlyāṃ pravṛttau tadupāyānatikrameṇaitadanubhavābhimāno kāṃaśṛṅgāraḥ* (p. 1144); *tadadhigamayogyatābhimāno mokṣaśṛṅgāraḥ*. (p. 1177). For the first phrase, *tadavāptyabhimāno* is my conjecture for the *tarākhyān* (?) [sic] *atimāno* of Raghavan's edition; for the last, *tadadhigamayogyatābhimāno* is my conjecture for *tadadhiga-* <lacuna> *tābhimāno* (cf. p. 840.2).
58. For dharma, *bhāratī vṛtti, paurastyā pravṛtti, pāñcāī rīti* (p. 1080); for artha: *ārabhaṭī vṛtti, uḍhramāgadhī pravṛtti*, and *gauḍīyā rīti* (p. 1106); for kāma, *kaiṣikī vṛtti, dākṣiṇātyā pravṛtti*, and vaidarbhī rīti (p. 1144); for mokṣa, *sāttvikī vṛtti, āvantyā pravṛtti*, and *lāṭiyā rīti* (p. 1178).
59. ŚP, p. 917 (cf. 746.10 and 1083) for the general account of *dhairya*; the four heroic types are discussed on pp. 1083, 1108, 1145, and 1180 respectively.

60. *Kāvyādarśa* 1.21–22; cf. Ratnaśrī, who makes it clear that Daṇḍin accepts the *prakāradvayam* (p. 14).
61. Hereafter (ŚP, 741.9–11) is printed what to my eyes is a clear dittography (from *nāyakasya ... na doṣaḥ*). I conjecture: *tasyānucchedyatvāt* followed by ko hi. For *puruṣārthaviṣayatvena* (line 20) we should read *puruṣakāra-*.
62. RG, pp. 62–63.
63. Burke, 1973: 296, 304.

Works Cited

Primary Sources

Abhidhāvṛttamātṛkā of Mukulabhaṭṭa. Edited by Revaprasad Dvivedi. Vidybhavana Samskrta Granthamala, 1973.

Aucityavicāracarcā of Kṣemendra. Edited by Brajmohan Jha. Caukhambha Orientalia, 1982.

Dhvanyāloka (DĀ) of *Ānandavardhana with the Locana of Abhinavagupta*. Edited by Pattabhirama Shastri. Chowkhamba Sanskrit Series Office, 1940.

Kāvyānuśāsana of Hemacandra. Edited by Rasiklal C. Parikh and V. M. Kulkarni. Sri Mahavira Jaina Vidyalaya, 1964.

Kāvyalakṣaṇa [= *Kāvyādarśa*] *of Daṇḍin*. Edited by A. Thakur and Upendra Jha. Mithila Institute, 1957.

Kāvyaprakāṣa (KP) of *Mammaṭa*. Edited by Vamanacharya Jhalkikar. Bhandarkar Oriental Research Institute, 1965.

Kamalākarī, the commentary of Bhaṭṭa Kamalākara on the Kāvyaprakāśa. Edited by Babulal Shukla. Nag Prakashan, 1995.

Nāṭyaśāstra (NŚ) of Bharata, with the commentary of Abhinavagupta, Vol. 1. Edited by K. Krishnamoorthy. Oriental Institute, 1992.

Pratāparudrīya of Vidyānātha. Edited by V. Raghavan. The Samskrit Education Society, 1979.

Rasagaṇgādhara (RG) of Paṇḍitarāja Jagannātha. Edited by Mathuranath Shastri. Nirnaya Sagara Press, 1939.

Sāhityadarpaṇa of Viśvanātha. Edited by Durgaprasad. Bombay: Nirnaya Sagara Press, 1988.

Sarasvatīkaṇṭhābharaṇalaṅkara of Bhoja. Edited by Kedarnath Sarma and Wasudev *Laxman Sastri Pansikar*. Nirnaya Sagara Press, 1934.

Śṛṅgāraprakāśa (S'P) of Bhoja. Edited by V. Raghavan. Harvard University Press, 1998.

Vakroktijīvitā of Kuntaka. Edited by K. Krishnamoorthy. Karnataka University Press, 1977.

Vyaktiviveka (VV) of Mahimabhaṭṭa. Edited by Rewaprasad Dvivedi. Chaukhambha Sanskrit Sansthan, 1982.

Secondary Sources

Bhattacharya, Siva Prasad. 'Rasābhāsa in Alaṃkāra Literature', Calcutta Oriental Journal 2(7): 237–247, 1935.

Burke, Kenneth. *The Philosophy of Literary Form*. Berkeley: University of California Press, 1973.

de Sousa, Ronald. *The Rationality of Emotion*. Cambridge, MA: MIT Press, 1987.

Feagin, Susan L. 'The Pleasures of Tragedy', in Susan Feagin and Patrick Maynard (eds.), Aesthetics, pp. 305–313. Oxford: Oxford University Press, 1997.

Gerow, Edwin. 'Abhinavagupta's Aesthetics as a Speculative Paradigm', Journal of the American Oriental Society 114(2): 186–208, 1994.

Ingalls, Daniel H. H. *An Anthology of Well-Turned Verse: Vidyākara's Subhāṣitaratnakoṣa*. Harvard University Press, 1963.

Ingalls, Daniel H. H., Jeffrey Moussaieff Masson and M. V. Patwardhan. The *Dhvanyāloka of Ānandavardhana with the Locana of Abhinavagupta*. Cambridge, Harvard University Press, 1990.

Hanks, William F. Language and Communicative Practices. Westview, 1996.

Kosambi, D. D., and V. V. Gokhale. *The Subhāṣitaratnakoṣa*. Harvard University Press, 1957.

Krishnamoorthy, K. 'The Concept of Rasābhāsa in Sanskrit Literary Theory', in Essays in Sanskrit Literary Criticism, pp. 114–136, 1974 Dharwar: Karnatak University Press.

Malamoud, Charles. 'On the Rhetoric and Semantics of puruṣārtha', in T.N. Madan (ed.), Way of Life: King, Householder, Renouncer, Essays in honour of Louis Dumont, pp. 33–54. Delhi: Vikas, 1982.

McCrea, Lawrence. *The Teleology of Poetry in Medieval Kashmir*. Doctoral dissertation, University of Chicago, 1997.

Pollock, Sheldon. 'Bhoja's *Śṛṅgāraprakāṣa* and the Problem of Rasa: A Historical Introduction and Translation', Asiatische Studien/ Ètudes asiatiques 70(1): 117–192, 1998.

Pollock, Sheldon. 'New Intellectuals in Seventeenth-Century India', in Nita Kumar (ed.), The Dilemma of the Indian Intellectual. Special number of the Indian Economic and Social History Review 38(1): 3–31, 2001; and in book form, Beverly Hills/New Delhi: Sage.

Pollock, Sheldon (in press). 'Sanskrit Literature from the Inside Out, in Sheldon Pollock (ed.), Literary Cultures in History: Reconstructions from South Asia. Berkeley: University of California Press.

Raghavan, V. "The History of Aucitya in Sanskrit Poetics," in *Some Concepts of Alaṃkāraśāstra*. Adyar Library, 1942.

Raghavan, V. Bhoja's *Śṛṅgāraprakāśa*. Punarvasu, 1963.

2

What is New and What is Navya

Sanskrit Poetics on the Eve of Colonialism

Yigal Bronner

A remarkable trend of innovation seems to characterize Sanskrit Poetics on the eve of colonialism. Like intellectuals in other Sanskritic disciplines, *ālaṃkārikās*—from about mid-sixteenth-century onward—adopted a new discursive idiom, composed in novel genres, demonstrated a fresh interest in the history of their tradition, and worked across disciplines at a hitherto unknown rate. Moreover, they often had a clear sense of themselves as breaking new ground and were thus conceived by their colleagues. But of what exactly did their innovations consist? The new poeticians may have identified themselves and their fellows as new (*navya*) in contrast to their antecedents (*prācīna*), an act which, as Sheldon Pollock puts it, "appears to signify not just a different relationship with the past but a different way of thinking."[1] Yet they seldom presented their theories as innovative, let alone as general theoretical breakthroughs, and mostly worked from within the conceptual frameworks of their predecessors. Indeed, many modern scholars see their work as simply redundant. One Indologist maintains that by the sixteenth century "the age of really original or thoughtful writers was long gone by."[2]

The utter discrepancy between the emic sense of innovation emanating from the works of post-sixteenth century *ālaṃkārikas* and the etic evaluation of them as superfluous, is of less interest to me here. Modern judgments stem more from a biased picture of the history of Sanskrit poetics, with the ninth-century thinker Ānandavardhana as its only apex, than from a careful and impartial examination of the late-precolonial texts. Far more interesting is the fact that even to a sympathetic reader, the sense of novelty is rarely accompanied by the ability easily to detect innovative agendas. New statements are often in the form of answers to age-old questions, and they are commonly grounded in some older-day view. Indeed, the new *ālaṃkārika*s invoke and discuss the views of the "ancients" more often than ever before, and in ways not seen earlier—a novel practice which concomitantly leads to a confusing sense of *déjà vu*. In short, what novelty actually meant to poeticians of the period, and how it was related to a newly shaped interest in their tradition's past, are highly complex questions for which no ready-made answer can be found.

Moreover, as soon as we ask the question of what is neoteric in late precolonial *alaṃkāraśāstra*, this discipline's unique history and specific concerns immediately give rise to further complications. I shall briefly consider these here, even at the obvious risk of opening up more questions than I can possibly answer in this short paper. This is because the complexity of the general investigation must be borne in mind before a smaller set of case-studies can be examined.

Three unique aspects of *alaṃkāraśāstra* merit mention here. First, it has an exceptionally multifaceted nature. This tradition never possessed a core *sūtra* text of unquestioned authority, nor commentaries and subcommentaries branching out from it, which would have created distinct schools of clear ancestry. In the earlier period (mid-seventh to mid-ninth centuries), we find several unsuccessful attempts to compose such core texts, each taking a somewhat different approach and rarely engaging in direct conversation with one another. The groundbreaking thesis of Ānandavardhana (c. 850)—declaring that suggestion is poetry's soul and that all other poetic phenomena are subordinate to it—provoked a serious controversy lasting roughly two centuries. Thereafter, the universal acceptance of Ānanda's thesis was not accompanied by a uniform practice of "Ānanda poetics." On the contrary, between the twelfth and sixteenth centuries we find an explosion of topics (those stemming from Ānanda's thesis along with more traditional ones), discussions (some supra-local, others regional), and genres of composition. This great variety, which itself has not yet been fully charted, certainly complicates our search for new tendencies in the later period.

Secondly, there is the potential openendedness of the discipline's subject-matter. For *Mīmāṃsā*, the paradigmatic text-oriented *śāstra*, the Vedas are a fixed corpus. But Sanskrit literature, to which *alaṃkāraśāstra* relates—however obliquely—continued to evolve and reinvent itself throughout the period of early modernity. Did contemporaneous trends in practice of poetry have an impact on the new practice of theory?

Finally, unlike other systems of knowledge, *alaṃkāraśāstra* did not remain the monopoly of Sanskrit: By the sixteenth century there were *alaṃkāra*-like discourses in many South Asian languages, which borrowed, adapted and modified Sanskritic notions. Did the regional discussions leave any imprint on the Sanskritic one, or was the direction of the influence always from the cosmopolitan to the vernacular?

As I have already mentioned, I cannot address all of these questions here, but they should be kept in mind as we turn to discuss the question of novelty in *navya-alaṃkāraśāstra*. This we shall do by examining the works of three key scholars who, between them, cover almost the entire time-span of new scholasticism: the South-Indian polymath Appayya Dīkṣita (1520–1593[3]), Banaras's highly prominent thinker and poet Jagannātha Paṇḍitarāja (c. 1650), and the prolific, Almora-based writer Viśveśvara Bhaṭṭa (c. 1725). As I believe Appayya's discussion exerted great influence on those of his successors, the first and larger portion of my paper will be devoted to an exploration of a small selection of his writing. I shall then turn to discuss more briefly the contributions of Jagannātha and Viśveśvara in its light.

Appayya Dīkṣita's Contribution to Alaṃkāraśāstra

Tradition has ascribed to Appayya 108 books in various disciplines—obviously a rounded-up figure, but one which is nonetheless indicative of his immense productivity. Three of these are dedicated to poetics, the earliest of which is probably a small work titled "The Exposition of Linguistic Powers" (*Vṛttivārttikā*), which sets out to explain and distinguish between the denotative and figurative operations of poetic language.[4] This treatise belongs to a relatively minor sub-genre of Sanskrit literary theory dedicated to a general overview of linguistic capacities in poetry.[5] It has been the least influential of his contributions to the discipline of poetics, although the book does much more than recapitulate old arguments.

His second work, "The Joy of the Water Lily" (*Kuvalayānanda*), is a manual meant to familiarize beginners with one of the basic subjects of the field: the sense-based figures of speech (*arthālaṃkāras*).[6] Although this work is of rather limited scope—setting aside, as it does, all other topics of the discipline—and despite its commentarial nature—it claims to supply illustrations in verse and brief explanations in prose of definitions already found in the earlier *Candrāloka* of Jayadeva—Appayya's "Joy" quickly became the most popular *alaṃkāra* textbook in the subcontinent, a status it retains even today. In fact, the "Joy" became something like *alaṃkāraśāstra*'s number one "bestseller." Major manuscript collections often possess more copies of this work than of any other treatise in the field.[7] Although the rate at which the work gained such popularity has yet to be investigated, my guess is that this happened rather rapidly.[8] It seems that within a generation after Appayya's death most scholars interested in speech-figures were familiar with his primer, and the majority of later *ālaṃkārikas* were introduced to the field by studying it. However, the reasons for the work's amazing success have never been explored.

The immense popularity of *The Joy* notwithstanding, Appayya's main contribution to the field of poetics is his unfinished magnum opus, "The Investigation of the Colorful" (*Citramīmāṃsā*). This in-depth interrogation of the same sense-based speech-figures, which he merely introduced in his primer, had a remarkable influence on later writings. To a large extent, the post-Appayya debate in Sanskrit poetics takes up the discussion begun in the *Investigation*, either in the form of approval or disapproval. It therefore seems only reasonable to examine a section from this work for the purposes of the present study.

Defining the Simile: Appayya's Refutation of Earlier Formulations

I have selected the discourse on the simile–the very first *alaṃkāra* Appayya turns to, and one which he discusses at great length. For Appayya, like so many before him, the simile, or *upamā* (fem.), is the prototype *alaṃkāra*. He thus envisions it as "the one and only actress on the stage of poetry, who delights the heart of those who know her, by assuming variegated roles."[9] While Appayya is not the first to grant such a status to the simile, he seems to take this idea further than his predecessors and seriously to entertain its logical implications.

He likens the status of the *upamā* in the figurative realm of to that of brahman in the phenomenal world. Just as one understands reality in its totality (*viśvam*) by understanding its only source and cause, the brahman, so one can only grasp the entire figurative domain (*citram*) by knowing the simile. This being the nature of the *upamā*, it merits the most thorough exploration—one which includes all of its types and subtypes (*nikhilabhedasahitā*).[10]

As a result, Appayya's exploration of the simile is matchlessly comprehensive and thorough. While the *upamā* was by no means a neglected topic before him, no thinker had dedicated so much space and energy to its analysis. His unique meditation on the simile and the crucial status he himself grants it, make it a particularly important case-study for his overall contribution to Sanskrit poetics.

Two surprises await the reader at the outset of the *Investigation*'s simile section. The first is the lack of a definition. Until Appayya's intervention, there had been a universally respected, unwritten rule in *alaṃkāraśāstra*, that when one introduces a figure of speech one does so by defining it. Appayya departs from this millennium-long tradition, thereby sending a message: The definition of the quintessential *alaṃkāra* is not yet in our possession, nor can it be easily extracted from the work of previous thinkers. A definition, in other words, can by no means act as the starting point of the discussion, but rather must serve as its end, and it soon becomes clear that it has to be arrived at through a fairly elaborate process.

This process is the second surprise. In his work's introduction, Appayya states that his definitions (*lakṣaṇa*s) and illustrations (*lakṣya*s) are mostly those given by the "ancients" (*prācīna*).[11] But as soon as his discussion begins, we learn that it consists first and foremost of *refuting* the definitions of these "ancients."

Indeed, Appayya examines five definitions (one anonymous, the others by Mammaṭa, Vidyānātha, Bhoja and Ruyyaka), and each is shown to be ill-conceived. The main concern of Appayya's five antecedents was to characterize the simile in order to distinguish it from various figures which closely resemble it. Yet Appayya is skeptical precisely about their success in setting the simile aside from its "kin."

We will sample one small section from Appayya's lengthy procedure, where he criticizes the renowned Andhra-based thinker Vidyānātha

(c. 1300). Vidyānātha defines the simile as "a singularly expressed, substantial similarity, which the entity being described shares with a separate, approved and self-established entity."[12] At first, Appayya seems to approve of this definition, closely following Vidyānātha's own exposition.[13] Thus, we are told, the stipulation that the similarity must be with a *separate* entity rules out *ananvaya,* that is, a comparison of an entity to itself (e.g. the battle of Rāma and Rāvaṇa is like that of Rāma and Rāvaṇa). Likewise, the modifier expressed eliminates over-extension with respect to suggested similes. The word substantial eliminates a possible overlap with *śleṣa,* where the similarity pertains to the language used to describe the entities rather than to the entities themselves. The demand that the other entity be self-established does away with *utprekṣā,* where the object of comparison is not real but imagined (e.g. the king is like the moon come down to earth).

Yet none of these neat distinctions, maintains Appayya, can withstand serious scrutiny. Take, for instance, the stipulation that in a simile, the tenor has to be measured against a standard *separate* from it, unlike in an *ananvaya,* where the tenor and the standard are the same. Appayya undermines this adjective, *separate,* gradually, first citing Kālidāsa's famous description of Mt. Himālaya:

> Source of unending treasures, none of his splendor
> is lessened at all by the snow.
> A single fault will vanish under a mass of virtues,
> as the spot on the moon is lost in rays of light.[14]

Appayya's point has to do with the comparison in the latter half of the verse. This is clearly a simile, yet, according to Appayya, Vidyānātha's definition cannot apply to it. The moon's spot and rays are particular instances of the more general categories of faults and virtues respectively. And since a specimen cannot be said to be separate from its class, Vidyānātha's provision of a similarity "with a *separate* entity" fails to apply to this instance.

Now this may seem like a rather cheap shot. Indeed, Appayya concedes that there may be a way to distinguish between what appears to be an inseparable pair of a specimen and its category, and allows his imagined opponent to suggest one. The interlocutor appears to be a logician, as his *navyanyāya* jargon reveals. The simile's standard (*upamāna*), he argues, is an entity delimited by the delimiting characteristic (*avachedaka*) of "standardness," whereas the simile's tenor (*upameya*) has an altogether different delimiting characteristic, namely "tenorship." What we have here, then, are not a class and a specimen but two different groups: faults (the tenor), of which faultiness is the delimiting characteristic, and the moon's spot (the standard), of which "spotness" is the defining factor. These two groups are mutually exclusive, and in that sense *separate*.[15]

But this interpretation of the definition's word "separate" leads to a new difficulty. For now the definition cannot extend to include chain-similes (*raśanopamā*), such as the one found in the second part of the following praise of a king:

> You who have hordes of petitioners drenched in water,
> poured on your hand, when you give away endless gold,
> your mind is equal with your speech, your action with your mind,
> your fame with your action, in being utterly spotless.[16]

In this chain of equations, 'mind' is the tenor of the first clause (mind equals speech), and then the standard of the second (action equals mind). So it is impossible to say that here the delimiting characteristic of the tenor ("tenorship") and the delimiting characteristic of the standard ("standardness") are mutually exclusive.

Again, this may seem to be a rather specious argument. Obviously, the delimiting feature of the standard separates it from the tenor in *its own clause*. In other words, there is no problem with the definition if every "link" in the chain of similes is taken *individually*. But as Appayya reminds us, this would force the interlocutor to concede that the adverb "singularly" in Vidyānātha's definition is redundant, since its role is taken up by the full import of the adjective "separate."[17]

Now comes the main argument. Let us accept that the word "separate" posits the standard and the tenor as two mutually exclusive entities in a single clause. There are still similes in which the very same entity serves as *both* the tenor and the standard, and which are nonetheless not considered *ananvayas*. Take, for example, the following verse:

> The Thousand-Rayed Sun holds his bright parasol for him,
> newly crafted by Tvaṣṭṛ.

Its sloping rim of cloth nearly touches his crest,
so as to make him appear like the One on whose head the Gaṅgā is falling.[18]

Here Śiva with a bright parasol, the rim of which nearly touches his head, is compared to his own self at the moment river Gaṅgā fell on his locks. The verse is understood to express similarity between the two iconic representations of Śiva, and not to imply that Śiva is beyond comparison. This is therefore not an *ananvaya* but a simile. But since Śiva cannot be said to be separate from his own self, this is a simile which Vidyānātha's definition fails to include.

The definition likewise falls short with respect to the following example:

Knocking on door after door, a beggar,
preaches the following rather than plead:
"Don't give, and you'll be like me,
give, and you'll be like yourself!"[19]

In the last portion of this ironic stanza, the beggar's addressee is compared to his own self. Here, as above, argues Appayya, the standard and the tenor cannot be said to be mutually exclusive, even if one uses the *navyanyāya* idiom. And as the adjective "separate" does not allow this example into the domain of the simile—where it belongs—the definition (*lakṣaṇa*) fails to delimit the defined phenomenon (*lakṣya*) in its entirety.

One could argue with Appayya on this issue, as did many in the generations to follow. One could say, for instance, that in the above verse the tenor and the standard are indeed separate in time, location and so forth. But one also has to admit that Appayya raises a nontrivial point. He demonstrates that not all of the similes consist of easily separable entities, such as the stock face and moon. Rather, there seems to be a continuum of separateness among entities in poetic propositions. On one end we find sets of highly distinct entities, while on the other there are pairs of self-same entities. In between these two extremes, we find a whole gamut of relatedness: a type is compared to its own specimen, an entity is both a tenor and a standard (in a chain of similes), and a person is compared to his/her own future or past self. Appayya maintains that the language used by Vidyānātha fails to draw the line which is meant to break up this continuum and distinguish between a simile and an *ananvaya*. The adjective "separate" is simply too insensitive; it is a crude *lakṣaṇa* which betrays the intricacy of its *lakṣya*.

Arriving at a Definition

Appayya examines virtually *every word* in each of the five definitions he cites. No matter how hard thinkers tried to craft their *lakṣaṇas*, meticulously choosing their words, Appayya demonstrates that they failed to accurately delimit the simile. So perhaps such precision in the description of speech-figures cannot be achieved? Maybe the poetic landscape is so intricate and dense that for any definition there will always be an exception or counter-example; maybe each solution only generates new difficulties? Indeed, Appayya concludes his long section of refutation by plainly stating that the "definition of the simile [in such a way that is free of faults] is impossible (*durvacam*)."[20]

This is a shocking conclusion. The discipline's bread and butter had always been the identification and characterization of distinct speechfigures. Can it not define its most paradigmatic trope? Despite his statement, though, Appayya is not really willing to give up. He does come up with a definition, but one which is very different from anything the tradition had seen in over a thousand years. A simile, he says, is "the act of comparison, if intended up to the full completion of the action."[21]

That is all there is: a brief and cryptic statement which appears to explain nothing. Upon first reading, there is a strong feeling of anticlimax—the definition seems to amount to little more than a tautology. However, a closer inspection reveals it to be subtler. It consists, we realize, of two parts. First, the simile is purposely characterized rather inclusively as an *act of comparison*, or a "description of similarity" (*sādṛśyavarṇana*), of any kind.[22] Why try and specify the simile formally, when *any* description of similarity may fall under its scope? A simile may entail either substantial or insubstantial similitude, its entities may be clearly separate or one and the same, contextual or extraneous to the context, repeated once or twice. A simile is a description of similarity which cannot be limited by any of these formal considerations.

The first part of Appayya's stanza thus supplies a necessary requirement, which is not in itself sufficient. For clearly, it applies to numerous other *alaṃkāras*; there is "an act of comparison" in a *vyatireka* (A is superior to B) or an *ananvaya* (A is like itself). It is the second part of the definition which bars such poetic devices, by stating that the act of comparison has to be "intended up to its full completion." This means, first, that nothing should prevent the act from being fulfilled. Hence the figure of *vyatireka,* where a similarity is described but negated, is excluded from the domain of the simile. In the statement "the spotless face is superior to the moon," the face is explicitly said to lack what the moon is known to possess (namely a spot). This prevents the act of comparison from being fulfilled. As for *ananvaya,* here the issue of intention is crucial. For in statements such as "your face is like your face," the poet intends to highlight the uniqueness of the face and to deny the possibility that there exists a standard against which to measure it. The act of comparison is thus *not meant* to be completed in an *ananvaya*.

What is New about Appayya's Discussion?

It should be clear by now that Appayya, who begins his discussion by claiming merely to recycle old formulations, radically differs from his predecessors, and does so quite consciously. But again, of what exactly does his innovation consist?

There are several answers to this question. First, Appayya's discursive style is remarkably new. By this I mean not just his criticism of older writers—unprecedented in both scope, tone and systematic nature—but also what I see as his breaking of various genre-distinctions and his novel style of composition, somewhat in the mode of a general scholarly "essay." I discuss these stylistic innovations elsewhere.[23] Then, of course, there is the unique, almost puzzling formulation of the simile's definition, the novelty of which we have already witnessed, though not yet fully explained.

Another possible answer to the question of novelty in Appayya's writing—one which may partly explain those mentioned above—is a new sense of historicity traceable in it, a sense which, according to Pollock, is a central feature of scholarship on the eve of colonialism.[24]

For even if, unlike the seventeenth-century scholars cited by Pollock, Appayya does not classify his colleagues into ancients (*jīrṇa*), elders (*prācīna*), followers of the elders (*prācīnānuyāyin*), moderns (*navīna*), most up-to-date scholars (*atinavīna*) and so forth, an important distinction between two historical phases of literary theory is strongly implied by his discussion.

The first consists of the earlier, pre-Ānanda authors: Bhāmaha, Daṇḍin, Udbhaṭa, Vāmana and Rudraṭa. While these thinkers are frequently quoted and treated as authorities, their definitions of the simile are not cited and hence not criticized. Whenever Appayya's discussion runs contrary to the views of these earlier scholars, the contradiction is explained away. We are never told that they are wrong, but rather that the apparent meaning of their statements was not the intended one.[25]

A second phase combines the later thinkers—those who return to discuss *alaṃkāras* as part of a modified domain of poetics in the wake of Ānandavardhana's essay on suggestion. The treatment of these authors—Bhoja, Mammaṭa, Ruyyaka and Vidyānātha—is distinct. Their definitions are cited and unequivocally refuted as "wrong" (*ayuktam*), even as their views on other matters may be quoted respectfully.

Now Appayya is not the first to distinguish between pre- and post-*dhvani* thinkers. The paradigm shift led by Ānanda's theory on suggestion had already been noticed by Ruyyaka.[26] Yet Appayya's tacit understanding of his tradition's past is subtler than Ruyyaka's and serves two further purposes. First—and this is part of what is really new about Appayya's discussion—in a tradition which never possessed a root-text nor a figure of unquestioned authority, a small group of early thinkers is, for the first time, instituted as something of a collective founding father. These pre-Ānanda writers, and Daṇḍin in particular, are now viewed as authorities, and therefore cannot—by definition—be wrong.[27]

Secondly, Appayya's differential treatment of pre- and post-Ānanda writers is informed by- and hence serves to highlight the differences in their definitional practices. Earlier writers, while clearly shaping their definitions so as to reflect what they viewed to be the distinctive features of separate poetic ornaments, seemed far less worried than their followers about possible overlap between them, and paid much less attention to this possibility in wording their definitions. Their main concern was to characterize speech-figures positively, not to set them apart from one another. It is in later generations that we find, perhaps under the influence of the logical discourse (*nyāya*), a growing preoccupation with questions of over- and under-extension. The desire to avoid the shading of categories now becomes *the* driving factor behind definitions, and each definition had to take into consideration the figurative-system in its entirety. Vidyānātha's definition and his self-supplied justification for it perfectly exemplify this trend.

Appayya's position *vis-a-vis* these two groups of authors is complex. Similar to later writers, he is concerned about the danger of overlapping figurative domains, and shares their premise that a good definition must avoid over- and under-extension. Yet he views the kind of solutions proffered by this second group as solving nothing. Indeed, each clarification only created a further complication. In this sense, Appayya is siding with what he tacitly identifies as the older school. For instance, his insistence on not specifying the type of similitude in his definition of the simile echoes Daṇḍin's definition of it as "a similitude which arises in whatever manner."[28]

Viewed in light of this new historicity, Appayya's definition of the simile is better understood. Like his most immediate predecessors and perhaps even more so, Appayya is driven by the need to craft a definition that would delimit the simile with utmost precision; nothing more and nothing less. But unlike authors such as Vidyānātha—and perhaps closer in spirit to writers of old, such as Daṇḍin—Appayya is pessimistic about the possibility of formally characterizing it with any accuracy. He drops the technical analysis in favor of a more conceptual one.

Note that prior to Appayya, *ālaṃkārika*s all identified the simile (*upamā*) with similitude (*sādṛśyam* or *sāmyam*). This forced them to take into consideration both the structure of its proposition—similitude had to be of one entity (*upameya*) with another (*upamāana*), the two had to be separate from one another, and so forth—as well as its truth value—the two entities had to be *truly* similar.[29] Appayya was the first to altogether avoid the structure and truth value of the simile as a proposition, and to adopt a vision of it as a verbal action. A propositional definition of the simile proved insufficiently flexible to include all the various types of poetic similitude-making and nothing but them. It is this traditional type of definition which Appayya believes to be impossible (*durvacam*). But defining the simile as a kind of poetic speech act is free from such problems. For acts are defined not by their formal structure and truth value, but rather by the intentions behind them and their success in being fulfilled.

The parameters of intention and effect allowed Appayya to solve the dilemma of his more immediate predecessors, namely the crafting of a definition capable of covering all similes and nothing more, and, at the same time, facilitated his tapping into the older notion of the *upamā*, as found in the work of Daṇḍin and the other elders. Moreover, his new, notional definition is closely related to the old view of most (or all) speech-figures as variations on the theme of the *upamā*, insofar as they either qualify or negate its expression of similitude. Only when the poet intends no such qualification—just the expression of similitude, fully stated and unhindered—is there a simile. This brings to mind the image with which Appayya begins his discussion. A simile, we may conclude, is a successful poetic act, wherein the poet means for us to see the real actress on stage, unobscured by makeup or costume.

Jagannātha and Viśveśvara

Let us now turn to two of Appayya's important successors and see how his innovations were received by them. It should be stated at once that both Jagannātha and Viśveśvara were harsh critics of Appayya. Jagannātha is particularly known for his animus against him. He dedicated an entire work, *The Critique of the Investigation of the Colorful* (*Citramīmāṃsākhaṇḍana*), to debunk his forerunner; his attack on Appayya often carries personal and even ethnic overtones.[30] Moreover, the *Critique* merely summarizes Jagannātha's criticism of Appayya, which is omnipresent in his larger work, *The ocean of Rasa* (*Rasagaṅgadhara*). Naturally, then, in examining Jagannātha's definition of the simile, one is attuned to find differences between it and the formulation of his predecessor.

And indeed, reading Jagannātha's brief definition of the *upamā*—"a charming similarity, which beautifies the meaning of the sentence"[31]—one immediately realizes that he switches back from Appayya's identification of the simile with the act of comparison to the more traditional equation of it with the similitude itself. Jagannātha makes sure his readers do not miss this move. As soon as he is finished with explaining and defending his own definition, he tackles a series of older formulations, beginning with Appayya's. His predecessor's conception of the simile as a verbal act, or rather a "description" of similarity (*varṇana*), is at the heart of his critique.

Jagannātha claims that the use of the verbal noun *description* in characterizing the *upamā* is ill-advised, for by 'description' one either refers to the employment of a specific vocabulary, or to some knowledge arising from it, neither of which is equal to the unique expressivity typifying a sense-based ornament.[32] Furthermore, the phrase "description of similarity" may equally apply to non-poetic acts of comparison. There is, after all, such a description in matter-of-fact utterances such as "the cow resembles the ox," and even in scientific statements which point out the similarity between two grammatical cases.[33] Clearly, then, Appayya's radical attempt to define the simile as an act of comparison is seen by Jagannātha as flawed.

But this important difference between Appayya and Jagannātha should not obscure the overall agreement in their concerns, style of discussion and definitions of the simile. Jagannātha too, like Appayya, seems pessimistic about the possibility of formally defining the simile with any accuracy, and shares the same sense of historicity as his predecessor. This is clear from the following two features of his simile discussion. First, after criticizing Appayya's definition, Jagannātha goes on to quote the very same post-Ānanda thinkers cited by his predecessor. He proves their endless effort formally to define the simile to have been futile by finding virtually the same faults as Appayya.[34] Secondly, Jagannātha's definition is as 'notional' as Appayya's. Note that like Appayya, Jagannātha is brief, cryptic and shies away from any formal characterization. Like his antecedent's formulation, Jagannātha's definition has minimal specifications. He qualifies his identification of the simile with similitude by requiring that the latter be charming and beautify the meaning of the sentence.

Indeed, Jagannātha defends his minimal stipulations in a way that closely resembles Appayya's defense. My definition excludes *ananvaya*, says Jagannātha, because in that figure beauty is not the result of similitude but rather of its absence. An *ananvaya*, after all, negates the very possibility that an entity similar to the tenor exists. Likewise, there is no overlap with a *vyatireka*, for in it the negation and not the similarity is responsible for the charming effect.[35] There can be little doubt, then, that Jagannātha, like Appayya, wishes to differentiate the simile from its closely related figures not by any formal features but through its unique poetic effect, and that the two are in full agreement as to what accounts for that effect and how it differs from both *ananvaya* and *vyatireka*. Moreover, both scholars share the desire accurately to define the simile, and the view that the formalistic definitions of Vidyānātha's generation failed to achieve such accuracy. In short, both agree on what the problem is and on the general way to solve it, and differ only as to the actual solution. Appayya emphasizes the intention and completion of the act of comparison, while Jagannātha insists on the charm of the similarity as the defining factor.

If all of this is not sufficient to prove just how closely Jagannātha follows on the heels of his predecessor's discussion, it should be noted that the kind of criticism he employs against Appayya is quite "Appayyalike." Indeed, the very warning that the definition of the simile must exclude scientific and matter of fact statements of similarity, was earlier issued by Appayya himself.[36] In short, Jagannātha's discussion and definition are closely modeled after Appayya, with the major difference being Jagannatha's attempt to outdo him.

The irony in the overall agreement between the two famous rivals is not missed by Viśveśvara, who half-jokingly pegs Jagannātha as "the follower" of Appayya Dīkṣita (*dīkṣitānuyāyin*).[37] Distinguishing himself from both, Viśveśvara first defines the simile in a rather conventional manner, as the "similarity of two separate entities which is expressed by a single sentence."[38] Yet this definition, which is much closer to Vidyānātha's than to Appayya's and Jagannātha's, is entertained for no longer than two lines and never mentioned thereafter. In its place, Viśveśvara introduces its "realized purport" (*phalitārtha*), which serves as his actual definition for the remainder of the discussion.

This "realized" definition is completely written in navyanyāya's formal metalanguage. It is thus impossible to translate, but I shall nonetheless attempt to render it into English so as to allow the reader to get a sense of its complexity. "When there is the state of being a counterpart in whichever relationship of similarity," says Viśveśvara, "that [relationship of similarity] is a simile given two absences: (1) of the counterpart being delimited by the delimiting characteristic of tenorship, and (2) of co-referentiality [of the counterpart] with a property which exists merely in the counterpart, excepting any such property which serves as a delimiter of it [i.e. of the counterpart]."[39]

This basically means—to use the set example of face and moon for purposes of clarification—that when the moon is the counterpart [i.e. standard] in a relationship of similarity, that relationship is a simile unless: (1) the moon is also the tenor (which would make it an *ananvaya*), (2) the moon's properties (such as a spot) exist only in the moon (but not in the face, otherwise this relationship would be a *vyatireka*), except, of course, for the moon's defining property, namely moonness, which necessarily exists in it, and in it alone.

In what must be viewed as a strong reaction to the notional definitions of his predecessors—both Appayya and his "follower," Jagannātha—Viśveśvara resorts to the extremely technical idiom of logic. Not identifying the simile with similitude (as do all early *ālaṃkārikas,* and as does Jagannātha) nor with the act of describing it (as does Appayya), Viśveśvara chooses to describe it as a relationship between part and counterpart, which *navya-nyāya* has already defined with great sophistication. The importation of *nyāya* concepts and vocabulary allows Viśveśvara access to its tools. These tools alone, he implies, are capable of characterizing the simile with precision.

Thus Viśveśvara very consciously distances his definition from what he sees as the similar formulations of Appayya and Jagannātha. Yet despite this obvious distancing, he shares several important features with the definition and discussion of his two predecessors: 1. All are largely in agreement as to what the phenomenon under discussion, namely *upamā,* really is. Their argument is first and foremost about the definition and not the thing defined—the *lakṣaṇa* rather than the *lakṣya.*[40] All three scholars are driven by the need for absolute accuracy in the characterization of the *upamā*—they wish to craft a definition of the *upamā* which would include all of its instances and nothing but them. More specifically, all three definitions are crafted so as to distinguish the *upamā* from the same two figures—*ananvaya* and *vyatireka,* which are seen as particularly problematic from the perspective of *lakṣaṇa*-making. 3. All three thinkers seem to agree that the ancient *ālaṃkārikas* correctly understood the basic notion of the simile. 4. Yet all find the attempts of Vidyānātha and his colleagues to define it as not fully satisfying. This position is more explicitly expressed by Appayya and Jagannātha, who openly criticize Vidyānātha, and is only implicit in Viśveśvara's work. In fact, Viṣveśvara defends Vidyānātha from Appayya's criticism, but this seems to be more out of opposition to the latter than from satisfaction with the former. After all, his own realized (*phalitārtha*) definition is very distinct from Vidyānātha's formulation.

Viṣveśvara totally differs from Appayya and Jagannātha in his unwillingness to accept their pessimism regarding the possible accuracy of a formal definition. This pessimism, which Appayya expresses most straightforwardly, is replaced in Viṣveśvara 's work by an enthusiastic adoption of *nyāya*'s concepts and terminology, indeed a complete "nyāyization" of *alaṃkāraśāstra*. This new vocabulary, for Viṣveśvara, enables the tradition to delimit the phenomena observed by the elders with hitherto unknown tools.

Novelty and Navyatā: Concluding Remarks

Despite the admittedly limited scope of the above discussion, we are now in a position to draw several conclusions about *alaṃkāra* discourse on the eve of colonialism. First of all, it should be clear that in this period *alaṃkāraśāstra* was highly innovative. Probably the most visible break from the past consisted of the actual simile-definitions we have examined. The differences between the formulations of Appayya, Jagannātha and Viśveśvara not withstanding, none of these is even remotely similar to what tradition had yielded in nearly a millennium of intensive discussion of its quintessential figure. All three definitions smack unmistakably of ingenuity, both in tone and thinking.

Secondly, and perhaps more importantly than the visible innovations in the field of definition-making, is the new relationship to the tradition's past from which they seem to stem. This new historicality is characterized first and foremost by *ambivalence*. On the one hand, we find a newly expressed admiration for the discipline's earliest known figures—Daṇḍin, Bhāmaha and their followers. There is a sense that these ancients succeeded in identifying the basic ornamenting components of Sanskrit poetry—*upamā, ananvaya, vyatireka, utprekṣā, rūpaka, śleṣa,* etc.—and in realizing the true nature and effect of each. This profound understanding enabled them to differentiate the *alaṃkāra*s from one another. Thus they were capable of conceiving a system of figures—an exhaustive survey and analysis of poetic "morphemes," in the numerous combinations of which the poet's tongue can be said to consist. The achievement of these *ālaṃkārika*s is not deemed less significant than Ānanda's discovery of suggestion.

Yet, accompanying this profound respect for the elders one also senses anxiety concerning their very accomplishments. This anxiety seems to derive from a new look at the second generation of *ālaṃkārika*s—the post Ānanda thinkers such as Mammaṭa, Ruyyaka and Vidyānātha. These writers tried to further strengthen the figurative system by providing each *alaṃkāra* with a more accurate, formal definition, emphasizing the differences between it and similar poetic phenomena. Yet, at least for Appayya Dīkṣita, there can be no doubt that such efforts amounted to an enormous failure. Appayya's criticism of the *upamā*-definitions of this later group of writers makes it clear that all of the *lakṣaṇa*s examined failed to delimit their *lakṣya*s in their entirety, and what is more, they overextended to other *lakṣya*s as well. Appayya's discussion therefore implies that the entire well-ordered system of *alaṃkāra*s was in imminent danger of collapsing. This notion is more openly expressed by Jagannātha who, as Pollock notes, occasionally warrants the rejection of a particular position, "out of what seems to be the sheer anxiety that the [ancient] 'taxonomy' would be 'destroyed' or even 'weakened'."[41]

Poeticians from the sixteenth-century onward thus viewed the old taxonomy as valid, but, at the same time, as fragile. They therefore tried first and foremost to protect it. The paradox inherent in this project is that one had to amend the system in order to preserve it. Even if the ancient taxonomy succeeded in capturing the essence of poetic figuration, it was necessary to modify and refine it—by adding new categories and sub-categories, by merging others and by redefining the figures—in order to assure its overall survival. Thus, although the earliest scholars were often invoked as authorities, they were just as frequently sidestepped when new categories were invented or borrowed from later thinkers (Mammaṭa, Ruyyaka, etc.), and when remarkably new definitions were crafted.

Now the old system was rather amorphous, and each new scholar envisioned it somewhat differently. Likewise the category of the ancients often seemed quite open-ended and was used with considerable flexibility. As we noted in the very beginning, the *alaṃkāra* tradition never possessed founding figures of unquestioned authority nor clearly defined schools following them. The fact that even after a category of 'ancients' was created it remained fuzzy, alongside the inconsistent attitude towards these ancients—at times venerated, at others disputed—may lead one to think that the new scholars constantly contradicted themselves.[42] But it is important to remember that this apparent contradiction is rooted not in some logical inconsistency. Rather, it is the result of their newly found ambivalence towards the past, and of the drive, shared by all of the three scholars we have examined, to protect an overall excellent system from its own destabilizing faults.

The new historicality of late precolonial *ālaṃkārika*s is, to my mind, the most important feature of their writing, and what they all seem to have in common. Besides this, however, their new practice of poetics lacked a shared agenda, and they spoke in many and often conflicting voices. In this respect it should be noted that *navyatā* in the *alaṃkāra* discipline can by no means be identified with the period's widespread use of *navya-nyāya* idiom. The use of this vocabulary and tool kit was seen twice above—as the position of the imaginary disputant of one scholar (Appayya) and in the actual position of another (Viśveśvara). It was, then, just one possible path taken by scholars of the period to improve upon the definitions of older generations. But, as we have seen, there were also other ways to reach the same goal, such as the 'notional' definitions of Appayya and Jagannātha, and it has yet to be determined which way, if any, was the more dominant.

Our discussion should have clarified why the outstanding innovations of the scholars we have examined were so easy to ignore. The fact that these innovations are based upon a fresh perspective of the past—that the new is so intimately connected to reestablishing the old—must have obscured their novelty. When Appayya Dīkṣita knowingly breaks with his tradition in the Investigation—a pivotal work which inaugurated a whole new way of writing Sanskrit poetics—he begins by claiming that he is only setting out to paraphrase the words of the ancients. There is certainly irony in such a statement, but it is perhaps also emblematic of the complex relationship between new and old in his work.

It is, for instance, telling that the most visible index of change we have seen consisted of new definitions to age-old categories. The innovations of the new *ālaṃkārika*s involve novel answers to old questions, rather than asking questions which have never been asked. Neither Appayya nor his followers showed the slightest interest in challenging the millennium old basic concepts of their discipline. These proved to be extremely resilient, and continued to be seen as valid as far as the discussion went.

Thus, *navya ālaṃkārika*s after Appayya do not present us with radically new agendas, theories or questions, about language, poetic expressiveness and so on. In this and other senses, then, we may view these scholars as "innovative traditionalists." This, combined with the lack of a single, unified voice in the "new poetics," makes it difficult to pinpoint its novelty, and partly accounts for the ease with which late *ālaṃkārika*s were unfairly labelled unoriginal and redundant.

Finally, I would like to briefly consider the possible effects of the three unique features of *alaṃkāraśāstra* mentioned at the beginning of this paper on the late precolonial discussion. The tradition's exceptionally multifaceted nature, and particularly its lack of founding figures, has definitely influenced the discussion on the eve of colonialism. The need to recognize the "founders," the fuzziness of such a group, and the equivocal attitude towards it, all exemplify the importance of this unique feature.

Regarding the two remaining aspects, however, the picture is more complicated. On the one hand, since the discussion of Appayya and his successors is almost entirely theory-driven—propelled by internal concerns about the system of figures itself—there seems to be little scope for influence of the two evolving external traditions we mentioned above—poetry in Sanskrit and poetics in the vernacular.

On the other hand we should be careful not to dismiss these possible influences altogether. New *ālaṃkārika*s follow Appayya in the practice of criticizing older formulations by citing numerous counter examples, for which purpose any piece of poetry seems useful. Verses by Kālidāsa may be cited along with much later and less famous ones. The result is that each chapter of a work such as the *Citramīmāṃsā* is like a mini-anthology consisting of numerous Sanskrit stanzas from varied sources. This widening of the canon is in itself worth noticing, and may not be insignificant, although its magnitude and possible consequences require further investigation.

As for poetics in the vernacular, we have seen no direct indication that they exerted any influence on the Sanskritic discussion. Still, it is not altogether impossible that the resurrection of Daṇḍin by Appayya is not somehow related to the former's lasting prominence in non-Sanskrictic circles, particularly in the South. Moreover, understanding the potential relationship between Sanskritic scholars and intellectuals of vernacular and Persian cultural spheres cannot be carried out as long as the social dimension of new scholasticism is left uncharted. Indeed, only once this social dimension begins to unfold—through the research project of which this paper is part—will we be able to gain a better understanding of the fascinating movement of new scholasticism.

Acknowledgments: I am grateful to Lawrence McCrea, Sheldon Pollock, Catherine Rottenberg, and Galila Spharim for their helpful comments on an earlier version of this paper. I am also indebted to H.V. Nagaraja Rao who initiated me into Appayya's *Citramīmāṃsā*.

Notes

1. Pollock, 2001: 5.
2. De, 1960, Vol. 2, p. 252.
3. The dates of Appayya given here are based on V. A. Ramaswami Sastri's edition of the *Tattvabindu* by *Vācaspatimiśra*, pp. 94–103.
4. On the relative dating of Appayya's works see De, 1960: Vol. I, p. 223, as well as the new edition of the *Vṛttivārttikā*, edited and translated by Edwin Gerow in collaboration with H. V. Nagaraja Rao
5. On this genre see McCrea, 1998: 286ff.
6. It seems reasonable to assume that Appayya composed both the *Kuvalayānanda* and the *Citramīmāṃsā* simultaneously, completing the former and leaving the latter unfinished.
7. I list, as an illustration, the number of copies of the *Kuvalayānanda* copies in three major collections (Madras, Varanasi and Poona), compared to those of

Mammaṭa's extermely popular work, the *Kāvyaprakāṣa*. The Government Oriental Manuscripts Library in Madras has, according to its descriptive catalogue, 25 copies of the *Kuvalayānanda*, out of a total 195 *alaṃkāra* manuscripts (nearly 13 percent). In comparison, there are only 12 mss. of the *Kāvyaprakāśa* (6%). The *Kuvalayānanda* seems as popular, if less dominant, in the North. The descriptive catalogue of the Sarasvati Bhavan collection in Varanasi lists 48 mss. of this work (with or without a commentary), and 27 additional mss. of separate commentaries or summaries (the exact percentage is not available since the catalogue lists both *kāvya* and *alaṃkāra* works). In comparison, there are 51 copies of the *Kāvyaprakāśa* (with or without a commentary), and 15 more works that summarize, amend or criticize Mammaṭa's treatise. However, there also 82 mss. of separate commentaries and sub-commentaries on the *Kāvyaprakāśa*, an area in which Mammaṭa's treatise vastly outnumbers the *Kuvalayānanda* or, for that matter, any other work in Sanskrit poetics. Indeed, commentaries on the *Kāvyaprakāśa* seem to be the most productive genre in poetics during the period under discussion. The collection of the Bhandarkar Oriental Research Institute in Poona yields a similar picture. Its descriptive catalogue lists 13 copies of the *Kuvalayānanda* (with or without commentaries), and additional 8 copies of commentaries, summaries etc. (about 7 percent of its *alaṃkāra* collection). As for the *Kāvyaprakāśa*, there are 19 mss. of that work (with or without a commentary, a similar percentage), but 44 separate commentaries.

8. On the swiftness of circulation of books and ideas in this period one learns much from Christopher Minkowski's yet unpublished paper on Nīlakaṇṭha's commentarial work.
9. Or the roles of all other figures, *citra* denoting both "variegated" or "colorful," as well as the entire figurative domain. *Citramīmāṃsā*, p. 33.
10. *Citramīmāmsā*, p. 35.
11. Ibid., p. 30.
12. Ibid., p. 42, Cf. *Prataparudrīya*, p. 253: *svataḥ siddhena bhinnena sammatena ca dharmataḥ| sāmyam anyena varṇyasya vācyaṃ ced ekadopamā ||*
13. Compare *Citramīmāṃsā*, pp. 42–43, to *Pratāparudrīya*, pp. 253–256.
14. *Citramīmāṃsā*, p. 48, cf. *Kumārasaṃbhava* 1.3. The translation, with a slight modification is by Hank Heifetz, 1985: 21.
15. *Citramīmāṃsā*, p. 48.
16. Giving is accompanied by pouring water on one's hand.
17. This is an oversimplification of Appayya's argument about the adverb "singularly" (*Citramīmāṃsā*, p. 48). It later becomes clear, however, that what negates the opponent's point here is the impossibility of viewing every clause of the chain simile individually for the purpose of the definition. For the same logic forces one to take an *upameyopamā* (A is like B, B is like A) as a combination of an *upamā* (A is like B) and a *pratīpam* (B is like A) (p. 62).

18. Ibid., p. 48. Tvaṣṭṛ is the architect of the gods.
19. Ibid., p. 48.
20. *Citramīmāṃsā*, p. 68, on which the commentator Dharānanda says: *upasaṃharati—tasmād dhetor asyā upamāyā lakṣaṇam. doṣarahitam iti śeṣaḥ durvacaṃ vaktum aśakyam iti* (ibid., p. 69).
21. Ibid., p. 69: *vyāpāra upamānākhyo bhaved yadi vivakṣitaḥ | kriyāniṣpattiparyantam upamālaṃ kṛtis tu sā||*
22. A phrase Appayya seems to prefer later on, when offering a pair of alternative definitions (ibid., p. 78).
23. See "Arriving at a Definition: Appayya Dīkṣita's Meditation on the Simile and the Onset of New Poetics" (forthcoming in David Shulman and Shaul Shaked, eds., *Language, Myth and Poetry in Ancient India and Iran*), where the themes presented here are discussed more elaborately.
24. Pollock, 2001: 8–19.
25. See, for example, *Citramīmāṃsā*, pp. 54–55, when an apparent contradiction with Rudraṭa is explained away.
26. *Alaṃkārasarvasva*, pp. 3ff. For the term "paradigm shift" in this context, see McCrea, 1998: 21ff.
27. My initial findings suggest that even the opponents of Appayya respected the newly acquired status of Daṇḍin and his colleagues. See, for example, how Viśveśvara refutes Appayya's use of Daṇḍin's example of *asambhāvitopamā* (*Citramīmāṃsā*, pp. 44–45, cf. *Kāvyādarśa* 2.39). Viśveśvara does not say that Daṇḍin was wrong (in classifying this as an *upamā* rather than *utprekṣā*), but rather that his true intention was misunderstood by Appayya (*Alaṃkārakaustubha*, p. 11). In addition to Daṇḍin and the other pre- Ānanda writers, Ānanda himself seems to be granted a similar authority in Appayya's work and later.
28. *yathākathaṃcit sādṛśyaṃ yatrodbhūtaṃ pratīyate* | *Kāvyalakṣaṇa* (2.14)
29. A position which Appayya rejects. In statements like "a face is like the moon," he says, the brightness of the moon cannot, in truth (*vastutas*), be the same as that of the face. (*Citramīmāṃsā*, p. 77, cf. my forthcoming paper mentioned above, in note 23).
30. E.g. *draviḍaśiromaṇibhir abhidhīyata, Citramīmāṃsākhaṇḍana*, p. 25.
31. *sādṛśyaṃ sundaraṃ vākyārthopaskāram upamālaṃkṛtiḥ|Rasagaṅgādhara* Vol. II, p. 211
32. Ibid., p. 226.
33. The example for the latter is Pāṇini 1.2.57. An earlier *sūtra* stated that teaching some basic grammatical notions is unnecessary. This *sūtra* adds that "[the meanings of the terms] 'tense' and 'secondary' too are *likewise* [not to be taught]."
34. Ibid., pp. 233 ff.
35. Ibid., pp. 211–212.

36. *Citamīmāṃsā*, p. 37.
37. *Alaṃkārakaustubha*, p. 21.
38. *tatraikavākyavācyaṃ sādṛṣyaṃ bhinnayor upamā* | p. 4.
39. *yatsādṛśyapratiyogitāyām upameyatāvacchedakāvacchinnatvasvāśrayamātravṛttisv ānavacc—hedakadharmasāmānādhikaraṇyobhayābhāvaḥ sopamā* | Ibid., p. 5. I am grateful to Lawrence McCrea for his useful comments on my "translation" of this definition.
40. There are, however, occasions where the *lakṣya* itself is being debated, as in the case of *śleṣa*. See, again, my forthcoming paper mentioned in note 23.
41. Pollock, 2001: 15.
42. See, for example, the contradictions noted by Pollock, 2001: 15–16.

Works Cited

Primary Sources

Alaṃkārakaustubha of Viśveśvara. Edited by M. M. Sivadatta and Kashinath Pandurang Parab. Delhi: Chaukhamba, 1987.

Alaṃkārasarvasva of Ruyyaka with the Sañjīvanī comm. of Vidyācakravartin. Edited by S. S. Janaki and V. Raghavan. Delhi: Meharchand Lachmandas, 1965.

Citramīmāṃsā of Appayya Dīkṣita with the Sudhā comm. of Dharānanda. Edited by Jagadīśa Chandra Miśra. Varanasi: Chowkhamba, 1971. Kashi Sanskrit series 207.

Citramīmāṃsākhaṇḍana of Jagannātha Paṇḍitarāja with the comm. Marmaprakāśa of Nāgeśa. Varanasi: Kṛṣṇadās Academy, 1986.

Kāvyalakṣaṇa [=Kāvyādarśa] of Daṇḍin with the comm. Ratnaśrī of Ratnaśrījñāna. Edited by Anantalal Thakur and Upendra Jha. Darbhanga: Mithila Institute, 1957.

Kumārasaṃbhava of Kālidāsa with the comms. of Mallinātha and Sītārāmā. Edited by Kāśīnātha Pāṇḍuraṅga Parab. Bombay: Nirṇaya Sāgara Press, 1893.

Kuvalayānanda of Appayya Dīkṣita with the Alaṃkārasurabhi Hindi comm. of D. Bholashankar Vyas. Varanasi: Chowkhamba, 1994 (fourth edition).

Pratāparudrīya or Vidyānātha with the comm. Ratnāpaṇa of Kumārasvāmin. Edited by V. Raghavan. Madras: The Sanskrit Education Society, 1979.

Rasagaṇgādhara of Jagannātha. Vol. 2. Edited by Madana Mohana Jha. Varanasi: Chowkhamba, 1995 (fourth edition).

Secondary Sources

De, S. K. (1960). History of Sanskrit Poetics. Calcutta, Firma K. L. M., 2 vols., second edition.

Descriptive Catalogue of the Government Collection of Manuscripts Deposited at the Bhandarkar Oriental Research Institute. Edited by Parashuram Krishna Gode. Vol. 12, Alaṃkāraśāstra,Saṃgīta and Nāṭya. Poona, 1936.

Descriptive Catalogue of the Sanskrit Manuscripts Acquired for and Deposited in the Sanskrit University Library (Sarasvati Bhavan), Varanasi, During the Years 1791–1950, Volume XI, Sahitya MSS., Complied by the staff of the Manuscripts Section of the Sanskrit University Library, Varanasi, 1964.

Descriptive Catalogue of Sanskrit Manuscripts in the Government Oriental Manuscripts Library, Madras. Vol. 22: Rhetoric and Poetics, Music and Dancing, and ´Silpaśāstra. Edited by S. Kuppuswami Sastri. Madras, 1918.

Heifez, Hank (1985). The Origin of The Young God: Kālidāsa's Kumārasaṃbhava. Berkeley: University of California Press.

McCrea, Lawrence (1998). The Teleology of Poetics in Medieval Kashmir. University of Chicago dissertation. Pollock, Sheldon (2001). "New Intellectuals in Seventeenth-century India." The Indian Economic and Social History Review 38(1): 1–31.

Tattvabindu of Vācaspatimiśra with the comm. Tattvavibhāvanā by R. s. iputra Parame´svara. Edited by V. A. Ramaswami Sastri. Madras: Annamalai University, 1936 (Annamalai University Sanskrit Series No. 3).

Vṛttivārttikā or Commentary on the Functions of Words, of Appaya [sic] Dīkṣita. Edited and translated by Edwin Gerow in collaboration with H. V. Nagaraja Rao. New Haven: American Oriental Society, 2001.

3

Tamil Sangam Poetry

The Plebeian in the Classical Tradition

Mini Chandran

The term 'classical' generally evokes the image of tradition and refinement, especially in the context of art and literature; classical literature is considered to be the esoteric privilege of the upper classes, and in the Indian context, upper castes. This can be seen as largely correct with respect to classical Sanskrit literature because Sanskrit was considered the literary or priestly language associated with the *dvijas* (twice-born, consisting mostly of the Brahmins and other upper caste-classes like the Ksatriyas and Vaisyas). Although scholars like Johannes Bronkhorst argue that Sanskrit is 'accessible to all, it being the only 'real' language' (223), it was generally an acquisition which was denied to the Shudras and females. Moreover, the themes of classical Sanskrit literature—particularly in dramatic genres like the *nātaka, prakarana* or *kāvya*—reflected this predilection for the upper classes/castes of society, if not kings and gods. The major poet Kālidāsa's oeuvre—*Abhijnānaṣākuntalam, Vikramorvaṣiyam, Kumārasambhavam, Malavikāgnimitram,* or *Raghuvamṣam*—is a case in point. Even Śudraka, who wrote 'secular' plays like *Mricchakatikam,* dealt with Brahmins like Chārudatta.

Classical Tamil literature, on the other hand, does not seem to be similarly focused exclusively on the upper castes or classes. This paper argues that most of the literary works in this tradition can be seen inscribing the common man into the classical canon. The beginnings of this orientation towards the commonplace and the ordinary can be discerned in Sangam poetry, and it seems to continue with epics like *Cilappatikāram* and *Manimekalai,* which do not focus on royalty or great wars. It could also have paved the way for the egalitarian Bhakti movement which evolved later from the Tamil-speaking regions. In this sense, Sangam poetry can be perceived as a classical tradition that contains the seeds of two divergent paths—one (mainly through the *akam* poems that dealt with human emotions and feelings) that portrayed lived realities, and a related but different path (through the *puṟam* poems that extolled wars and martial exploits of chieftains and brave warriors) that concealed heterodox tendencies. Thus, although Sangam poetry cannot be thought of as a counter-culture in itself, it can be seen as a centrifugal impulse, an impetus to break free of conventions and stereotypical literary or cultural moulds.

This paper describes this 'plebeian' element in the classical Sangam tradition, and goes on to explore its two associated aspects—one, the 'democratic' spirit that is discernible in later works like the twin epics and Bhakti poetry; and the other, the subterranean heterodox element that gestures towards the possibilities of subversion in poetic composition. Tamil, which is as ancient as Sanskrit in India, was a language spoken predominantly in what is today the state of Tamil Nadu in the south of India. David Shulman defines Tamil as '...first, the name of an ancient language, spoken today by some eighty million people in south India, Sri Lanka, and a large diaspora that includes Malaysia, Singapore, Fiji, South Africa, Paris, Toronto, and many other sites throughout the world... Among the South Asian languages, Tamil is perhaps the only case of a very ancient language that still survives as a vibrant mother-tongue for tens of millions of speakers' (2). The corpus of classical Tamil consists mainly of Sangam poetry and the early medieval epics of *Cilappatikāram* and *Manimekalai*. The Sangam corpus (composed around 100BCE–250CE) consists of *Eṭṭutokai* (8 anthologies, some of which are *Kuruntokai, Akanānuru, and Ainkurunūru*), *Pathupāṭṭu* (Ten long poems), and the treatise on Tamil grammar and poetics, the *Tolkāppiyam*. Sangam, or Cankam, indicates a group or fraternity; according to A.K. Ramanujan, 'Cankam means "an academy or fraternity": a seventh-century commentator applied the term to poetry and spoke of three academies or Cankams, lasting 4,400, 3,700, and 1,850 years respectively' (2006: xiv). Although poets like Kapilar, Perunkaṭunko, Auvaiyār and Nakkeerar are known, the identity of the poets, male and female, who composed these poems are largely unknown. The poems which vary in length from as few as three lines to over eight hundred, are broadly classified as *akam* and *puṟam* poems, or poems which deal with the home and the world respectively.

The *akam* poems are mindscapes dealing with the private space of emotions and feelings which outsiders are not privy to. What marks this category is the complete absence of proper names, be it of the landscape or people. The landscape is generic and the characters are either a 'she' or a 'he'. According to Ramanujan:

> The dramatis personae for *akam* are idealised types, such as chieftains representing clans and classes, rather than historical persons. Similarly, landscapes are more important than particular places. The reason for such absence of individuals is given in the word *akam*: the 'interior' world is inexpressible, there are no names there; it has neither geography nor history(2004: 199).

The categorisation of the landscape into five *tinai*s or categories in both *akam* and *puṟam* genres conforms to this tendency to anonymity, foregrounding universal human emotions and states of mind rather than the people concerned. The range of landscape spans a wide variety of emotions from hopeful love to the despair and pain of separation or spurned love. The very fact that landscape is used as objective correlative is indicative of a community that lived close to nature, following the change of seasons which correspond to the highs and lows of their personal or emotional lives. The mountain slopes where bees make rich honey from the black-stalked kurinji flowers (*Kuruntokai* 3, Ramanujan, 2006: 5), a rain cloud that sits on sapphire hills, or flowering hilltops (Kapilar, *Ainkurunuru*, Ramanujan, 2006: 12–13)—these indicate young and eager love. Grazing milch cows returning at sunset, or the reddening white flowers of the jasmine are enough to remind the girl of a lover who is not with her (*Kuruntokai* 108, Ramanujan, 2006: 74). The images are almost entirely taken from village life, the city being significantly absent, suggesting an agrarian, rural community where the bonds of family (mother-daughter, foster mother, husband-wife, husband-wife-child) are predominant. For instance, poem 410 of Peyanar in *Ainkurunuru* celebrates the bliss of domestic ordinariness, where, with his wife, 'his companion on the short-legged cot in their front yard' and infant son crawling on his chest, a man experiences incomparable joy (https://sangamtranslationsbyvaidehi.

com/ettuthokai-ainkurunuru/). This is an image from an ordinary household which could be found anywhere, anytime.

The landscape and the mind are seamlessly woven together in what Sharma terms 'eco-poetics' or poetic ecology of the mind.

> ... this notion of 'eco-poetics' is virtually based upon a system of eco-semiotics, bearing many-layered meanings and values arising from the interrelations of nature and culture, landscape and feeling, and internalized by a whole community of poets and their readers. It is a landscape which becomes culture before it can be viewed as nature—a construct of a 'secular' symbolic imagination (Sharma 23).

The symbolic value attributed to the landscape naturally focuses our attention on the essence rather than the materiality of place and person; thus the world it depicts is *out of time*, or always *in time* and contemporary.

The Female Domestic Space

The *akam* poems are almost entirely female-centred where an important role is played by the girl friend, or *thōzhi*, of the woman, who becomes a trusted confidante, sensible adviser in hour of need, and occasionally the spokesperson. It is almost as if the anonymity of the characters extends to the situation as well; the *akam* poems insinuate the reader into that world by making her by default an eavesdropper on the most intimate thoughts of those who people that realm. As Ramanujan explains: 'No poet here speaks in his own voice; and no poem is addressed to a reader. The reader only overhears what the characters say to each other or to themselves or to the moon. A poem in this tradition implies, evokes, enacts a drama in a monologue' (Ramanujan, 2004: 209). The poems are preceded by what Shulman terms a 'colophon' that '...provides basic information about the context of composition: in the case of *akam*, the name of the poet and the particular situation or theme (*kiḷavi*) in the prototypical love sequence suited to the poem; in the case of *puṟam*, the names of the king, hero, or patron celebrated in the poem and of the poet who sang of his deeds ...' (68).

The framing narrative of the colophon in the case of the *akam* poem, never has names. 'What her Girl Friend said, seeing her friend suffer in silent dignity over her husband's suffering' or 'What He said, to his charioteer on his way back', are examples of the contextual explanation provided by such colophons.

The images which abound in these poems are naturally from the domestic space dominated by the woman who works at home and in the fields. For instance,

> The millet plants in your field will
> not get too dry. His sapphire hued, tall mountain
> covered with clouds appears like
> meat covered with fat.
> (Kapilar, *Ainkurunūru* 207, Kurinji thinai; https://sangamtranslations byvaidehi.com/ettuthokai-ainkurunuru/).

The analogy of the cloud on the tall mountain to fat on meat is startling as it defies our concepts of the poetic. However, its propriety becomes apparent when one thinks of how naturally these images would occur to girls who habitually handle both agricultural tasks as well as cooking. Bangles on wrists, kohl lining blue-black eyes, garlands which adorn the hair are all images which recur in these poems, indicating female beauty and sexuality in all its aspects. Female desire is expressed obliquely, a trait which is believed to be intrinsic to the feminine psyche which has inhibitions about exposing the *akam* or the intimate and private world of emotions. The cryptic eco-poetics of Sangam poetry is thus best suited for the articulation of female passion, as in:

> Please listen!
> In his country,
> the muddied water that deer
> drink and leave behind
> beneath dried leaves in the pits,
> is sweeter than the milk mixed
> with honey from our grove (*Ainkurunūru*, 203, Kapilar, https://sangamtranslationsbyvaidehi.com/ettuthokai-ainkurunuru/).

The preference for muddied water expressed by the girl indicates the sexual nature of the passion she feels for her man; the muddied water also hints at the loss of innocence of the girl who had till then subsisted on milk and honey.

The loss of love is also similarly evoked through the lines spoken by a friend to the heroine:

.... Why is your body
without luster, like a plucked
tender sprout that has wilted?

Is it because of your lover
from the country where a big,
murderous male tiger with short
front legs hides in the dense shade
of a jackfruit tree bearing fruits,
and stalks a young tottering calf
of an innocent female elephant
in the forest with tall bushes? (*Ainkurunūru* 216, Kapilar, ibid.).

The menace of the landscape hints at the treachery of the man who is capable of abandoning her and emotionally crippling her.

Even an open expression of desire is depicted through a very ordinary and prosaic image; the following poem is an instance:

Since my pallor vanishes
whenever my lover touches
me, and spreads whenever
he leaves me,
it is like the moss floating on
the town's drinking water well.
(*Kuruntokai* 399, Marutham tinai, https://sangamtranslationsbyvaidehi.com/ettuthokai-kurunthokai-201-400/)

This interior world of *akam* poetry is thus almost exclusively female-centric, drawing upon nature and the domestic realm to imply and insinuate what cannot be expressly said, but has to be said nonetheless. This is a radical departure from the classical world of Sanskrit where the agon pertains only to the male world, and the reader is hardly aware of the thought-processes of the female characters.

The Male Domain

The *puṟam* poems, which are mainly about the exploits of kings and military victories, deal with specific battles and kings who are named, also noticeably lack in images of the city. According to Ramanujan, 'Usually *puṟam* poems are about good and evil, action, community, kingdom; it is the "public" poetry of the ancient Tamils, celebrating the ferocity and glory of the kings, lamenting the death of heroes, the poverty of poets. Elegy, panegyric, invective, poems on wars and tragic events are *puram* poems' (Ramanujan, 2004: 199). *Puram* is thus the complement of *akam*—the male space dominated by activity outside the home and the hearth. However, these are not rigidly demarcated areas but fluid entities which seep into each other, reflecting a way of life and a thought process peculiar to a tribal society '…pregnant with the incipience of a folk religion' (Sharma, 2014: 24). Sharma points to Kamil Zvelebil's argument that when poetry '…reflects some kind of religion, it is mostly the rites and ceremonies connected with the daily life of the people (such as marriage ceremonies, etc.) or in bardic war-poetry, reflections of tribal cults and their survivals' (qtd by Sharma, 2014: 24). Thus the *puram* poems also reflect the ethos of the *akam* category even when they are elegiac or laudatory.

The laudatory poems are generally about specific kings, like Auvaiyār's poems about Anci, or Kapilar's about Pāri. The 'kings' in these poems might very well have been chieftains of small tribes but that does not in any way detract from the reverence in which the bard holds him. Nonetheless it is also true that the King here is not the distant imperial figure on the throne but a protective father figure who is concerned about the well-being of his subjects: 'If he had even a little rice/he shared it/in many plates' sings Auvaiyār lamenting Anci's death, calling him 'father, mainstay, king' (*Puranānuru* 235, Ramanujan, 2006:170). The (perhaps unintentional) hierarchy of words is significant here, where 'king' comes last. Likewise the 'king' in other laudatory poems is valorous, compassionate, fiercely protective of his subjects and a generous giver to bards who sing songs of praise for him. Ālattūr Kiḷār urges bards to go to Kiḷḷi Vaḷavaṇ:

> If you go and see Killivalavan who wears a fine garland and lovely gold ornaments that flash like fire, you will not have to wait at his tall gate without seeing him donate chariots at harsh noon time in his court. You will not fail to gain a golden lotus flower upon which bees that swarm on flowers do not buzz. (*Puranānuru* 69, Poet: Ālathūr Kizhār sang for Chozhan Kulamutrathu Thunjiya Killivalavan, Thinai: Pādān, Thurai: Pānātruppadai Link: https://sangamtranslationsbyvaidehi.com/ettuthokai-purananuru-1-200/).

However, hidden in these panegyrics is the lament for lost lives and the even more desperately sad lives they have left behind. Through the image of a horse that never came back, the poet Erumai Veḷiyaṉār brings out the pathos of a widowed house:

His horse has not come back!
His horse has not come back!
Everyone else's horses have come back!
The horse he is riding, the man who gave
a son with a dull hair knot to our house,
has not come back!
Has the horse that he was riding, fallen like
a fallen tree that blocks two huge merging rivers?
(*Puranānūru* 273, Poet: Erumai Veliyanār, Thinai: Thumpai, Thurai: Kuthirai Maram; https://sangamtranslationsbyvaidehi.com/ettuthokai-purananuru-201-400/)

Another poem poignantly brings out the widow's austere life deprived of even simple pleasures:

These small white waterlilies are pitiful!
When I was young, I wore them!
Now that my prosperous husband has died,
their seeds are the miserable food that I have
to eat at wrong hours daily, with suffering!
(*Puranānūru* 248, Poet: Okkur Masāthanār, Thinai: Pothuviyal, Thurai: Thāpatha Nilai; https://sangamtranslationsbyvaidehi.com/ettuthokai-purananuru-201-400/).

Even if they seem to glorify their war heroes or kings, many of the *puṟam* poems thus carry an implicit critique of war that widows women and the land.

The Influence of the Everyday

Images of a feudal agrarian society notwithstanding, it has been pointed out how both *akam* and *puṟam* poems are essentially elitist. Tolkappiyar, the author of the work on Tamil poetics, stipulated that the characters in both the categories are '...invariably from the upper/leisure classes, and that slaves, servants, errand men are not to be portrayed in them' (Sharma, 2014: 24). Devapoopathy Nadarajah points out how '...the hero in classical literature, be it Tamil or Sanskrit, comes from a good, noble family with at least a reasonable amount of wealth' (35). Even if we concede an obvious preference for the upper class (it is not very clear if it was also upper caste), we see the reflections of everyday life with all its banalities in both *akam* and *puṟam* poems.

Ramanujan points out how the *akam* and *puṟam* poems are linked together in a larger network: 'Every poem resonates with the absent presence of others that sound with it, like the unstruck strings of a sitar. So we respond to a system of presences and absences; our reading them is not linear, but radial' (Ramanujan, 2004: 15). Thus we find that the aspects of the quotidian, the images of family, village life, nature and so forth find their way into both categories.

The description of the havoc wreaked on the battlefield by a war hero in a *puṟam* poem borrows from a typical kitchen activity in a rural household:

> He is the beloved son of a fine old lady with
> white hair without fragrant oils, her breasts
> dried and nipples shriveled like *ilavam* seeds.
> Like the few drops of curds that a herder woman
> flicks with her sharp finger nails into a pot of milk,
> he spreads among enemies, causing them distress!
> (*Puranānūru* 276, Poet: Mathurai Poothan Ilanākanār, Thinai: Thumpai, Thurai: Thānai Nilai; https://sangamtranslationsbyvaidehi.com/ettuthokai-purananuru-201-400/).

In an *akam* poem, unrequited love is compared to milk spilt on the ground:

> It is like a fine cow's sweet milk
> being wasted on the ground
> without feeding its calf or being
> milked into a pail.
> (*Kurunthokai* 27, Velliveethiyār, Pālai Thinai—What the heroine said to her friend. https://sangamtranslationsbyvaidehi.com/ettuthokai-kurunthokai-1-200/).

Other examples of images drawn from a rural surrounding are: 'Ears of grain cluster on the paddy grass maned like horses', 'Kitchen smoke from frying fish wafting through the streets' (*Narrinai* 311, Ramanujan, 2006: 48), or

> This town,
> ……… where fishermen with huge nets
> ……… struggle in the powerful ocean
> ……… and haul abundant fish that they
> ……… dry on fresh sand,
> ……… the uproarious streets reek of
> ……… flesh,
> (*Natrinai* 63, Ulōchanār, Neythal Thinai—What the heroine's friend said to her, as the hero listened nearby https://sangamtranslationsbyvaidehi.com/ettuthokai-natrinai-1-200/).

or 'As they carry the white paddy of their land/to barter it for the salt of another' (*Narrinai* 183, Ramanujan, 42). These poems are alive with the sounds, smells and sights of a rustic hard-working community which understands and respects the value of manual labour, is in harmony with the cycles of nature and values the cow, horse and even the wild, jungle animal as extensions of the same life force that is pulsing through them.

The *puṟam* poems, even while they describe the extraordinary, are rich in imagery drawn from the ordinary. Auvaiyār compares Atiyamāṉ Anci to 'a chariot wheel' crafted thoughtfully by a skilled carpenter (*Puṟanāṉuṟu* 87, Ramanujan, 2006: 137). Kapilar, describing the bounty of Pāri's kingdom, talks of four things which are unique to that land—wild rice which grows among bamboo leaves, sweet jackfruit, sweet potatoes, and beehives rich with honey (*Puṟanāṉuṟu* 109, ibid: 143). Thus although the characters are drawn from the upper classes, the poems abound with the nature and culture of the society with all its stratifications.

The Bhakti Tradition

This 'everyday' aspect became a feature of post-Sangam period Tamil literature, and is directly manifested in the two major epics and the Bhakti poetic tradition. P.N. Venkatachari observes: 'Sangam works provide us with valuable information regarding religion, social life, government, commerce, arts, music, dance, courtship, manners and customs, and the daily life of the Tamils ... From the equanimity of the Sangam poets came the sermons of equality' (605). The two epics of *Cilappatikāram* and *Manimekalai*, composed around the fifth or sixth centuries, are, unlike epics in general, not about gods or godmen. In fact, Kamil Zvelebil is of the view that the conception of the epic is '...is based totally on the Sanskrit tradition, and cannot and does not apply strictly to Tamil epics' (129). The *Cilappatikāram* is a Jain epic about an ordinary couple Kovalan and Kannagi, and the tribulations they face due to complications on the domestic front. It is true that the purely domestic trouble escalates to largescale destruction and havoc of the kingdom, but the epic is singularly lacking in the description of war that usually marks epics like the *Iliad*, the *Rāmāyaṇa* or the *Mahābhārata*. *Manimekalai*, which is considered the Buddhist sequel to this Jain epic, centres on Manimekalai, daughter of Kovalan (the hero of *Cilappatikāram*) and Madhavi, a courtesan. R. Parthasarathy, who has translated *Cilappatikāram*, has drawn out the pattern of what he terms a 'poetic sequence' which evolved in three phases, beginning with the Sangam anthology of *Pathupāṭṭu* (The Ten Long Poems) and the epics which comprised the second phase. The *akam*/*puṟam* poetics of the Sangam poems also resonate in these epics. Parthasarathy describes how Kannagi's waiting for her husband Kovalan's return is described in language that has '...motifs from the *mullai* (forest) *tiṇai*: cowherds returning from their pastures on the edge of the forest, the evening filled with the sound of their flutes, and the smell of jasmine in the air' (290).

This utilisation of the ordinary to represent even the extraordinary continues beyond the phase of the epics in Tamil literature, to the Bhakti tradition. 'Bhakti' is described by Ramanujan as a 'great, many-sided shift [that] occurred in Hindu culture and sensibility between the sixth and ninth century' (1993, 103). Bhakti, which can be loosely translated as 'devotion', was marked by an individualistic turn, an attempt to break away from the ritualistic practices dictated by caste norms within Hindu religious belief. This was not a monolithic mass movement as the name tends to indicate, but a multiplicity of sectarian streams of thought that were iconoclastic and egalitarian in terms of caste as well as gender. Bhakti poetry also spoke the language of the common person, avoiding classical Sanskrit and the images that were common to religious poetry in that language. It thus became a people's movement where god became your personal friend or lover whom you dearly loved but could rebuke or insult without fear of reprisal. What was essentially a religious movement manifested itself in literature, especially the poems written by the pioneers of the movement. The first bhakti poets—the Saivite Nāyanmārs and the Vaishnavite Ālwars—appeared in the Tamil-speaking region, which, according to Ramanujan is no cause for surprise: 'Tamil alone had a full-grown literary courtly tradition as well as oral and village folk traditions—which "qualified" Tamil as a real alternative, in the culture of the time, for popular religious compositions' (1993:128). The relation between god and the bhakta is not that of a master and servant; as Ramanujan points out, the god is 'like a local Tamil chieftain and playboy—powerful yet accessible' (139). So the terms used by the *ālwar* saint is reminiscent of the *akam* poems. She berates the lord for telling lies, and like the arch artificer that he is, of 'play acting' and 'sweet talk' (qtd by Ramanujan 1993:139). The god is like an errant lover rebuked by a jealous girl. This motif which recurs in almost all bhakti poetry like that of Kabir or Mira, can be seen as a strand that emanates from Sangam poetics.

The *Praśasti* and the *Puṟam* poem

Thus both the *akam* and the *puṟam* poems managed to draw the commonplace into the classical world. However, with the quotidian came a rather dangerous, subversive tendency in the *puṟam* poems that tended to conceal itself like a worm in the woodwork.

The poets of the *puṟam* category were also composers of eulogies (the Sanskrit equivalent to this would be the *praśasti*s). The eulogist-poet was an indispensable component of a king's associates because the eulogies 'legitimized the status of the ruler, and this was primarily necessary when the rule of primogeniture had been broken; it underlined the expectations from a just king; it bestowed immortality on the ruler... and it recognized the role of poets as part of the royal entourage' (Thapar 27). Upinder Singh points out that a similar, mutually-validating bond between poet and patron or poet and king can be found in the early Tamil kingdoms as well. The poet who composed the eulogy was dependent on the king for material support and very often, livelihood. The king, in his turn, recognised the valuable contribution made by the poet in the construction of a public image (bombastic titles like Devanampiya Piyadasi for Emperor Ashoka, Gangaikonda Cholan for the Chola King Rajendra Chola or Imayavaramban for the Chera King Nedum Cheralathan, are examples) and the perpetuation of that construct through his verses. If the poet could not afford to displease the king, the reverse was also true because the king's extra-material greatness was sculpted entirely through the poet's efforts. So Upinder Singh notes: 'The relationship between ruler and poet was often very close and intense, based on strong bonds of loyalty, even friendship' (387). Ramanujan notes that the '*pāṭān tinai*' or the genre of praise is one of the seven sub-genres recognised by the *Tolkāppiyam*, and observes 'A large portion of the poems included in the *puṟam* anthologies are classified under the heading *pāṭān*, and even *puṟam* poems classified under other *tinai*s often include words of praise for a warrior or a king' (Ramanujan, 2004: 235).

The mutually beneficial bond between king/chieftain and bard is evident from the *puṟam* poems. Auvaiyār exhorts the poor bard to go and meet the King Anci to fill his bowl for 'He has the strength/ to protect and care/though the times are troubled./Bless him and his works' (Ramanujan, 2004: 130). The generosity of their kings is praised by Kākkaipāṭiyanār Nacalleiyar, Kapilar and others. In fact, like Anci through Auviayār, the King Pāri is mainly known through Kapilar's numerous poems. The *puṟam* poems unlike the *akam* do not appear to be overtly enigmatic but they nudge the reader in the direction of another layer of meaning, mainly because of the diverse roles assumed by the poet. The bard, besides eulogising, also has a Cassandra-like function in cautioning the king or chieftain from rushing headlong into rash acts. For instance in one of the poems, Killi Valavan is warned about the consequences of having his enemy's children publicly trampled to death by elephants. After reminding him of the illustrious line he belongs to which is that of a Chola king who gave his flesh for a pigeon in danger, the poet exhorts: 'Look at these children/the crowns of their heads are still soft/as they watch the elephants/they even forget to cry'. The poem ends thus: 'Now that you've heard me out/Do what you will' (Ramanujan, 2004: 122). Here is a public intellectual who is speaking truth to power. The poet's word proves to be more powerful than the king's sword.

The poet who wrote both *akam* and *puṟam* poems then seems to be fulfilling a dual role—the singer of the private realm of emotions, and the public life of courtier-politician. For example, Kapilar who wrote *Ainkurunuru* also contributed plentifully to the *puṟam* category with his fulsome praises of Pāri.

Latent Heterodoxy

What is the implication we have to read into these laudatory verses which often also become celebrations of the land ruled over by the king? Leo Strauss in his *Persecution and the Art of Writing*, has observed that writing in unliberal societies generally tends to be exoteric, by which he means 'writing between the lines' or cleverly concealing the purport of the text so that it can be deciphered only by a few discerning readers (24). The classical Sanskrit concept of *dhvani* and the *ullurai* and *irraici* of *Tolkappiyam* point to a tertiary meaning which lies beyond the denotative and connotative power of words. Dhvani is the ability of the word to suggest meanings beyond 'the conventional meaning, which is standardized by universal acceptance' and 'the idiomatic sense in particular expressions, sanctioned by usage...' to evoke 'certain emotions which are universally present in men' (Krishnamoorthy, 1974: 106). According to the *Tolkappiyam, irraici* 'is a meaning that is obtained beyond and besides the plain meaning of the words in the poem' (Tol. Por. Por.229) (qtd by Abraham Mariaselvam, 136). Tolkappiyar explains that the subtle messages contained within *irraci* are apparent only to 'those who are capable of understanding the true nature of them' (136–137). Mariaselvam makes a distinction between *irraici* and *ullurai*, in that *ullurai* is seen only in *akam* poems where the landscape becomes a metaphor for the state of the mind. Ramanujan describes *ullurai* as 'inner substance' and 'a technique of using the scene (in Kenneth Burke's terms) to describe an act or agent...' (2004: 206).

Considering that the poems of the Sangam age extensively make use of these poetic techniques, can we or should we assume that the anonymous poets or the poets who wrote under pseudonyms were telling us a truth that we perhaps have not heard or cared to hear?

George Steiner, in the different context of translation, emphasises the importance of 'listening' when the process of comprehension of a literary work is not lateral but 'ingressive' (375). This involves a rigorous disciplining of our attention, and a concerted attempt to 'discard the static of ready explanation, of scattered association, of personal commentary' if we have to 'listen totally' (375). Perhaps it is time to 'listen' to these poems.

Akam poems can be excluded from the purview of this particular enquiry because they have already taken the precaution of anonymity. As pointed out earlier, lack of specificities shroud them with a safety net. However, the poet of the *puṟam* poems, especially the bard of eulogies is in a more precarious position because s/he names and is named. Besides being tributes to the king and his munificence, these eulogies also became indirect tributes to the poetic genius of the composer: the king would never die because the lines in which he is immortalised would outlive time itself, or in other words, the poet's genius ensured immortality which could not be guaranteed by all the worldly might of the king. The poet of the eulogy, like Shakespeare, had enough confidence about the power of his verse to immortalise his patron: 'Nor shall death brag thou wander'st in his shade/When in eternal lines to time thou grow'st' (Sonnet 18). Auvaiyār's claim, for instance, that

> He was like the glowing sun and his white
> umbrella was like the moon with cool rays.
> His fame will never die!
> (*Puranānūru* 231, Poet Avvaiyār sang for Athiyamān Nedumān Anji, Thinai: Pothuviyal, Thurai: Kaiyaru Nilai; https://sangamtranslations byvaidehi.com/ettuthokai-purananuru-201-400/).

This was composed after the King's death and can also be seen as a rather egoistic boast that her verses will outlast other man-made monuments.

In a comparative analysis of the different forms of panegyric like the Sanskrit *praśasti,* Arabic qasida and the Chinese *fu*, Rebecca Gould draws upon Aristotle's *Rhetoric* to underline the self-referentiality of this genre. She argues that it had a 'double goal': 'to praise the patron who occasions its existence, and to confer glory on itself and its author' (257).

Ramanujan points out the different *'turais'* or specific thematic situations which are characteristic of *puṟam* poetry. *Centuraippatan pattu* or 'poem in praise of might, mien and glory' or *iyanmoli valttu* 'theme of extolling a hero by attributing to him all the noble deeds of his ancestors' also become a performative speech act in the Austinian sense, because the king/chieftain becomes what the poet says he is. Perceived this way, the question remains as to what the *puṟam* poem is validating—the king's might or the poetic genius which is a major causative aspect of that imperial might.

In a poem extolling Anci's generosity, Auvaiyār cautions her own mind to be not too greedy, and wait patiently for the gifts which the King was sure to give. She reassures herself that the gifts are waiting with the king to be dispensed of, like fodder.

> ... When we receive gifts from Athiyamān who owns
> fine chariots and elephants adorned with ornaments,
> they are there, whether it takes more or less time.
> The gifts are in our hands like a ball of food placed
> between the tusks of an elephant.
>
> He will not fail us, my heart that desires food!
> Do not worry! May his efforts prosper!
>
> (*Puranānūru* 101, Poet Avvaiyār sang for Athiyamān Nedumān Anji, Thinai: Pādān, Thurai: Parisil Kadā Nilai)

The last lines become an ironic coda which hints that she is praising the king only for the gifts which result from such an act, and not because he has any intrinsic merit.

Kapilar's apparent tribute to Pāri holds sarcasm for such self-seeking poets:

> Pāri! Pāri, they utter, and poets
> with eloquent tongues praise him.
> There is not just Pāri!
> There is also the rain that gives
> and protects this world!
>
> (*Puranānūru* 107, Poet Kapilar sang for Vēl Pāri, Thinai: Pādān, Thurai: Iyan Mozhi; https://sangamtranslationsbyvaidehi.com/ettuthokai-purananuru-1-200/).

Kāppiyāṟṟukkāppiyaṇār's tribute to a king who is victorious in battle begins with the line 'Great King, you shield your men from ruin' (*Patirruppattu* 35, Ramanujan, 2006: 115). Nevertheless the poem goes from one horrendous image after another about the battlefield, ending with the picture of loose chariot wheels lying haphazardly along with elephant tusks (125). And further to 'flocks of male eagles/eat carrion/ with their mates', 'headless bodies/dance about/before they fall', 'blood glows,/like the sky before nightfall' and 'demons dance there' before ending with 'And your kingdom/is an unfailing harvest/ of victorious wars' (125.). This seems to be a tribute to a pyrrhic victory, an implicit critique of a war that wreaked widespread destruction on men and animals.

These poems seem to bear out the truth of Gould's observation of the panegyric:

> In resisting purely denotative language, premodern literary cultures constituted the panegyric as a discourse *about, within,* and sometimes *against,* sovereign power. Although such stances would appear to imply contradiction, the panegyric as a literary genre is relevant to our political present precisely because it managed, as few literary genres can today, to hold all three relations to power in tension with one another, in a single poetic gesture (263; emphasis mine).

This is bodied forth by/in Auvaiyār. Self-designated as a *virāli* or minstrel poet she was powerful enough to be respected by the kings of her day. Sharma points out that she was sent as an envoy of her patron Anci to the court of Tondaiman to negotiate a military alliance. He describes her as a 'political/social activist, perhaps a dissident at large' and states that '...she was much admired by the feudal lords of the era for her political acumen and was invited by them to attend 'a grand Rajasuya sacrifice performed by a Chola king' (69).

Vaidehi in her translation of Sangam poems has noted that 'Auvaiyār and King Athiyaman Neduman Anji [sic] were great friends' (www.sangamtranslationsbyvaidehi.com). Auvaiyar's poems about Anci are undeniably about sovereign power written from within it, but on occasion some of them display a subtext which if not subversive, displays a frustration which is not named or accounted for. For instance, one of the poems portrays the disturbance of a soldier who is forced to attack unsuspecting people; his mind is buffeted as if caught in the 'swirls' of a moving wind. Interestingly, the 'suffering' here is of the attacker and not those who are attacked (qtd in Sharma 69).

There is no doubt as to the nature of the emotion expressed here; however, we can only speculate as to what occasioned it. It could admittedly be a personal feeling of annoyance with non-sympathetic fellowmen who cannot sense the emotional turbulence within her; conversely, it could be a very public statement of frustration with citizens who refuse to act against an injustice.

Interiorised Meaning

The ambiguity in these lines might be hiding a meaning which has been 'interiorised', waiting to be prised out by discerning readers. Ayyappa Paniker in his discussion of the Indian narrative technique of interiorisation observes how a text can have 'layer upon layer of signification' and the reader who is not alert to these multiplicities of meaning might get carried away by a charming exterior (5). He in fact warns that the simpler an exterior is, the greater the chances that it hides a highly complex interior. In this context he posits the '*nalikerapakam*' which is the model of the coconut with a hard outer covering hiding a soft and sweet interior. This is borne out by the model of Sangam poetry as well, with its complex polysemic structure; however, the reverse of it seems to apply here—a soft and sweet exterior conceals a hard message of defiance to authority and non-conformity. Could this poetic corpus then have interiorised a seed of counter-culture which has to be coaxed into displaying its full range of possibilities?

It also has to be debated if *dhvani* and *irraci* were the means by which ancient Indians forged their own Aesopian language or language of the 'literary underground', as Sue Curry Jansen describes it. She points out how during the seventeenth and eighteenth centuries, which were the years of Enlightenment but also the time of state suppression of heterodox thought in Europe, writers like Swift, Voltaire and Montesquieu were advocates of an 'outlaw language', which was marked by 'dissimulation, double entendre, and satiric irreverence' (81). The distinctive trait of this style is an Iago-like double-facedness: 'I am not what I am'. So, expressive prohibitions might actually be eager invitations, apparent praise could be oblique criticism. For instance, Mōsi Keeranār's *iyan moli* or eulogy for Kilān reads more like a breezy claim for his own poetic prowess which builds up the King's morale and reputation:

> Whether you give or not, I can easily sing of your
> manhood that is such that you do not run away from
> weapons thrown at you in battles, and of your
> Konkānam Mountain with many cool waterfalls that
> flow down from its summits, like pure cloth that
> drapes down/ (https://sangamtranslationsbyvaidehi.com/ettuthokai-purananuru-101-200/).

This is different from the *vyājastuti* of Sanskrit poetics which is defined as 'literal expression of blame the actual effect of which is congratulatory, and inversely, a statement that is phrased as praise, but actually delivers a harsh critique' (Bronner 179); this was but an *alamkara* or a poetic device which embellished the poem proper. The beauty of the language forged by the Sangam poets on the other hand, is that it became an elaborate arcane cryptogram which could not be deciphered till you were initiated into it. A heterodox idea could be smuggled into a poem in the garb of seemingly innocuous words. This also had the potential to be the weapon of the weak, the powerless and the marginalised who had to compose words and sentences which interiorised meanings waiting to be discovered.

However, this is not to argue that the *puṟam* poems were deliberately and intentionally subversive. There is no denying the fact that poetic devices like *dhvani* or *irraici* are contingent on the immediate cultural environs of the reader, which in turn is shaped by spatio-temporal aspects. Consequently, reading premodern texts in a different(ly) political present can be dangerous for precisely the reason that we might interpret and over-interpret, or quite simply, misread. Nevertheless the 'occupational hazard' that any writer has to confront is a reader who will read and interpret according to her interpretive community and the Sangam poetic corpus cannot be exempt from this 'readerly' privilege; these poems then will continue to challenge the reader, inspiring different readings which might not have been originally intended.

Such interpretive challenges notwithstanding, what this ancient poetic tradition convincingly did was to inscribe the commons in the annals of classical literature, blurring the boundaries of the classical/plebeian divide. They stand as reflections of lived realities, as well as reflections about political and poetic power.

Works Cited

Bronner, Yigal. "Change in Disguise: The Early Discourse on Vyājastuti", *Journal of the American Oriental Society*,2009, (129.2): 179–198.

Gould, Rebecca. "The Much Maligned Panegyric: Toward a Political Poetics of Premodern Literary Form." *Comparative Literature Studies*, 2015. Vol. 52, No. 2: 254–288.

Jansen, Sue Curry. *Censorship: The Knot that Binds Power and Knowledge*. New York: Oxford University Press, 1991.

Mariaselvam, Abraham. *The Song of Songs and Ancient Tamil Love Poems: Poetry and Symbolism*. https://www.google.co.in/books/edition/The_Song_of_Songs_and_Ancient_Tamil_Love/9TULZX3SY18C?hl=en&gbpv=1&dq=the+song+of+songs+and+ancient+tamil+love+poems&printsec=frontcover. Accessed September 10, 2020.

Nadarajah, Devapoopathy. *Love in Sanskrit and Tamil Literature: A Study of Characters and Nature (200 BC–A.D. 500)*. New Delhi: Motilal Banarssidas, 1994.

Paniker, Ayyappa. *Indian Narratology*. New Delhi: Indira Gandhi National Centre for the Arts with Sterling, 2003.

Parthasarathy, R. *The Cilappatikāram: The Tale of an Anklet*. Translated, with introduction and postscript. Penguin, 2004.

Ramanujan, A.K. *The Collected Essays of A.K. Ramanujan*. Ed. Vinay Dharwadker. New Delhi, New York: Oxford University Press, 2004.

——. Translated. *Hymns for the Drowning: Poems for Viṣṇu by Nammāḻvār*. Penguin, 1993.

——. Trans. and ed. *Poems of Love and War*. New Delhi: Oxford University Press, 2006.

Sharma, T.R.S. *Dialogics of Cultures in Ancient Indian Literatures*. Indian Institute of Advanced Study, 2014.

Shulman, David. *Tamil: A Biography*. Cambridge, Massachusetts; London, England: The Belknap Press of Harvard University Press 2016.

Singh, Upinder. *A History of Ancient and Early Medieval India*. New Delhi; Upper Saddle River, NJ : Pearson Education, 2008..

Strauss, Leo. *Persecution and the Art of Writing*. Chicago: University of Chicago Press, 1988

Steiner, George. *After Babel: Aspects of Language and Translation*. New York: Oxford University Press, 1975.

Thapar, Romila. *Cultural Transaction and Early India, in History and Beyond.* Oxford University Press, 2006.

Vaidehi. *Sangam Poems translated by Vaidehi.* https://sangamtranslationsbyvaidehi.com/Accessed June 17, 2016.

Zvelebil, Kamil Veith.*Tamil Literature. A History of Indian Literature. Vol X*. Ed. Jan Gonda. Otto Harrassowitz. Wiesbaden, 1974.

4

What To Do with the Past?

Sanskrit Literary Criticism in Postcolonial Space

V.S. Sreenath

Throughout its history of almost a millennium and a half, Sanskrit *kāvyaśāstra* was resolutely obsessed with the task of unravelling the ontology of *kāvya* (literary prose and poetry). It believed that it was the presence of certain special linguistic features such as poetic suggestion, figures of speech, figurative deviation, etc. that attributed literariness to a work of art. Therefore, Sanskrit *kāvyaśāstra* was exclusively preoccupied with the task of identifying and analysing the formal devices generating literariness in a work of art. Considering *kāvya* as a 'specialized' mode of language marked by the 'ingenious' use of certain distinctive linguistic devices, *kāvyaśāstra* always made it a point to delimit *kāvya* from other uses of language such as *śāstra*, the Vedas, and workaday language. Literary theoreticians in Sanskrit, irrespective of their spatio-temporal locations, unanimously agreed that *kāvya* was a special mode of expression (distinctly different from the ordinary form of speech) characterized by the presence of certain unique linguistic elements. According to Gerow, "the problem of *kāvyaśāstra* was then seen in differentiating that particular expression we call poetic from other verbal means, *śāstra*, and narrative" (224), and *kāvyaśāstra* "never ever strayed away from this central problem" (219).

Nonetheless, this did not imply that *kāvyaśāstra* was an intellectual tradition unmarked by disagreements. The most important and long-standing of all the points of contention among the practitioners of Sanskrit literary theory was the prioritization of certain formal elements as the 'soul' of literature. This strong sense of intellectual disagreement on the question of what constituted the 'soul' of *kāvya* eventually paved the way for the emergence of new frameworks of criticism and an in-depth analysis of various formal elements, thus playing a vital role in keeping this tradition alive and contemporary.

Although *kāvya* originated as early as the beginning of the Common Era and flourished through the works of writers like Aśvaghoṣa (2 CE), Bhāsa (4 CE?), Kālidāsa (4 CE), et al., there was no attempt to systematize the knowledge about the art of composing *kāvya* until 700 CE. According to the available historical evidence, Bhāmaha's *Kāvyālaṅkāra* (7 CE) is the earliest available text in the *kāvyaśāstra* tradition.

For Bhāmaha, the earliest known exponent of *kāvyaśāstra*, it was primarily *alaṅkāras* (figures of speech) that transformed a piece of writing into *kāvya*. Therefore, in his *Kāvyālaṅkāra*, Bhāmaha was chiefly concerned with the identification and analysis of *alaṅkāras*. According to Bhāmaha, what made an *alaṅkāra* different from other uses of language was its figurative deviation (*vakratā*) from ordinary speech. He opined that a poet should always be diligent in honing his skills in the art of figurative deviation, the vital force of all *alaṅkāras*. Bhāmaha pointed out that prosaic statements such as 'the sun has set,' 'the moon shines' or 'the birds fly back to their nest' were a mere 'report' or *vārtā*, not *kāvya* (II.87). He noted that *vakrokti* by which linguistic expressions are rendered beautiful is found in all *alaṅkāras*, and poets should be assiduous in cultivating it.

The exponents of the theories of *guṇa*. (poetic merit) and *rīti* (style) refuted the primacy that *ālaṅkārikas* such as Bhāmaha and Daṇḍin had given to figures of speech. Vāmana (8th century) noted that *rīti* (poetic style) where *guṇas* are properly knit together served as the soul of *kāvya* (I.2.3).[1] For him, *guṇas* such as *ojas* (grandeur) and *prasāda* (perspicuity) were primarily responsible for the unique nature or literariness in *kāvya*, and *alaṅkāras* could only enhance the charm, already beautified by the presence of *guṇas* (*Kāvyālaṅkārasūtravṛtti*, III.1.1). Ānandavardhana (9th century), who was Vāmana's successor, vehemently opposed the primacy given to both *alaṅkāras* and *rītis* by his predecessors as the vital components of literature. For Ānanda, *dhvani* or poetic suggestion was the 'soul' of *kāvya*. Ānandavardhana criticized his predecessors who "contend that poetry is nothing more than what is embodied in word and meaning".[2] He was of the view that "It was persons unable to analyse the true nature of poetry ... who propounded the doctrine of "styles" (*Dhvanyaloka*, 3.46 K).

Kuntaka, a tenth-century Sanskrit literary critic from Kashmir, considered *vakrokti* (figurative deviation of speech) as the chief source of literariness. According to Kuntaka, "*Kāvya* is that combination of *śabda* (signifier) and *artha* (signified) which shines forth with *vakratā* (figurative deviation of speech) to impart pleasure to readers" (61). According to him, "*Vakrokti* signifies that kind of a beautiful signification (*abhidhā*) which is different from common usage ("*prasidhābhidhānavyatirekiṇī*"; 91). Kuntaka says, "These two [*śabda* and *artha*] are things to be ornamented. The only ornament that beautifies them is *vakrokti*, and *vakrokti* issues from a poet's expertise in using language beautifully" (*Vakroktijīvita*, 91).

Samudrabandha, a tenth-century commentator on Ruyyaka's *Alaṅkārasarvasva*, gives us a glimpse into the history of this debate in the following passage.[3]

> A literary work is marked by certain special words and meanings. The speciality of these two [i.e. *śabda* and *artha*] can be analysed in three ways—through some language feature [*dharma*] or through some function [*vyāpāra*] or through aesthetic suggestion [*dhvani*]. The first group contains two sects—the one that gives importance to figures of speech and the one that lays emphasis on poetic qualities. In the second sect, some pay attention to beautiful expression and the others to the capacity to produce aesthetic pleasure [in readers]. Of these five groups, the first one is accepted by Udbhaṭa and others; the second one is accepted by Vāmana, the third one by the author of *Vakroktijīvita*, the fourth by Bhaṭṭa Nāyaka and the fifth by Ānandavardhana. (*Alaṅkārasarvasva* 4)

This strong sense of critical thinking continued to exist in *kāvyaśāstra* even in the medieval period which is often wrongly dubbed as the dark age by imperialist historiographers. Bronner's observation on this matter is worth mentioning here. Bronner opines,

> A remarkable trend of innovation seems to characterize Sanskrit Poetics on the eve of colonialism. Like intellectuals in other Sanskritic disciplines, *ālaṃkārikās*—from about mid-sixteenth-century onward—adopted a new discursive idiom, composed in novel genres, demonstrated a fresh interest in the history of their tradition, and worked across disciplines

> at a hitherto unknown rate. Moreover, they often had a clear sense of themselves as breaking new ground and were thus conceived by their colleagues (441).

It is significant to note that Sanskrit literary theoreticians in the medieval phase often called themselves *navyas* (new intellectuals) to mark their intellectual departure from their predecessors (who they often addressed as *prācīnas* or old-fashioned ones). A case in point is Jagannātha's (17th century) debate on the causes of *rasābhāsa* or the semblance of *rasa* in *kāvya*. According to *prācīnas*, a woman with multiple male partners was not a cause of *rasābhāsa*, provided she was married to them. But for *navyas* like Jagannātha, this was a clear case of *rasābhāsa*. Therefore, he argued that Draupadī's love for her five husbands was a case of *rasābhāsa*. Distancing himself from the old school and calling himself *navya* or new, Jagannātha declared: "Here Draupadī's love for her husbands is definitely an instance of *rasābhāsa* or semblance of *rasa*. This is the view of the new intelligentsia. But the ancient scholars do not see this as an instance *rasābhāsa*" (*Rasagaṅgādhara*, 101).[4] Similarly, Jagannātha's *Citramīmāṃsā-khaṇḍana* is a repudiation of Appayya Dīkṣita's (16th century) *Citramīmāṃsā* which had previously criticised scholars such as Bhoja (11th century), Mammaṭa (11th century) Ruyyaka (12 century) and Vidyānātha (13th century). Siddicandra's (16th century) *Kāvyaprakāśa-khaṇḍana* was self-evidently a criticism of Mammaṭa's *Kāvyaprakāśa* which attracted a series of commentaries from the practitioners of literary criticism all over Sanskrit cosmopolis.[5]

Sanskrit Poetics and the Colonial Period

It is interesting to note that even during the colonial period scholars continued to produce treatises in Sanskrit poetics. A few cases in point in this respect include Cirañjīva Bhaṭṭācārya's (18th century) *Kāvyavilāsa*, Hariprasāda Māthura's (18th century) *Kāvyārthaguṃpha*, Garaḷapurī Śāstrī's (19th century) *Kṛṣṇabhūpalīyam*, Caṇdamārutācārya's *Citramīmāmsodhara* (19th century), Rama Pisharody's (19th century) *Dhvanyalokalocanākhyāyikā*, *Kuvalayānandavyākhyāyikā* and *Citramīmāmsāvyākhyāyikā*; Acyutācārya's (19th century) *Sāhityasāra*, and Gulāba Rāva Mahārāja's (19th century) *Kāvyasūtrasaṃhita*.[6]

But towards the turn of the 20th century, Sanskrit *kāvyaśāstra* tradition underwent a serious epistemic rupture. During this phase, the vigour in which new treatises in Sanskrit poetics were produced dwindled. This does not imply that all discussions about Sanskrit poetics came to a close during this period. One should note that scholarship about Sanskrit literature and literary theory continued to exist, but in a different form and shape. During this phase, the scholars of Sanskrit poetics were primarily interested in faithfully recording the intellectual history of this epistemology, as opposed to creating new texts in Sanskrit poetics and carefully criticizing the observations of their predecessors. This does not mean that *pāṇḍitya* in Sanskrit poetics and the production of literary works in Sanskrit disappeared from the scene altogether.[7] What is really significant about this period is the fact that the dynamism of Sanskrit knowledge system to create history drastically diminished. Pollock underlines this decline: "The two centuries, before European colonialism decisively established itself in the subcontinent around 1750, constitute one of the most innovative epochs of Sanskrit systematic thought (in language analysis, logic, hermeneutics, moral-legal philosophy and the rest) ... Concurrently with the spread of European power, however, this dynamism diminished so much that by 1800, the capacity of Sanskrit thought to make history had vanished" (1). One would be surprised to note that well-known scholars of Sanskrit *kāvyaśāstra* in the 20th century such as S.K. De, P.V. Kane, C.D. Narasimhaiah, M. Hiriyanna, Krishna Chaitanya, K. Krishnamoorthy, Raghavan and so on did not produce a single new treatise in Sanskrit poetics. This is primarily because by the twentieth century the traditional ontological notions about literature (to which Sanskrit *kāvyaśāstra* greatly conformed) started undergoing a radical transformation, and the style and language of literary works became similar to everyday speech.

In the olden days, literature was a special form of language which could be created only after a careful and dedicated practice in *alaṅkāraśāstra* which treated *kāvya* as a 'special' use of language, distinct from the ordinary form of speech. This was primarily motivated by the hope that understanding the textual elements responsible for the unique nature of *kāvya* will contribute greatly to the creation of good art (Sivarudrappa and Seshagiri Rao 78; Pollock 44). Many Sanskrit literary theoreticians talked in extenso about the role that proper training in poetics played in the production of literary texts. Daṇḍin's observation about the importance of education in *kāvyaśāstra* is a representative case in this regard. According to Daṇḍin, "Just as a blind person cannot distinguish between different colours, so also a poet untrained in poetics cannot differentiate between poetic merits and faults" (*Kāvyādarśa* I.8). He went on to say that a poet, irrespective of whether he is naturally endowed with poetic genius or not, can master the art of poetry simply by learning and practicing *kāvyaśāstra* (I.104). According to Bhāmaha, an aspiring poet should venture into composing *kāvya*s only after achieving mastery over all the *śāstra*s related to *kāvya* (I.10). Vāmana held that a poet should understand the *guṇa*s and *doṣa*s of *kāvya* by getting educated in *kāvyaśāstra*. Even if a person is naturally endowed with poetic talent, s/he should definitely undergo training in poetics (*Kāvyālaṇkārasūtravṛtti*, I.1.4.5). In his *Kāvyamīmāṃsā* (10 CE), Rājaśekhara emphasised the importance of education in *kāvyaśāstra* by saying that "[t]he prior knowledge of *śāstra* is essential for the appreciation of *kāvya*." According to him, "Just as nothing is visible in the dark without the aid of light, so also no poet can create [poems] without the knowledge of *śāstra*" (20). All these observations attest to the fact that mastery over *kāvyaśāstra* was as important as *pratibhā* (inborn genius) for a person to become a *kavi*. Familiarity with the technicalities underpinning a literary artefact was also necessary for the readers of Sanskrit *kāvya* to appreciate literary works. This conception remained unchanged even when vernacular literature took shape during the medieval period. The very existence of texts in vernacular poetics—*Līlātilakam* in Malayalam, *Kavirājamārga* in Kannada, or *Kavikulkalptaru* in Brajbhāṣa—attests to this fact.

But, by the mid-twentieth century, a new conception about literariness (which already began in the 19th century under the influence of Western literature) started taking deep root in the Indian subcontinent. This new approach tried to replicate the style and cadence of everyday speech in literary works and consequently stood in contrast to the Formalistic notions about literature to which Sanskrit *kāvyaśāstra* conformed. In other words, the erstwhile conception that one needs to know the lessons of Sanskrit poetics before attempting to compose a literary work altogether disappeared. By this time, the literary world in India was also making a transition from Sanskrit to English and the vernacular languages which mostly embraced and championed this new conception of literature through new genres like novel, short story, autobiography, etc.

It is also significant to note that there was a strong feeling among many vernacular critics that the parameters of Sanskrit criticism were not adequate enough to judge and appreciate the new literary works founded on a new sense of literariness. In connection with Malayalam literature, K.M. George observes,

> In the olden days, literature was essentially in verse and in India the language was Sanskrit. In order to enable the average *sahṛdaya* to enjoy literature, there was a need for commentaries and interpretations. It was therefore natural that external apparatus like rhyme, rhythm and figures of speech was expounded by scholars: this was an accepted aspect of criticism, construed by some as the be-all and end-all of criticism. When works came in nālikera pāka (like a coconut), the hard shell had to be broken and the kernel shown. So this kind of criticism developed in Malayalam and it was quite relevant when classics appeared in the maṇipravāla style. Even in the modern period when we deal with the poems of Kumaran Asan and Vallathol, though the shell is not hard, a similar analytical approach had some relevance. But criticism had to take a fresh turn, to explore and explain the spirit of the work, which was more elusive than the external aspects. And when fiction came to the force, a completely different approach was called for. The form itself was Western and works were mostly in draksha paka (like grapes) and hence the analysis of the external structure had no relevance. What was necessary was to unravel the spirit of the work and to arouse the reader's dormant sensibility to full participation. Who wants a commentary for Thakazhi's *Chemmeen*, written in the colloquial language? (86)

Many literary critics in Malayalam vehemently criticized the Sanskritic influence upon drama and sought for the employment of a new set of parameters for the appreciation and analysis of modern literary works which shared the style and sensibilities of everyday speech and life.[8] Satchidanandan in his "Dilemmas of Indian Literary Criticism" observes, "The new textures of urban living with its contradictory aspects of penury and luxury, the intensification of the alienation among the intelligentsia; the angst of the new awareness of space and time; the growing consumer instinct; the loss of traditional values and the growth of the new post-industrial ethos made possible by new technologies", etc. proved that "traditional critical frameworks are hopelessly inadequate to meet the needs of literary criticism which declared their independence from Sanskrit centuries ago, even while retaining aspects of it that they found useful to their flowering and growth." According to him, "this crisis which is often unacknowledged had already begun with the maturing of Indian languages."

What engendered a radical break off from this conventional notion of literariness was obviously the educational policies of colonial government. An important aspect of colonial education was the introduction of Western literature in schools and universities. The new genres of literature from the West such as the novel, short-story, essay, etc.[9] which stood closer to the style of workday language, played a vital role in replacing the old conception of literariness with a new one.

The erstwhile ontological notion of literature on which Sanskrit *kāvyaśāstra* was founded could never again recapture the terrain of literature. Today literature is no longer an ontological category, as it used to be in the past. It has now completely become a functional category. In other words, according to the modern parameters of literariness, any piece of writing (be it a news item in a daily or a hoarding on wayside or a railway catalogue) can become a literary work, provided the reader reads it poetically. Terry Eagleton talks about this paradigmatic shift to a functional, reader-oriented view of 'literariness:

> There is no 'essence' of literature whatsoever. Any bit of writing may be read non-pragmatically, if that is what reading a text as literature means, just as any writing may be read 'poetically.' If I pore over a railway timetable not to discover a train connection but to stimulate in myself general reflections on the speed and complexity of modern existence, then I might be said to be reading it as literature (10).

This changed perception about literariness also stalled the production of new texts in Sanskrit poetics which traditionally believed in the ontological definition of literariness.

A New Direction for Sanskrit Poetics

Despite the general feeling that Sanskrit poetics is outdated to appreciate modern literary works, a group of critics during the 1980s attempted to apply Sanskrit *kāvyaśāstra* to evaluate the merit of modern literary works from India. This shift which can be labelled a 'revivalist trend' was spearheaded by Indian literary theoreticians such as K. Krishnamoorthy, Krishna Rayan, Ayyappa Paniker, C.D. Narasimhayya, and so on. This tendency in the first instance was the result of a strong desire to decolonize Western critical sensibilities and to "reconstitute a sense of Indianness of the texts considered, and assess their virtue by the standards and assumptions of indigenous aesthetics" (Bill Ashcroft, et al. 173). Bill Ashcroft (2002), et al. talk about this tendency in literary criticism in their *Empire Writes Back*,

> Indian scholars and critics have been locked in debate as to how far these traditions can be adapted to the needs of modern criticism for Indian literature. The debate centres on whether or not the 'highly sophisticated theories' propounded by the Sanskrit 'schoolmen' can be, or, indeed, ever were 'applied in the evaluation of works of art' (Krishnamoorthy 1984) and, more specifically, whether the terms of this tradition: *rasa, dhvani, alaṅkāra*, etc., are more relevant and suitable than imported terms to the description of contemporary literatures in the Indian vernacular languages and, to a lesser extent, to Indian literatures in English. (116)

The seminal event which inaugurated this movement was a seminar held at the Literary Criterion Centre at Dhvanyāloka in Mysore, on the theme of 'the formulation of a Common Poetics for Indian Literature Today.' The seminar paid considerable attention to the practical use of Sanskrit poetics as a common critical framework to effectively understand and judge the literary merit of Indian literary texts in modern times. The conference concluded that the *rasa-dhvani* approach, being the most dominant critical system in the Indian literary context, could be used as a common critical framework to evaluate literary texts of Indian origin.

The book *The Burning Bush* (1988), edited by Krishna Rayan, was an immediate output of this thought. This book analyses seventeen literary works from seventeen different Indian languages through the lens of *rasa-dhvani* approach in order to understand the practical applicability of these theoretical positions in modern criticism. The blurb of the book says,

> With literature in the various Indian languages interacting more vigorously today than ever before, it has become all-important that critical practice

> in them shares a common theoretical framework, so that the assumptions, analytical tools, and evaluative criteria used are roughly uniform. Obviously, there are major advantages in evolving this framework from existing Indian theory rather than sources elsewhere. The most widely dominant Indian critical system is the Rasa-dhvani theory formulated in the 9th century. But before adopting it, it must be revised in the light of other Indian and Western theories, and it must also be tested on texts in Indian Languages. It is this latter that Krishna Rayan's book [*The Burning Bush*] seeks to do.

Krishna Rayan's "*Rasa-Dhvani* and Present-day Literary Theory and Criticism"; Ayyappa Paniker's "The Renovation of Rasa-theory"; Krishnamoorthy's "The Relevance of Rasa Theory to Modern Literature"; R.B. Patankar's "Does the Rasa Theory Have Modern Relevance?"; Umashankar Joshi's "The Relevance of Sanskrit Poetics to Contemporary Practical Criticism," etc. are some of the major works in this direction.

Though these two approaches to Sanskrit poetics, namely the Intellectual historiography and revivalist trend, were crucial in introducing modern readers to the complexities of Sanskrit literary science, they were caught up in ontological certitude.[10] In other words, neither of these two directions attempted to study these theoretical positions from a standpoint other than that of literary theory. Although it is important to record how classical knowledge systems were canonically understood and practised, it is also significant to re-read and reinterpret these theoretical positions from newer perspectives. Each time we re-interpret or re-read these theoretical frameworks from a new position, we are in fact creating new knowledge about them.

In other words, we necessarily need to come out of our fetish for the frameworks of canonical reading with which we have so far been dealing with these theories. To borrow a Barthian terminology, we need to treat Sanskrit poetics as a 'Text,' instead of a 'work.' According to Barthes, while the idea of 'work' imposes a permanent signification and a specific generic label on a discourse, the concept of 'Text' does not limit a discourse to any permanent categorization or any fixed order of signification. Barthes notes,

> The Text is plural. Which is not simply to say that it has several meanings, but that it accomplishes the very plural of meaning: an *irreducible* (and not

> merely an acceptable) plural. The Text is not a co-existence of meanings but a passage, an overcrossing; thus it answers not to an interpretation, even a liberal one, but to an explosion, a dissemination. The plural of the Text depends, that is, not on the ambiguity of its contents but on what might be called the *stereographic plurality* of its weave of signifiers. ("From Work to Text" 159)

We should also note that 'work' and 'Text' are not two separate entities. It is our attitudinal difference that makes a certain discourse either a 'work' or a 'Text.' If we attribute a definite meaning and a generic label to a discourse, then we are considering it as a 'work,' whereas if we hold that a discourse can have multiple meanings and generic labels, then we are treating it as a 'Text.' It is to mark this radical attitudinal shift from the idea of monolithic signification to multiplicity of signification that Barthes employs the term 'Text.' To open up Sanskrit poetics to newer possibilities of reading, we necessarily need to treat this epistemology as a 'Text.'

Just as a poem or a drama or an article can be interpreted from multiple perspectives, so also the texts that constitute Sanskrit poetics can be revisited from a variety of vantage points. I do not mean to propose that all kinds of readings that a reader or a researcher makes about this epistemology should be considered valid. Only those readings that are backed by proper textual evidence should be taken into account in this process. Hence, we should, as Derrida has famously put it, 'play' with these texts. The Derridian idea of 'play' is always a reader-oriented position in the sense that it gives freedom to readers to deal with a text without aiming at any teleological point of completion or permanently adhering to any specific framework of reading. The idea of 'play,' as Derrida conceives it, aims to explore a text's potential to produce an infinite number of significations.

That said, I do not mean to propose that the existing approaches to Sanskrit poetics—Intellectual historiography and revivalist trend—are invalid and one should not understand these texts in the canonical way they were practised and understood. Along with this praxis, we also need an 'interventionist historiography of ideas' which will critically examine these theoretical positions from different vantage points thereby preventing them from becoming static categories. Each new reading of a text dislodges it from our taken-for-granted conceptions about it and leads us to the production of new knowledge about/ from that text. This is the only way in which we can make sure the live continuum of the existing frameworks of ideas. Each time we deconstruct or 'play' with a text, we are in fact creating new knowledge about that text. An approach of this sort has often given a new lease of life to many philosophical positions that were considered exhausted and out-dated. A case in point is Nicholas Royle's re-interpretation of Freud in *The Uncanny*. In *The Uncanny*, Royle gives "a series of close-readings of different aspects of the topic" [the uncanny] (Royle: vii), thereby breaking free from the canonical reading prescribed for the understanding of the idea of uncanny. The following section of the paper is an exemplification of this methodological praxix vis-à-vis Ānandavardhana's famous *avivakṣita-vācya-dhvani*.

Dhvani and Play

In Sanskrit poetics, Ānandavardhana is the first literary theoretician to approach the idea of *dhvani* or poetic suggestion systematically. Ānanda divides the whole realm of poetic suggestion into two, namely *avivakṣita-vācya-dhvani* (*dhvani* where the literal meaning is not intended) and *vivakṣitānya-paravācya dhvani* (*dhvani* where the literal meaning is understood in a different way). While *vivakṣitānya-paravācya dhvani* deals with aesthetic emotion and stylistic aspects, *avivakṣita-vācya-dhvani* deals with semantic aspects. The conventional notion about *dhvani* is that it is an essential formal element for a piece of writing to be called a *kāvya*. Therefore, Ānanda calls *dhvani* the soul of literature. But in my analysis of *dhvani*, I would like to take a non-canonical approach towards the idea of *avivakṣita-vācya-dhvani* by calling it a mechanism which resists the rigid, conventional relationship between signifier and signified. Here I argue that *avivakṣita-vācya-dhvani*, as conceptualized by Ānandavardhana, opens up a signifier to new significations that are not conventionally associated with it. In this process, I also argue by extension, that *avivakṣita-vācya* becomes a liberating experience for the author, reader and the sign.

Convention exists everywhere and even the language we speak is ultimately a product of it. As far as the realm of language is concerned, convention prevails in the form of lexicon, grammar, style, orthography, etc. In any language, convention is a necessary evil. It is necessary in the sense that it is important for the production of meaning. It is an evil in that it curbs one's freedom to use the language in whatever ways one wants. For example, if one says 'he study hard before his exam' or 'you sings well', s/he will be considered wrong in their usage of English, as it is directly at war with the conventions of the English language. The same holds true for the relation between the signifier (the word that represents a concept) and the signified (the concept represented by the signifier). As far as the relation between the signifier and signified is concerned, convention imposes a semantic ambit upon a signifier. What I mean by semantic ambit is the range of significations that a particular signifier is allowed to signify. Because of this semantic ambit, a signifier is not allowed to designate significations that are outside the limit of the semantic ambit. For example, the word 'cat' cannot normally represent the idea 'rat' or 'bat' or 'tree.' This semantic ambit not only structures the signifier, it also forces the language user, be it a reader or a listener or a speaker or an author, to approach a signifier in a specific fashion. In other words, conventional semantic ambit is a restrictive force upon the language user. Now let us see how *avivakṣita-vācya-dhvani* transcends the conventional semantic ambit imposed upon a signifier so as to liberate the position of the reader/listener and the writer/speaker.

According to Ānandavardhana, *avivakṣita-vācya-dhvani* is that sort of *dhvani* where a signifier abandons its primary meaning to suggest a new meaning that is not conventionally associated with it. To deterritorialize or transcend the semantic ambit, *avivakṣita-vācya* banks upon secondary usages like metaphor and metonymy (*Dhvanyāloka* 3.33 i *A*).[11] An example of *avivakṣita-vācya* given by Ānandavardhana in *Dhvanyāloka* will further show us how this particular form of *dhvani* transcends the conventional semantic ambit. This is one of the numerous examples of *avivakṣita-vācya-dhvani* that Ānanda gives.: "The sky filled with drunken clouds (*mattamegham gaganaṃ*)."[12] We know that the conventional meaning of the word 'drunken' is to be in a state of intoxication and the word 'drunken' is always associated with a sentient entity. In other words, only a sentient creature can get drunk. But here in the given context, the word 'drunken' is associated with a non-sentient entity which is a 'cloud.' So, the primary meaning of the word 'drunken' gets blocked here and the focus gets shifted to a quality conventionally associated with a drunkard, i.e. to wander around aimlessly. So, the word 'drunken' deterritorializes its semantic ambit to incorporate a new meaning that is not conventionally associated with it.

Now a question may arise—since secondary usages can also be part of linguistic convention, as in the case of dead metaphors like 'leg of a table, etc.' how can *avivakṣita-vācya-dhvani* ensure that it always pushes a signifier beyond the conventional meaning? To capacitate a signifier to transcend the conventional semantic ambit, Ānandavardhana eschews from the domain of *avivakṣita-vācya-dhvani* all the secondary usages that have become part of the existing linguistic convention. According to Ānanda, a secondary usage can become an instance of *avivakṣita-vācya-dhvani*, only if it is outside the purview of the existing linguistic convention. Ānanda opines, "To this we reply that here also there is no fault; because while the type of suggestion where the expressed meaning is unintended [*avivakṣita-vācya-dhvani*] relies on the path of secondary usage, it is not itself secondary usage. Secondary usage can also be found [in instances that are entirely] without suggestiveness" (3.33 j *A*).[13] For instance, the expression 'leg of a table' is technically a secondary usage because it is not possible for a table to have legs. But based on the function that a leg performs, the tool which shores up a table-top is called a leg. Technically it is a secondary usage, but it cannot become an instance of *dhvani* because 'leg of a table' is a dead metaphor—a secondary usage that has become part of the linguistic convention. So only those secondary usages, which are novel and innovative and are not part of the existing linguistic convention, can become a *dhvani*.[14] Ānandavardhana opines, "A denotative power is the very self of each word, for the word is never known without it. But suggestiveness is not bound to the word, but accidental, for our apprehension of it is conditioned by context, etc. and it is not apprehended in the absence of those conditions" (3.33 l *A*).[15] This impermanence of the boundaries of semantic ambit prevents *avivakśita-vācya-dhvani* from becoming another convention. In this mechanism, the author is forced to be more creative, in the sense that he is endowed with the task of pushing a signifier beyond the borders of its conventional semantic ambit. Ānanda notes that the meaning of a word in *avivakśita-vācya-dhvani* "is beyond the range of those who have taken pains only on the definitions of words and who have paid no attention to the poetic meaning, just as the character of the notes (*svaras*) and *śrutis*, etc. is beyond the range of those who know the definitions of music but are not good poet" (1.7 *K*). It goes without saying that a conventional semantic ambit so rigid that the author/speaker of a particular language cannot transcend the pre-given territory of signification. In the provisional semantic ambit created by *dhvani*, the speaker or the author can transcend the rigid boundaries traditionally imposed on a signifier by convention.

It is also important to note that Ānanda gives freedom to the reader/listener to experiment with the semantic ambit in their own stead. Ānanda observes that even if the author/speaker does not intend *dhvani* in his/her speech, the reader has the freedom to deterritorialize the semantic ambit. According to Ānanda, "Rather, it is a suggested element in any of the three forms, [*vastu*, *alaṅkāra* or *rasa*], *whether in the form speaker's intention or not*, if it is suggested as the final sentence meaning, that justifies the term *dhvani*, as we said in defining *dhvani* in terms of the aforesaid types of suggestiveness" (3.33 m *A*).[16] Ingalls, the translator of Ānandavardhana's *Dhvanyāloka*, further explains the words of Ānanda. Ingalls notes, "The *vyaṅgya* need not be intended by the speaker. A naive girl, to give an example not seldom used in Sanskrit poetry, may make a suggestion of which she is quite unaware and which she is so far from intending that she would avoid if she were" (n. 2 on 3.33 m *A*).

This non-canonical analysis of *dhvani* that I have shown now generates new knowledge and perception about Ānandavardhana's concept of *avivakśita-vācya-dhvani*. Similarly, one can also approach other theoretical positions from new standpoints hitherto untried. This approach can certainly take us beyond our blinkered conceptions about ancient knowledge systems. As I pointed out at the outset of this essay, it is important to constantly question and critically approach knowledge systems to ensure their continuum in the future. A strong sense of debate and resistance to uncritical reverence are what we need today.

Notes

1. *rītirātmā kāvyasya* | (*Kāvyālaṅkārasūtravṛtti* I.2.6).
2. Ānandavardhana is indirectly criticizing literary theoreticians like Bhāmaha, Daṇḍin and Vāmana who opine that *kāvya* is primarily a combination of *śabda*

and *artha* (sound and sense). For detailed reading, see Bhāmaha (I.16), Daṇḍin (I.10) and Vāmana (I.1).

3. I would like to point out the two opposing views regarding the evolution of Sanskrit poetics. While scholars like Kane and De follow the classification of Sanskrit poetics along the lines of *guṇa* and *rīti*, McCrea (2008) rejects it. For Kane and De's views, see respectively *History of Sanskrit Poetics*, p. 372 and History of Sanskrit Poetics Vol II, 32. For McCrea's view, see *The Teleology of Poetics In Medieval Kashmir*, pp. 30–31.
4. For a detailed reading of the debate between *navyas* and *prācīnas*, see "Vastutas tu: Methodology and the New School of Sanskrit Poetics" by Bronner and Tubb.
5. Highlighting the popularity of *Kāvyaprakāś*, Maheśvara (17 C.E.), the author of *Kāvyaprakāśādarśana*, says that although a commentary of *Kāvyaprakāśa* is prepared in almost all houses, it still escapes the grasp of intellectuals by its innovative nature (Jhalakikar 39). For a detailed reading of commentarial tradition, see *The Kāvyaprakāśa in the Benares-Centered Network of Sanskrit Learning* by Cummins (2020).
6. For a review of all the works in Sanskrit poetics ever published in India, see *An Annotated Bibliography of the Alaṃkāraśāstra* by Timothy C. Cahill. A note of warning should be sounded now: though Sanskrit kāvyaśāstra texts continued to get produced in the 19th century, the amount of original thought that went into these texts remains to be determined. Any categorical observation about the originality of these texts in terms of their interaction with the tradition requires a great amount of work. However, one thing we can say for certain is that none of these texts composed during the colonial period could become landmarks in the history of Sanskrit poetics as Jagannātha's *Rasagaṅgādhara* or Appayya Dīkṣita's *Kuvalayānanda* could do in the previous epoch.
7. For detailed reading of modern works in Sanskrit, especially of those from the 19th and 20th century, read Radha Vallabh Tripathi's "Modern Writings in Sanskrit: A Resume." Tripathi notes that "Modern Sanskrit writers made a departure from their age-old literary traditions by the way to looking towards vernaculars and European languages also" (169).
8. K.C. Anthappayi's *Bhāṣānāṭakapariśodhana* is a case in point. In this work, Anthappayi criticizes the predilection of Malayalam playwrights for Sanskrit dramas. He also opines that critics should do away with the *guṇanirūpaṇam* (analysis of literary merits) of Malayalam dramas based on the parameters of literariness set by Sanskrit poetics.
9. For a detailed reading of the role that Western literature played in the consolidation of colonial power in India, see Gauri Viswanathan's *Masks of Conquest Literary Study and British Rule in India*.
10. Ontological certitude is the act of reducing the identity of an entity to a set of fixed assumptions.

11. *vyañjakatvam hi kvacit vācakatvāśrayeṇa vyavatiṣṭhate| yathā vivakṣitānyaparavācye dhvanau| kvacittu guṇavṛttyāśrayeṇa| yathā avivakṣitānyaparavācye dhvanau| tadubhayāśrayatvapratipādanāyaiva ca dhvaneḥ prathamataram dvau prabhedāvupanyastau.* (Ibid., p. 427).
12. See the complete verse from *Dhvanyāloka. gaganam ca mattamegham dhārālulitārjunāni ca vanāni |nirahaṅkāramṛgāṅkā haranti nīlā api niśāḥ ||* (273).
13. *ayamapi na doṣaḥ| yasmād avivakṣitavācyo dhvanirguṇavṛttimārgāśrayospi bhavati, na tu guṇavṛttirūpa eva| guṇavṛttir hi vyañjakatvaśūnyāpi dṛśyate|* (432).
14. Ānandavardhana cites a lot of examples where *dhvani* does not occur even in the presence of *gauṇavṛtti* (secondary usage). A case in point is the word *lāvaṇya.* Ānanda observes, "Words such as *lāvaṇya,* which are used idiomatically in a sense other than their proper (etymological) sense, are never instances of *dhvani*" (184). *rūḍhā ye viṣayesnyatra śabdāḥ svaviṣayādapi | lāvaṇyādyāḥ prayuktāste na bhavanti padam dhvaneḥ ||* (Ibid., p. 147).
15. *ata eva vācakatvāttasya viśeṣḥ vācakatvam hi śabdaviśeṣasya niyatātmā, vyulpattikālādārabhya tadavinābhāvena tasya prasiddhatvāt | sa tv aniyataḥ aupādhikatvāt | prakaraṇādyavacchedena tasya pratīteritarathā tv aprātīteḥ |* (436–437).
16. *kintu tadeva kevalam aparimitaviṣayasya dhvanivyavahārasya na prayodanakam avyāpakatvāt | tathā darśitabhedatrayarūpam tālparyeṇa dyotyamānam abhiprāyarūpam anabhiprāyarūpam ca sarvameva dhvanivyavahārasya prayojakamiti yathoktavyañjakatvaviśeṣe dhvanilakṣaṇe nātivyāptiḥ na cāvyāptiḥ.* (443).

Works Cited

Abhinavagupta. *Locana.* In D. Ingalls, J. Masson, & M. V. Patwardhan, (Trans. and Eds.), *The Dhvanyāloka of Ānandavardhana with the Locana of Abhinavagupta.* Harvard University Press, 1990.

Ānandavardhana. *Dhvanyāloka of Ānandavardhana with the Locana of Abhinavagupta* (D. Ingalls, J. Masson, & M. V. Patwardhan, Trans. and Eds.). Harvard University Press, 1990.

Ashcroft, B., & Tiffin, H. *The empire writes back.* Routledge, 2002.

Bhāmaha. *Kāvyālaṅkāra.* (B. N. Sarma & Baldeva Upadhyay Eds.). Chowkhamba Sanskrit Series Office, 1998.

Bronner, Y. What is new and what is Navya. *Journal of Indian Philosophy, 305*(5), 2002. pp. 441–462.

Barthes, R. "From Work to Text." In *The rustle of language.* New Hill and Wang, pp. 56–64.

Daṇḍin. *Kāvyādarśa of Daṇḍin.* Ed. P. Tarkabagisa. Royal Asiatic Society.

Derrida, J. Structure, sign, and play in the discourse of the human sciences. In K. M. Newton (Ed.), *Twentieth-century literary theory*. Palgrave, 1997.

Eagleton, T. *Literary theory: An introduction*. University of Minnesota Press, 2008.

Gerow, E. *Indian poetics (A history of Indian literature)*. Harrassowitz, 1977.

George, K. M. "Literary criticism in Malayalam." *Indian Literature 16*(3), 1973.

Jagannātha. *The Rasagaṅgādhara of Jagannātha Paṇḍita with the commentary of Nāgeśa Bhaṭṭa*. D. Prasad, & K.P. Parab. The Nirnaya Sagara Press, 1888.

Krishnamoorthy, K. *Vakroktijīvita by Kuntaka*. Karnatak University, 1977.

Mammaṭa. *Kāvyaprakāśa of Mammaṭa*. Ed G. Jha. Bharathiya Vidya Prakashan, 1966.

Pollock, S. New intellectuals. *Indian Economic and Social History, 38*(1), 2001. Pp. 1–16.

Rājaśekhara. *Kāvyamīmāṃsā*. Ed. D.K. Sadhana Parashar. Print World, 2000.

Royle, N. *The uncanny*. Manchester University Press, 2003.

Samudrabandha. *Alaṅkārasarvasva of Rājānaka Ruyyaka with the commentary of Samudrabandha*. Ed. Ganapathy Sastri. Travancore Government Press, 1915.

Sreenath, V.S. *Avivakṣita-vācya-dhvani* and the deterritorialization of signifier: A liberating experience for author and reader. *Journal of Indian Philosophy, 45*(5), 2017. Pp. 817–836.

Satchidananda, K. "Dilemmas of Indian literary criticism." Frontline, March 21, 2014.

Vāmana. *Kavyalankarasutravrtti*. Ed. Nambootiri. Kerala Bhasha Institute, 2000.

Secondary Works

Kane, P.V. *History of Sanskrit Poetics*. Motilal Banarsidass, 1951.

McCrea, Lawrence, J. *The teleology of poetics in medieval Kashmir*. Harvard University Press, 2008.

Pathak, R.S. The Indian Theory of vakrokti in relation to the stylistic concept of deviance. *Annals of the Bhandarkar Oriental Research Institute, 63*(1), 1982. Pp.195–211.

Pollock, Sheldon. *The Rasa Reader*. Columbia University Press, 2016.

Pollock, Sheldon. "What was Bhaṭṭa Nāyaka Saying: The Hermenuetical Transformation of Indian Aesthetics." In *Epic and Argument in Sanskrit Literary Theory*, Manohar Publishers, 2010. pp. 143–184.

Pollock, S. Death of Sanskrit. *Society for Comparative Study of Society and History, 43*(2), 2001, 392–426.

Pollock, Sheldon. Sanskrit Literary Culture from the Inside Out. In *Literary Cultures in History: Reconstructions from South Asia*. University of California Press, 2003.

Ravishankar, Chinya V. *The Sons of Sarasvatī*. Suny Press, 2018.
Reich, James D. Bhaṭṭa Nāyaka and the Vedanta Influence on Sanskrit Literary Theory. *Journal of the American Oriental Society, 138*(2), 2018. pp. 533–557.
Rayan, K. Rasa and the Objective Correlative. *The British Journal of Aesthetics, 5*(3), 1965, 246–260.
Sastry, P. S. *Indian Poetics and New Criticism*. In *Indian Poetics and Western Thought*. Argo Publishing House, 1988.
Sivarudrappa, G. S., & Seshagiri Rao, S.L. An Essay from 'Kavyartha Chintana': Literary Criticism in Indian Poetics. *Indian Literature 28*, (5). 1985, 67–78.
Tripathi, R. "Modern Writings in Sanskrit: A Resume." *Indian Literature, 60*(1), 2016. pp. 168–183.
Vaghbhata II. *Kavyanusasana of Vaghbhata with His Own Gloss.* Edited by Pandit Sivadatta. Nirnaya Sagar, 1915.
Vaidyanatha. *Prataparudriya*. Ed. K.S Ramamurthi and S.R Matha. Oriental Research Institute, 1933.

Section Two

Beyond Classicism: Contemporary Aesthetics as Method

5

Critique of Popular Culture

Partha Chatterjee

In 1992, at a conference to mark a decade of cultural studies carried out by the Birmingham school, Stuart Hall spoke very critically of "the theoretical fluency of cultural studies in the United States." He was not, he said, demanding that American cultural studies become more like British cultural studies. The problem was not that American cultural studies was unable to theorize power in the field of culture or that it had formalized out of existence the relations of history and politics to culture. On the contrary. "There is no moment now, in American cultural studies," he said, "when we are not able, extensively and without end, to theorize power—politics, race, class and gender, subjugation, domination, exclusion, marginality, otherness, etc. There is hardly anything in cultural studies which isn't so theorized." But by carrying out this task through an "overwhelming textualization" of the material it studied, cultural studies was in danger of "constituting power and politics as exclusively matters of language and textuality itself." This allowed no room for cultural studies to become "a practice which always thinks about its intervention in a world in which it would make some difference, in which it would have some effect." Hall then went on to propose that Antonio Gramsci's "organic intellectual" and Michel Foucault's "specific intellectual" were alternative ways of thinking how the student of culture might intervene in the real world of culture. In any case, whatever the particular method by which this was done, Hall's plea was to "return the project of cultural studies from the clean air of meaning and textuality and theory to the something nasty down below." I take this to mean that cultural studies should not avoid making moral, aesthetic, or political judgments about the world of culture that it claimed to study (Hall, 1992, pp. 277–94).

But how did it come to be that a field of study that promised to investigate the production, consumption, and valorization of culture by connecting it to relations and practices of power found itself unable to make judgments about good and bad culture? Why did the scholars of culture have to restrict themselves to locating specific cultural acts within complex structures of power but refrain from becoming cultural critics? Let me approach this question by making a quick review of the study of popular visual culture as it has developed in India in the last three or four decades.

To take the case of cinema first: there is a framing debate, going back to at least the early 1960s, about the relation between cinema and the viewing culture of the public in India. On one side is the argument that the mass audience of the Indian cinema, steeped in traditional beliefs and practices and raised for generations in premodern viewing cultures, is simply incapable of understanding or appreciating the rational-realist cinema. As a result, not only has serious art cinema failed to take root in India's modern aesthetic life, but the film industry, too, has routinely churned out mythological and melodramatic rubbish that is cinematically infantile and ideologically retrograde. As Chidananda Das Gupta, one of the most articulate proponents of this view, claimed, the audience of the popular Indian cinema was unable to distinguish between fact and myth. This was shown by the political deification of film stars in the Indian states of Tamil Nadu and Andhra Pradesh and the persistence over half a century of Hindu mythological themes in the popular Hindi cinema. Das Gupta also pointed out that, unlike folk art that is produced organically within communities, the popular cinema is industrially produced, and "vast manipulative forces" are at work (Das Gupta, 1991, pp. 256–57). Reasserting the importance of taking a stand on social values, he rejected the trend of uncritically endorsing the popular cinema as popular culture. Culture could not be allowed to go uncriticized, he seemed to be saying, simply because it was popular.

On the other side was the provocative argument offered by Ashis Nandy, who insisted that the nonmodernity of the popular Indian cinema and its audience was a sign of the resilience of a tradition of viewing practices that still refused to cave in before the global onslaught of a culture of modern technological and commercial rationality.

The alleged failure of Indian cinemagoers to appreciate realist cinematic narrative was in fact a rejection of the cultural values of modern industrial life and an endorsement of the inherited virtues of tradition, faith, and community. Indeed, Nandy even insisted that the popular Indian cinema, though industrially produced, has "a built-in plurality that tends to subvert mass culture even when seemingly adapting to it passively" (Nandy, 1998, p. 13). It was neither classical nor folk, yet "now that modernity has become the dominant principle in Indian public life ... it is the commercial cinema which, if only by default, has been ... more protective towards nonmodern categories" (Nandy, 1995, p. 235).

This is a difference in viewpoints that still persists, at least in the public domain in India. There is no hesitation here in making aesthetic, moral, or political judgments about the cinema, whether high or popular. In the scholarly domain, however, things are quite different. As Ravi Vasudevan has reminded us in his survey of the analytical literature on the Indian cinema, the extreme terms of the debate between Das Gupta and Nandy have been largely superseded by the profusion of empirically rich and theoretically sophisticated studies that have appeared in the field of Indian film studies in the last decade and a half (Vasudevan, 2000). Both sides in that old debate had assumed a certain pregiven and fixed structure of the viewing practices of the allegedly premodern Indian audience. That structure, both positions assumed, could confront the modern technology of the cinema only on the terms allowed by their own inflexible practices; the structure could not adapt or change to accommodate the new. Most theorists and historians studying the Indian cinema today will reject this assertion and, hence, reject both of the views represented by Das Gupta and Nandy. The popular Indian cinema, they will say, has in fact modernized itself as well as its audience by adapting traditionally available narrative forms and performance techniques and inserting them into a modern technological medium. In the process, both the cinema and its audience have been transformed, albeit in complex ways that need to be documented and understood. This would be the prevailing common sense among students of Indian cinema today.

I believe this change in the terms of the debate is part of a larger change that has taken place in the last two decades in cultural disciplines such as anthropology and literary theory as well as in approaches to the study of cultural history. The older debate was fundamentally informed by a historical paradigm of modernization, whether Weberian or Marxian. The model was that of a modern sector, with modern economic, political, and cultural institutions, breaking into and transforming the traditional sector. It was with this model in mind that one set of scholars, impatient with the slow pace of transformation, complained of the rigidities of traditional practices and the lack of initiative, and perhaps even sincerity, within the modern sector to change the premodern. And the same model provoked the rival group of scholars to bemoan the loss of traditional virtues and celebrate the traces of resistance to modernization. What has happened in the last twenty years with the critique of anthropology as a colonial science, on the one hand, and with the emergence of postcolonial literary and cultural studies, on the other, is a realignment of the terms for the study of modernity.

I list just three elements of this realignment that are relevant for the next part of my discussion. First, it is no longer taken for granted that there is only one model or version of modernity that must be adopted by people all around the globe. The study of actual transformations of institutions and practices in different countries of the world in the modern period have prompted scholars to talk about different modernities, alternative modernities, and even multiple modernities. Not only that, but the history of Western modernity itself is being interrogated from this standpoint. It was always known that there were many countercurrents to the supposedly relentless sweep of modernity in Europe and North America, but the dominant ideologies of colonial modernization insisted on presenting an image of Western modernity as homogeneous, internally consistent, and universal. Now it is being argued that these countercurrents are not vestiges of some decadent past but integral, even if complexly structured, aspects of Western modernity itself. Further, Western modernity was not necessarily autonomously generated from within the parameters of European history, as all post-Enlightenment thinkers had assumed, but was itself the product of its encounters with non-European cultures, especially through the history of European empires. These arguments seriously complicate the earlier narrative of a modern sector, already formed by European historical processes, transforming through a pedagogical project the traditional structures of premodernity all round the world.

Second, it is now clear that even within the modern sector, transformations do not occur in the same way, or even in the same direction, in different institutional spaces. To cite an example I have used before, the spread of modern medicine in India was accompanied by a transformation of the institutions of traditional Ayurvedic and Yunani practices, which adopted patented drugs, standardized textbooks, university examinations, and public registration of physicians but did not thereby seek to become special branches of modern medicine and instead claimed their status as alternative medical practices. But nothing like this happened in the case of Indian chemistry or Indian mathematics (Chatterjee, 1995). To take an example from the cultural world, while the adoption of modern Western forms such as the novel or proscenium theater or oil painting led to fundamental transformations of Indian literature, drama, and art, the field of Indian music, even as it adopted instruments such as the harmonium and the violin, or techniques such as notation, or technologies such as the gramophone record, radio, and cinema, or institutions such as the music school, unquestionably retained its character as Indian music, distinguishable in systemic terms from Western music (Bakhle, 2005; Subramanian, 2006; Weidman, 2006). The dynamics of modernity, then, turn out to have different effective histories in different institutional sites, even in the same historical period and for the same people. This phenomenon cannot be understood as uneven development, because it is not simply a problem of different time lags or uneven dispersion over space. Rather, it becomes necessary to suspend the totalizing structural contrasts between the modern and the premodern and focus instead on localized, contingent, and often transient changes in actual practices.

Third, on the ethical-political question of the use of power, usually the coercive power of the state, to transform premodern institutions and practices, there has also been a change. At least in the cultural disciplines, if not in the social sciences as a whole, there is a much greater sensitivity today to the destructive social and cultural effects of large-scale, centralized, state-sponsored projects of modernization. Even in the domain of governance, there is greater emphasis on taking account of the heterogeneity of populations and the micromanagement of security and welfare policies to suit local conditions. If there has been a shift from the state to the market as the principal agency of global transformations, this has not resulted in the global homogenization of cultures; ever new localized spaces are being created for the production of cultural difference and the mobilization of identity politics. This has not made the operations of power regimes or, indeed, the resistance to them any more benign, but the ethical questions they raise no longer seem to be susceptible to universally applicable solutions. The political ethics of social change now tend to be evaluated within contextual, contingent, and strategically defined conditions.

This leads me to my final theoretical remark before returning to the subject of Indian visual culture. An important theoretical lineage of the new cultural studies inaugurated in Britain in the early 1980s went back to the remarkable writings on cultural politics by the Italian Marxist Antonio Gramsci. Hall specifically recalled this in the lecture I referred to above (Hall, 1992). Perhaps it is not a coincidence that almost at the same time, but with no direct connection, the writers assembled under the Subaltern Studies series began their critique of both the colonial and the nationalist historiography of India by drawing from the theoretical insights of Gramsci. I believe I am not wrong in saying that these two strands of recent scholarship have been influential in realigning the terms of debate on modernity, including that in the field of cultural studies. And since Gramsci's writings are a common source for these two strands, I wish to recall one intriguing sentence from Prison Notebooks in which Gramsci speaks of "the philosophy of praxis" as having become "a criticism of 'common sense,' basing itself initially, however, on common sense." He goes on to add that "it is not a question of introducing from scratch a scientific form of thought into everyone's individual life, but of renovating and making 'critical' an already existing activity" (Gramschi, 1971, pp. 330–31). I believe this sentence states in an aphorism a project that the new cultural disciplines—those that have emerged out of the critiques of theories of modernization—are struggling to formulate. The task is no longer to interrogate popular culture with the fully formed apparatus of a scientific worldview. Rather, it is to begin from the practices of popular culture, to immerse oneself in its forms, in order to develop its critique. The methods of such a critique remain elusive, which is why it is worth investigating those works of cultural production that not only inhabit and celebrate the modes of popular culture but self-consciously seek to transform them.

* * *

To illustrate some of these problems of method, let me turn to another field of popular culture in India that is only once removed from the field of cinema, namely, photography. Judith Gutman advanced the initial argument that Indian photographs, although they were products of the same modern Western technology, did not follow the Western realist aesthetic at all and instead reflected a completely different and distinctly Indian conception of reality (Gutman, 1982). Unlike a Western photograph, where the viewer is carefully led from one part of the picture to another according to a familiar set of realist-narrative conventions, in Indian photographs everything within the picture field seems to happen at once, as though in an idealized and timeless space. Using the painted photograph as her example, she argued that early Indian photographic artists used paint not to supplement but in fact to hide the technologically produced likeness to the real object.

Gutman's claim of a radically different Indian aesthetic was criticized for being hugely simplistic and overstated.[1]

But more recent scholars, such as Christopher Pinney, who have made more careful and nuanced studies of popular photography, have also tried to define the elements of the aesthetic conception that governs popular visual culture in India. For instance, there is the practice of the darshan, widespread in all parts of India, in which the devotee comes into visual contact with the image of the deity and secures, by the physical act of seeing and being seen, the blessings of the divine. The practice has extended from divine images to men and women with special qualities of holiness and even into the political field: from emperors to local chiefs, Hindu and Muslim, as well as modern political leaders such as Gandhi, all granted darshan to those who came to see them in the hope of gaining merit from visual contact with the holy and the powerful. Several scholars have argued that the conventions that govern the representation of divine or powerful figures in popular visual imagery in India are shaped by this idea of darshan. Pinney has cited the example of a widely available photolithograph of the saintly figure of Ramakrishna, much revered in Bengal, showing him seated with his wife Sarada and his disciple Swami Vivekananda in front of the image of the goddess Kali at the Dakshineswar temple in Calcutta (Figure 5.1).[2]

The image is a composite one, with photographs of the three human figures inserted in the foreground of a painted photo of the Kali idol, completely violating the norms of both narrative realism and historical plausibility (since the three could never have posed for the camera in this fashion). Curiously, however, the Kali idol at Dakshineswar is shown with two strikingly realist adornments: a framed and garlanded photograph of Ramakrishna on one side of the wall and a clock with the hands at nine o'clock on the other. The lithographed image seems to have been composed to give the viewer the chance to obtain a simultaneous darshan of all four powerful figures, divine and human, for, as it were, the price of one.

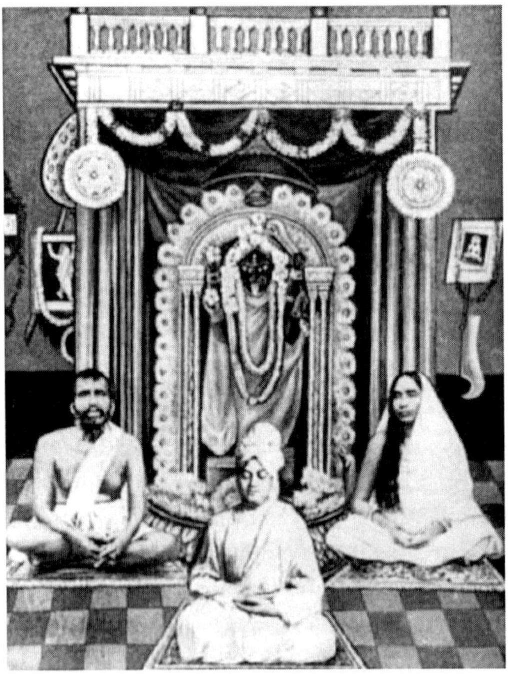

Figure 5.1: Photolithograph, c. 1920, from Pinney, Camera Indica. Courtesy of Christopher Pinney

To take another example: Ashish Rajadhyaksha, in a classic essay on D. G. Phalke, the pioneer of early Indian cinema, showed how Phalke evolved methods such as frontal staging and direct address into the camera, forms that are antithetical to the aesthetic styles of the Western film, by building into the new technology of the cinema prevailing popular conceptions of viewing such as darshan (Rajadhyaksha, 1993). Arvind Rajagopal has extended the argument to the much more recent phenomenon of the serially televised Ramayana, where the viewing of the epic was regarded by millions as a weekly darshan of the gods (Rajagopal, 2001). Similarly, Pinney has given us a fascinating analysis of the visual representation of bhakti or devotion to the god Shiva, whose power is commonly represented in the phallic form of the shivalinga. In a widely available calendar print, Pinney shows that "within the ling Shiv literally encompasses Parvati and hierarchy is denoted spatially. In this image we see the notion that within each consecrated image or murti there lives the pran [life] of the gods: the external form of the image contains the form of the god who contains the goddess" (Pinney, 1997, pp. 116–18) (Figure 5.2).

It is precisely this image that, Pinney then shows, is cleverly reworked in a photographic montage produced by a small-town studio in central India (Figure 5.3). Using complex printing techniques, this "marriage" photograph inserts a full-face portrait of the bride within a profile of the groom and then encloses both of those images within a larger shadow profile of the groom. "The montage clearly replicates the calendar image of the shivling."

It is clear that the modern technologies of print and photography, even as they penetrated deep into the everyday culture of ordinary people, did not mean the adoption of a realist visual aesthetic in the popular domain. Rather, as Pinney suggests with reference to the hugely popular lithograph images that have been produced since the late nineteenth century, the powers of Western realist art were mimicked and subverted into the "xeno-real"—"the form of colonially authorized realism that circulates outside its framework of origination: it is jettisoned into the colony, where it comes (primarily) to signify itself" (Pinney, 2004, p. 31) (Figure 5.4).

As several recent exhibitions and studies of so-called bazaar prints and calendar art have shown, many elements of Western realist art

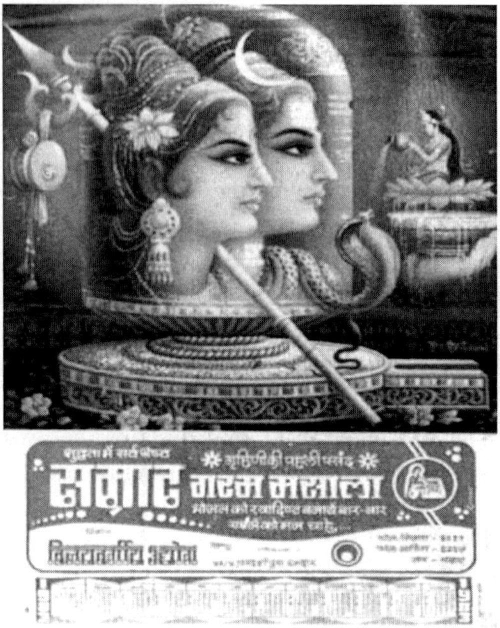

Figure 5.2: Calendar photo, 1983, from Pinney, Camera Indica. Courtesy of Christopher Pinney

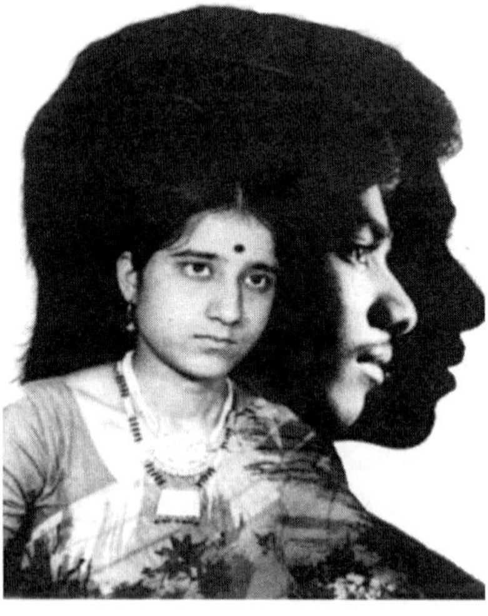

Figure 5.3: Photo composition, 1980, from Pinney, Camera Indica. Courtesy of Christopher Pinney

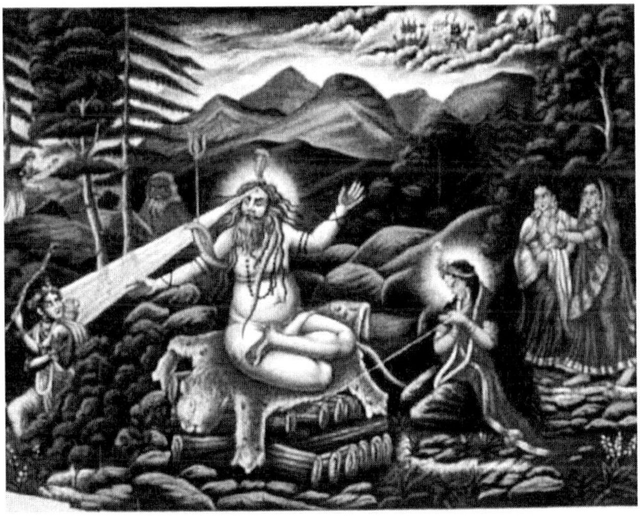

Figure 5.4: Madan bhasma, oleograph, Chorebagan Art Studio, Calcutta, c. 1890. Courtesy of the Centre for Studies in Social Sciences, Calcutta Archive

were freely adopted in these popular prints on mythological, historical, or social subjects, but emptied of their original meaning; there was no gesture of affiliation to any larger philosophical or aesthetic conception of "realism" (Figure 5.5). As Pinney explains: "Classicism and mythology supplied a system of references for the forms of their own idealized behaviour, whose translatability was dependent on their vacuity. In the xenoreal there is a double (and doubly productive) emptiness" (Pinney, 2004, p. 32).

Pinney has made one more point about the political significance of popular visual prints to consider in relation to this essay: the circulation of a large body of nationalist images suggests, he says, a rather different history from that described in the standard accounts of Indian nationalism drawn almost entirely from textual sources. First, the affective intensity of feeling evoked by the abstract idea of the nation seemed to be conveyed most powerfully by the visual representation of the nation as an actualized landscape.[3] Second, the most powerful image of the nationalist political struggle in the popular imagination was the depiction of armed revolutionaries (called "terrorists" by the

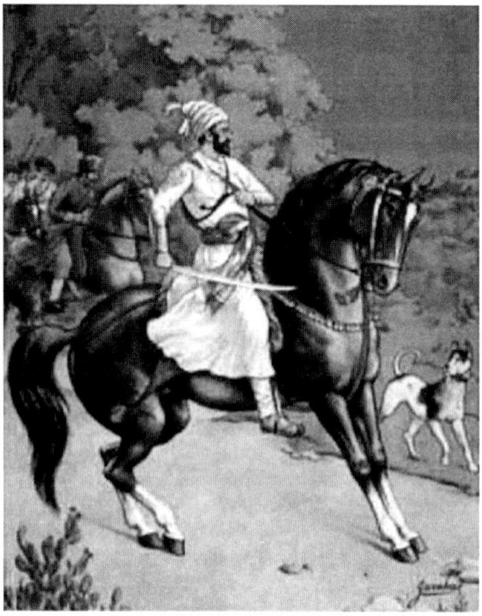

Figure 5.5: Shivaji, lithograph, Bharat Printing Works, Pune, c. 1890. Courtesy of the Centre for Studies in Social Sciences, Calcutta Archive

British) rather than the leaders of the nonviolent mass movement (Pinney, 2004) (Figure 5.6).

It is too early to pronounce on the validity of Pinney's specific hypotheses, but he has raised, it seems to me, a very important issue concerning the appropriate sources for the study of popular politics, especially in a country where most people do not read. Should visual sources be treated merely as providing illustrative supplements to a history constructed on the basis of the written or spoken word, or can they be allowed to rewrite that history? But to return to the question I raised at the beginning of this essay: Do these photographs or prints qualify as art? Can we make judgments on their aesthetic quality? On what grounds? By which criteria?

Even though such extreme distinctions as that between a modern high aesthetic and nonmodern popular tastes, or between Western and Indian ways of seeing, would be considered unacceptable in scholarly circles today, it is nevertheless noticeable that in explaining the distinctive features of popular viewing practices in India, even the

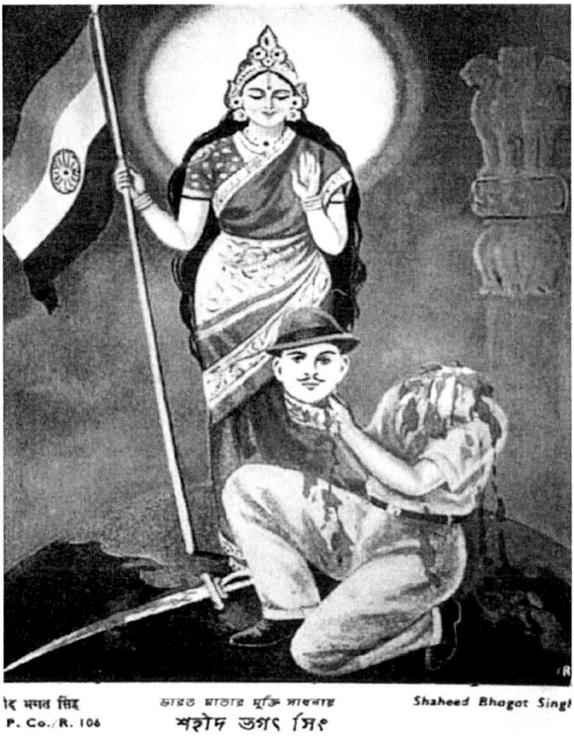

Figure 5.6: Bhagat Singh, c. 1950, lithograph, from Pinney, Photos of the Gods. Courtesy of Christopher Pinney

most careful scholars tend to fall back upon some conceptual distinction that is supposed to lie behind and thereby explain the differences in practice. For instance, looking at practices of photographic portraiture in India, Pinney has suggested that the Western aesthetic concept that the visible external body is anchored in an invisible internal ground of character does not obtain in the popular domain in India. Rather, "the external body is freed from the constraints with which it is shackled in the Western tradition of painted portraiture" (Pinney, 1997, p. 200).

Similarly, there is an influential body of literature on the popular Indian cinema that argues that the dominant conceptual framework that shapes its aesthetic modes is mythic-iconic, in contrast to the realist aesthetic of the Hollywood cinema.[4] Kajri Jain, in her valuable study of the production of calendar art or bazaar images, observes that the artists who design these iconic images of gods for the market themselves regard them as inferior art. But Jain attempts to redeem their aesthetic claim by suggesting that calendar images circulate in a different conceptual field of value from that of Western bourgeois art (Jain, 2003).

The problem with this form of explanation is that popular visual practices are being understood in terms of certain essential conceptual structures that must, in the end, be defined by reference to textual sources, whether it is darshan or the significance of the icon or the notion of the pran (life) that inhabits a body or the social valuation of the gift, and so forth. The assumption is that practices are external manifestations of concepts and beliefs that constitute the system of meanings that define a culture. This view of culture has a hoary lineage in the human sciences, especially in anthropology, and Clifford Geertz is probably its most recent, distinguished, and sophisticated explicator. But I believe this approach inhibits rather than facilitates the critical understanding of contemporary popular culture.

Have recent scholars seriously attempted to make judgments, whether aesthetic or ethical-political, on the products of popular culture they have studied? We may turn to Pinney, whose work I have considered at length in this essay. Speaking about the plethora of exotic backgrounds, supplied by painted backdrops or clever printing techniques in the studio, against which people choose to be photographed, Pinney says that they are "a space of exploration." There is also "the inventive posing that … is concerned with the transcendence and parody of social roles. The photographic studio becomes a place not for solemnization of the social but for the individual exploration of that which does not yet exist in the social world" (Pinney, 1997, p. 178) (Figure 5.7).

Again, speaking of the "wedding collage" compositions of photograph and paint, he speaks of "the compacted and constructed dream world, set free from any arbitrary frame, that this local photographic technology makes possible. Released from its habitual chronotopic imprisonment, these photographic images conflate time and place, so that at least several temporally discrete moments come to coexist within the same fabulous space" (Pinney, 1997, p. 134) (Figure 5.8).

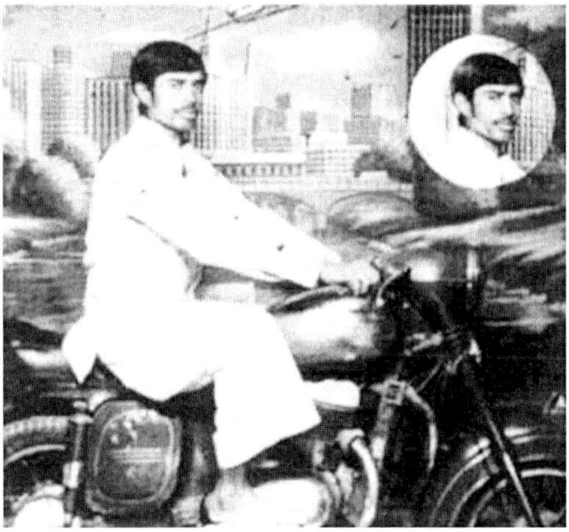

Figure 5.7: Man on a motorcycle, c. 1983, from Pinney, Camera Indica. Courtesy of Christopher Pinney

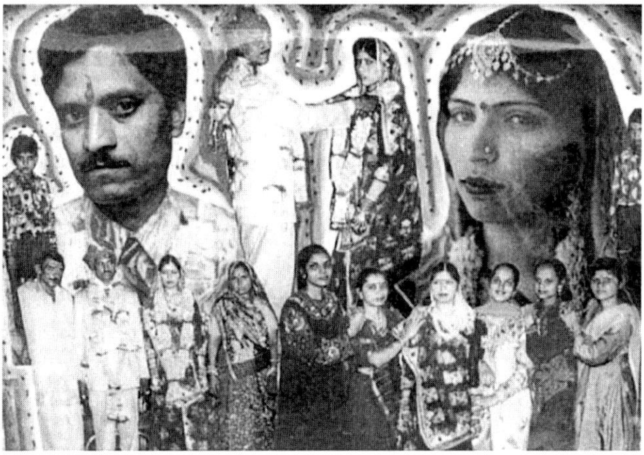

Figure 5.8: Vijay Vyas, color collage, 1996, photos, watercolor, and ink, from Pinney, Camera Indica. Courtesy of Christopher Pinney

The phrase that is repeated most often here is "freedom"—freedom to explore, to invent, to subvert, to dream—in contrast to the prisonlike confines of the realist conventions that come as a package with the Western technology of photography. This space of creative freedom, defined in contradistinction to the aesthetic norms of Western painting and photography, becomes the ground for making judgments about popular lithographs and photography in India. That is the space where they have recently gained a status as "popular art," as shown by the growing number of collections and exhibitions of such hitherto ignored images.[5]

The question is: Are we justified in attributing the quality of art to these products of popular consumption because we have persuaded ourselves that they have been created under conditions of "freedom"? Are we not imposing notions of artistic creativity that have come from very different historical and philosophical lineages that we have, in fact, identified as unrelated and opposed to the aesthetic world of the popular? Is this the only way in which we can claim this domain of popular cultural production as worthy of aesthetic appreciation—by declaring that they are products of the creative freedom of the popular artist? I am reminded here of the passionate intervention by Johannes Fabian, the anthropologist of African popular culture who wrote about popular painting and music in contemporary Zaire (now the Democratic Republic of Congo):

> There is no justification for using the concept of freedom quasi-logically, a priori, in distinguishing high from low, elite from popular culture.... Not mere exposure to power and oppression, but transformation of experience into communicable expressions, is at the origin of popular culture as resistance to colonial and postcolonial domination.... That freedom must exist for cultural creation to take place is, I believe, a position that needs to be maintained even if actual conditions in most postcolonial African countries, certainly in Zaire, seem to make it difficult to credit popular culture with much liberation. (Fabian, 1998, p. 18)

The problems with this position are apparent from the very tortuousness of its formulation. Beginning with an admirable gesture of refusal to restrict the concept of creative freedom to elite high culture, it ends up by declaring a dogmatic and metaphysical faith in the freedom of the popular artist, even if "actual conditions" indicate otherwise.

I wish to suggest a different method for approaching the question of artistic quality in the production of popular culture. This involves a move away from concepts and ideas to the practices of production and consumption. I do not insist that practices are external manifestations of concepts that constitute the structure of meanings that characterize a culture; rather, popular culture consists of practices. Of course, practices are shaped by institutional norms. Spaces for "creative freedom" may be available within a specific structure of norms; "freedom" may also lie in resisting those norms. In any case, the question of "freedom" here admits of no universal answer; its relevance and effect depend on specific, institutionally located, sets of practices.

The principal framework within which practices may be described and understood is, I propose, that of a discipline. A discipline is that set of authorized practices by which cultural products are made. It is, as Foucault has explained, a genealogically assembled set, whose elements may have been drawn from a variety of sources. But within an identifiable institutional space of cultural production and consumption, a discipline will specify authorities and authorized practices, techniques and skills, modes of training, norms of excellence, forms of use of cultural products, and judgments of taste. Disciplines usually invoke a tradition that authorizes, through a memorialization of their origins, whether historical or mythical, the specific practices of cultural production and use. Moreover, as Talal Asad has pointed out with respect to the religious disciplines, the aesthetic or ethical quality of the product is not necessarily a function of the degree of "creative freedom" exercised by the practitioner; on the contrary, the more strict and rigorous the adherence to discipline, the more valued may be the outcome (Asad, 1993).

The study of discipline in this sense is not unknown, whether in anthropology or in the specialized studies of arts and crafts. However, several features will be different in the study of the disciplines involved in contemporary popular cultural production. First, the usual assumption of an organic unity between the disciplines of cultural production and a community of users of culture must be abandoned. One must be prepared to find only a tenuous presence of such a community, or perhaps no community at all. The relation between producers and users of popular culture may be mediated by institutions such as the market or the media. Second, we must, I believe, stay away from the conservationist instinct of preserving the "dying arts and crafts." This effort has its place, and it may even make some difference to the real world of artisans and craftspeople. But it is not, I think, consistent with the method of investigating how disciplines of traditional artistic production have succeeded or failed to reinvent their practices to cope with the changing conditions of popular culture. Third, this must be a study of traditional disciplines in a process of change. The appropriate methods here would not be those of the old anthropology or studies of folk culture. Rather, one has to be more genealogical, identifying why and how specific elements of disciplinary practice are modified or abandoned and new ones adopted. No general framework of tradition versus modernity will work here. The question of the decline of old institutions and authorities and the emergence of new ones, as traditional disciplines innovate and reinvent themselves, will be a major topic of interest of these studies. Fourth, the criteria for making aesthetic judgments are to be found within the disciplines. This is unlikely to be a simple matter of identifying the norms and criteria that defined quality or taste in the traditional discipline, even though memories of such a tradition may continue to carry some weight in redefining quality and taste under the new conditions of popular culture. There will be contestations over authorities and norms, varying degrees of value attached to traditional skills and techniques, uncertainties about traditional methods of training, new evaluations of competence and virtuosity, searches for new sources of patronage, appeals to a new "public" and, finally, an active engagement with the idea of novelty. All of this will make the field of aesthetic judgment on any particular site of popular cultural production a highly contested one. But that is not to say that distinctions and judgments are not being made on those sites, or that disciplinary practices, even if new ones, are not being imposed on both producers and users. By looking more closely at disciplines, rather than at underlying aesthetic concepts, cultural studies may, I am suggesting, find a way of making distinctions among the products of popular culture, and thus of providing a critique of the judgment of popular taste.[6]

* * *

I use as my final example a range of cultural productions that come out of a single popular festival in the city of Calcutta, where I have lived from my birth. It is the annual Durga Puja, which is held in autumn on the occasion of the ritual worship of the goddess Durga (I use the word "worship" for puja, ignoring the difficulties of translation).

Through the twentieth century, the Durga Puja has emerged as the single most important cultural festival of Calcutta. Principally, it takes the form of about a thousand community pujas held for about a week in different neighborhoods of the city. Around the community pujas is a celebration by millions involving clothes, fashion, food, tourism, music, theater, and, most important for our purposes here, the mass viewing of Durga images in their specially constructed pavilions in each neighborhood (Ghosh, 2006, pp. 31–34). I am here drawing on the recent researches on the festival carried out at the Centre for Studies in Social Sciences, Calcutta, by a team led by the art historian Tapati Guha-Thakurta (2004). The huge variety of cultural productions associated with the Durga Puja gives us a chance to review several of the issues I have raised here concerning traditional disciplines, innovation, the loss and recovery of community, religion and art, the role of the market and the media, the distinction between artisans and artists, and, above all, the question of making aesthetic judgments in the field of popular culture.

I do not have the space here to elaborate on the religious significance and social history of the Durga Puja in Bengal, except to say that the current form of the urban community puja has developed in Calcutta over the last hundred years or so. It was originally funded by small contributions from residents of a neighborhood, but in recent years the major funding appears to come from corporate advertisers. Although the religious significance of the worship of Durga is tied with the mythical story of the annihilation of the buffalo demon by the goddess of power, in its popular form it is strongly associated with the idea of the married daughter, accompanied by her children, paying a brief annual visit to her natal home. The traditional Durga image is made of clay against a scaffolding of bamboo and straw, with clothes and ornaments of silk and tinsel. The image has to be made anew every year and ritually immersed in water at the end of the four-day period of worship. Moreover, there are a host of specialized disciplines of both craft and performance traditionally associated with different aspects of the Durga Puja and its accompanying celebrations, and it is these that have undergone the greatest transformations in recent years.

The most proximate dynamic shaping these changes is the emergence over the last four or five decades of a certain competitive spirit among the neighborhood pujas in Calcutta. A mass public, consisting of no less than a few million people, both residents and visitors to the city, moving from one pavilion (called pandal) to another at all hours of night and day for four or five days, is the target of this competitive effort. The size of the crowds is the most obvious measure of which *pandal* is the most popular. But there are also more formal competitions, with sponsors announcing awards adjudicated by celebrities. There is much pride attached to the drawing of crowds and winning of awards. The efforts of the organizing committees of the neighborhood pujas in selecting artists and designers are, not surprisingly, guided by those motives.

The competitive spirit has led, at one level, to a privileging of the spectacle. Familiar street corners and parks are suddenly transformed, albeit only for a few days, into famous historical or archaeological sites, or perhaps into structures that have recently been in the news. Thus, one could find puja pandals that are replicas of an Assyrian palace of Mesopotamia or St. Peter's of Rome or the Kremlin, or of the capsized Titanic (made in the year when the movie was released), or of the school of wizardry attended by Harry Potter, or (why not?) the burning World Trade Center towers. The sociologist Pradip Bose has described the space of the Durga Puja in Calcutta as a perfect example of Foucault's "heterotopia," where the real blends with the impossibly unreal and where several incompatible elements can coexist (Bose, 1997, pp. 3–9) (Figure 5.9).

It is spectacle that moves crowds here rather than piety. Of course, GuhaThakurta has made the point that the spectacle might create its own sacral aura, eliciting an engagement that is as intense as religious devotion. But, precisely because the spectacle produces its effect through the elements of novelty and the uncanny, it is difficult to relate this to our problem of the transformation of traditional disciplines. The matter is further compounded by the frequent resort to gimmicks in using the most unlikely material to erect giant pavilions to house the Durga image. Thus, one has seen pandals made of teacups, broken gramophone records, biscuits, medicine bottles, and sugarcane fiber (Figure 5.10).

It is arguable that there is some technical virtuosity involved in using such outlandish material to build structures that are both functional and recognizable. If so, the question of what sorts of disciplinary skills

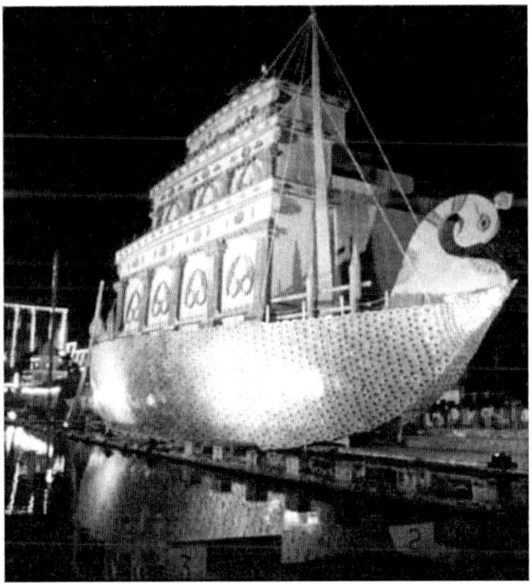

Figure 5.9: Golden barge at College Square, 2002.
Courtesy of Sambuddha Banerjee, Centre for Studies in Social Sciences, Calcutta Archive

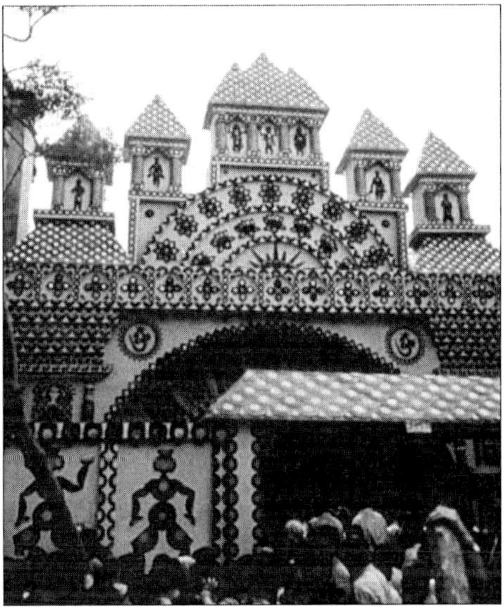

Figure 5.10: Temple facade made of broken gramophone records, 2002.
Courtesy of Sambuddha Banerjee, Centre for Studies in Social Sciences, Calcutta Archive

are mobilized to produce these gimmicks might become an interesting topic for research. But as far as I know, no one has yet attempted to answer this question.

The most important part of Guha-Thakurta's work is her study of the so-called "art" or "theme" pujas. These images and pavilions attempt quite self-consciously to achieve a more elevated aesthetic effect. There are several types here. On the one hand, we have designers from middle-class backgrounds, frequently with formal art school training, who conceptualize a theme that defines the stylistic unity of the entire display and direct various craftspeople to execute the separate items. On the other hand, we have a new crop of artists from an artisanal background, usually with training in a traditional craft but with exposure to the world of the modern arts, sometimes even having an art school degree, who may collaborate with an art director or, at times, design and execute the entire display with their own team of craftspeople. For both these types, of course, we have teams of persons having specialized craft skills who work under the direction of the main designing team. The degree to which such craftspeople enjoy independent authority in their own field varies. Let us look at some of the specific cases that Guha-Thakurta has described. One pandal was designed in the style of the well-known Madhubani frescoes of Bihar, with a Durga image built in the traditional clay but matching the Madhubani style (Figures 5.11, 5.12).

To clinch the claim of authenticity, an entire team of Madhubani men and women painters, representing the different caste groups with their distinct styles, was brought over from Bihar to paint the pavilion and, indeed, to exhibit their methods of work to the crowds during the course of the pujas. The design team for this pandal consisted of an art teacher who worked out the concept and an artist with a crafts background but with an art school degree who supervised the execution and built the Durga image. The traditional crafts theme has become quite popular in recent years.

But it is not only traditional arts and crafts from other places, presented with a claim of authenticity, that constitute new "themes" for the puja pavilions. Popular historical memory could also be invoked to endorse themes of current political interest. A particularly interesting theme a few years ago was that of interreligious communal harmony,

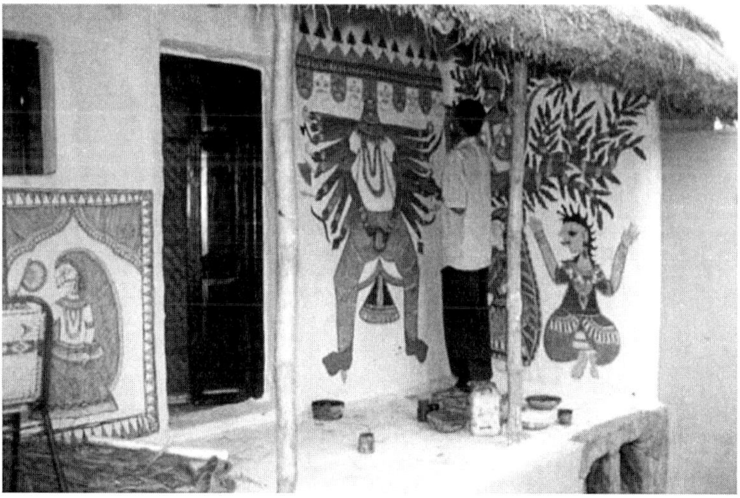

Figure 5.11: Madhubani-style pandal, 2002.
Courtesy of Sambuddha Banerjee, Centre for Studies in Social Sciences, Calcutta Archive

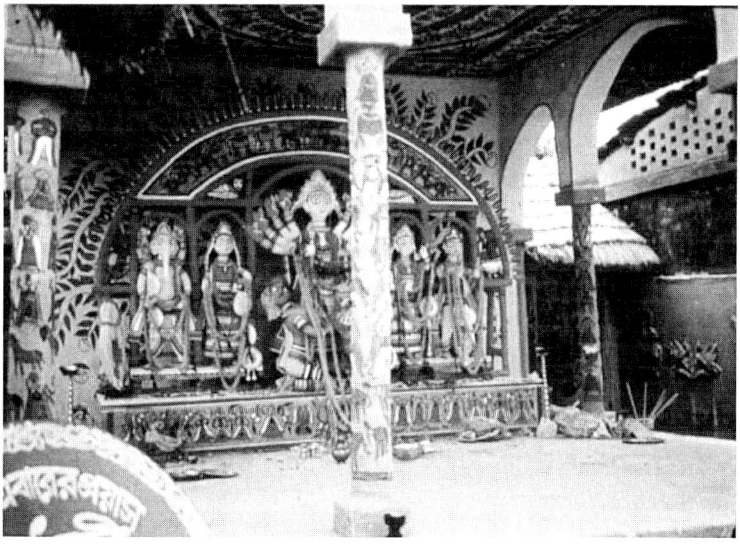

Figure 5.12: Madhubani- style Durga image, 2002.
Courtesy of Sambuddha Banerjee, Centre for Studies in Social Sciences, Calcutta Archive

that being the year of the deadly massacres of Muslims in Gujarat. One pandal was designed as the bamboo fortress of Titu Mir, an early-nineteenth-century leader of a peasant rebellion against the British in Bengal (Figure 5.13).

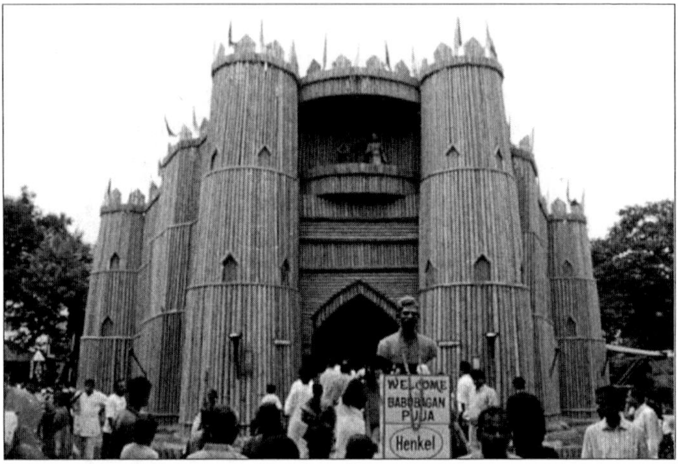

Figure 5.13: Titu Mir's fort at Babubagan, 2002.
Courtesy of Sambuddha Banerjee, Centre for Studies in Social Sciences, Calcutta Archive

The choice was particularly striking because Titu Mir was a fiery jihadi Muslim, inspired by the new Wahabi doctrine that had just reached Bengal from Hejaz through Delhi. He was the scourge of Hindu landlords and Muslim preachers accused of not being sufficiently orthodox. No one knows what his bamboo fortress looked like because, apart from a mention in the British official reports, there is no visual trace of it anywhere. But the choice of Titu Mir as the symbol of Hindu-Muslim accord, and the use of his imagined bamboo fortress as the site for the worship of a Hindu goddess, reflects a popular historical mythography in which, recalling Pinney's point, armed anticolonial resistance trumps everything else. Another pandal that year had the Durga image done in the style of Mughal miniature paintings (Figure 5.14). Yet another pavilion was modeled on the recently destroyed Bamiyan Buddhas of Afghanistan, with Durga carrying flowers instead of weapons in her hands.

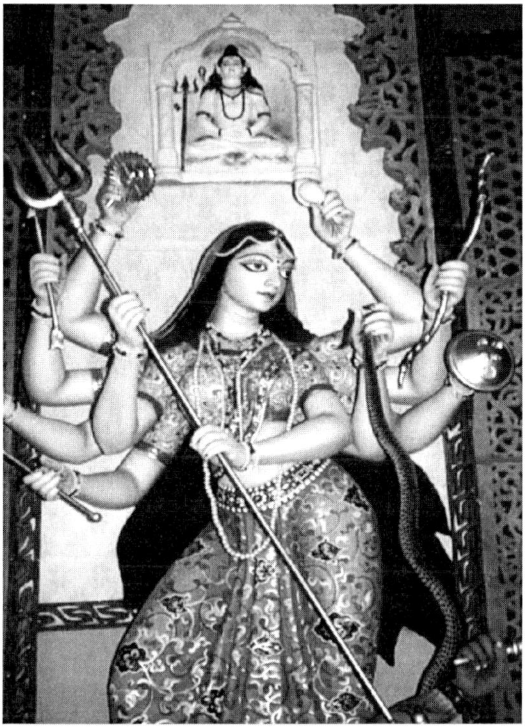

Figure 5.14: Mughal-miniature-style Durga image, 2002.
Courtesy of Sambuddha Banerjee, Centre for Studies in Social Sciences, Calcutta Archive

So what is the role of religion here? Many of the familiar accoutrements of the traditional Durga Puja have been dispensed with and entirely new elements, dictated by commercial or political motives, allowed entry. And yet there is always a core set of practices, involving the Durga idol and its worship, where prescribed religious ritual is followed. The method appears to be to demarcate a specific set of practices as subject to the exclusive direction of religious authorities, leaving other practices to be determined by other authorities. Thus, there is space available for intense religious piety, in the offering of puja to the goddess, for instance, or watching the ceremonies of arati, involving ecstatic chanting, drumming, and dance by trained practitioners. Other spaces, however, can be left open for spectacle and art.

One place where religion and art pull in different directions is around the status of the worshipped Durga image. Religious rules require that the idol be ritually thrown into water at the end of the puja. But some images now acquire enough of an aura as an art object to elicit proposals for preserving them in a museum. Sanatan Dinda, who grew up learning the traditional craft of imagemaking but then took a degree from art school, is a professional modern artist in his own right. He makes Durga images in a distinctly modernist style but, despite attractive offers from buyers, has refused to sell them, insisting that the worshipped image must be immersed in the river (Figure 5.15).

Bhabatosh Sutar, on the other hand, also with a crafts background and art school training, made a striking terra-cotta Durga image a few

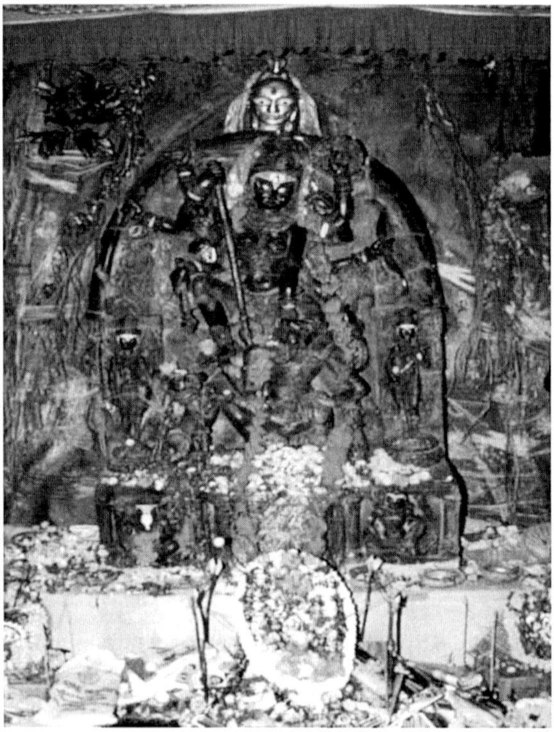

Figure 5.15: Sanatan Dinda, Durga image in stone idol style, 2002. Courtesy of Sambuddha Banerjee, Centre for Studies in Social Sciences, Calcutta Archive

years ago that is now permanently displayed on the lawns of a five-star hotel in Calcutta (Figure 5.16). There have been proposals to set up a park somewhere in the city to display Durga images that qualify as "art." Such museumization will require another set of debates and contests over the jurisdiction of religious authorities over popular cultural practices.

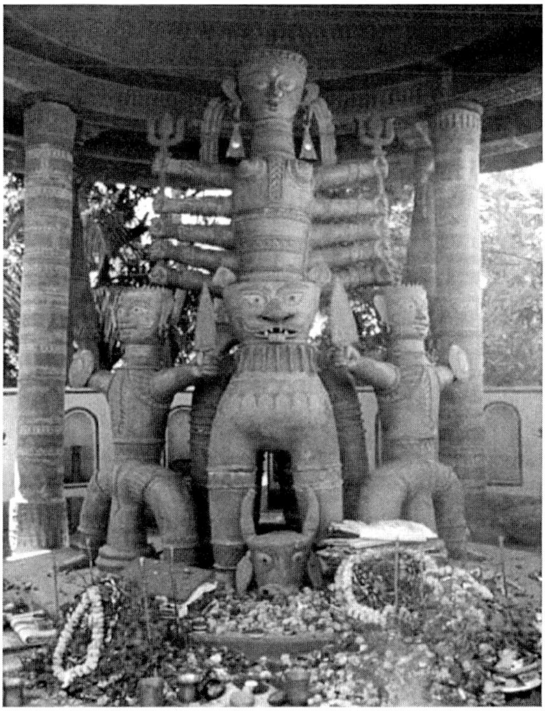

Figure 5.16: Bhabatosh Sutar, Durga image in terra-cotta, 2003. Courtesy of Abhijit Bhattacharya, Centre for Studies in Social Sciences, Calcutta Archive

To return to the question of the traditional disciplines and their ability to adapt and innovate, an interesting example has been provided by Guha-Thakurta's study of two generations of a family of traditional clay modelers. The father, Mohanbanshi Rudrapal, still operates from Kumartuli, the oldest and largest potters' quarter of Calcutta, using traditional designs and methods. His younger son, Pradip, works with his father but has a degree in fine arts from the prestigious Baroda school and is seeking to enter the "art" puja circuit. The elder son, Sanatan, has broken off with his father and moved out of Kumartuli to set up his own studio and establish a brand image of his own. Two factors seem to be relevant in this account of disciplinary innovation within a structure of inherited skills and training: first, the shift from one generation to the next and, second, exposure to a different disciplinary mode (in this case, art school training).

The crucial question is whether it is possible to make aesthetic distinctions and judgments of taste using criteria drawn from different, and possibly conflicting, disciplinary traditions. The judgments of modernist art will often conflict with the criteria of excellence used by the traditional image-maker. Yet, as the Durga Puja example shows, such conflicting judgments are actually being made in the field of popular cultural practices. The point to be emphasized here is one that cultural studies has made repeatedly in the last three decades, namely, that these contests and debates over cultural production are resolved not by disinterested philosophical analysis but by the acts of authorities and practitioners within fields of institutional power. Traditional disciplines have room for debates and change, albeit in varying degrees; whether they will adapt to new conditions or stagnate and die depends on the acts of the various authorities that decide on disciplinary practices. What the Durga Puja example shows, I think, is a point I cited from Gramsci: here is a set of traditional popular practices that have become selfcritical. They have not done so autonomously. On the contrary, they have innovated by responding to new opportunities and seeking new authorities drawn from very different disciplines.

It is in this context that it needs to be pointed out that cultural studies or, more specifically, the work of academic scholars of popular culture is already one of those new disciplinary authorities that are being invoked to authenticate and authorize these innovations in popular culture. No one can deny today the growing influence of the new work of scholarship on the popular visual arts or on different branches of the popular performing arts in countries like India. Such work is being drawn upon to open new institutional spaces of display and performance and to justify new practices. It is difficult in

Western academic contexts to appreciate the weight and significance that is attached to scholarly opinion on these matters in the local vernacular circles of popular artistic production. When associated with scholars located in prestigious national and international institutions, such opinions can catapult local popular artists and their work into the zones of attention of the media and the market, those crucial mediating institutions that foster contemporary popular culture. It is not uncommon for such scholars to suddenly discover, often to their annoyance, that what they had written about some local popular festival or product or artist in a faraway scholarly journal was being quoted, not always faithfully, to advertise the product or to attract tourists. Like it or not, scholars of popular culture are being, and will be, mobilized in the partisan wars over changing aesthetic practices. In this sense, to return to the topic I introduced at the beginning of this essay, cultural studies is already actually making a difference to at least some parts of the real world of culture, even if the effects have not always been intended. My plea is for the discipline to become aware of this role and to be both more self-consciously critical and responsible in its engagement with the changing cultures of the people.

Notes

1. E.g., by Christopher Pinney, Camera Indica: The Social Life of Indian Photographs (Chicago: University of Chicago Press, 1997), 95–96.
2. The photolithograph image printed for circulation around 1920 is reproduced in Pinney, Camera Indica, 105.
3. This is also suggested by Sumathi Ramaswamy in her study of the cartographic representations of an imagined and lost Tamil homeland, *Lost Land of Lemuria: Fabulous Geographies, Catastrophic Histories* (Berkeley: University of California Press, 2004).
4. E.g., Rajadhyaksha, 1993; Kapur, 2000.
5. Tapati Guha-Thakurta has made this point in her *Aesthetics of the Popular Print: Lithographs and Oleographs from 19th and 20th Century India* (Kolkata: Birla Academy of Art and Culture, 2006), 3–9.
6. It is hardly necessary to acknowledge that I am here invoking Pierre Bourdieu's investigations into popular taste in *Distinction: A Social Critique of the Judgment of Taste*, trans. Richard Nice (Cambridge, Mass.: Harvard University Press, 1984). Clearly, new methods have to be invented to uncover the disciplinary sources of judgment of popular taste in countries such as India.

Works Cited

Asad, Talal. *Genealogies of Religion: Discipline and Power in Christianity and Islam.* Baltimore Johns Hopkins University Press, 1993.

Bakhle, Janaki. *Two Men and Music: Nationalism in the Making of an Indian Classical Tradition.* New York: Oxford University Press, 2005.

Bose, Pradip Kumar. "Pujor kalkatar bikalpalok" ("Heterotopia in the Calcutta Pujas"), *Baromas* 19, no. 1 (1997): 3–9.

Bourdieu, Pierre. *Distinction: A Social Critique of the Judgment of Taste*, trans. Richard Nice. Cambridge Harvard University Press, 1984.

Chatterjee, Partha. "The Disciplines in Colonial Bengal," in *Texts of Power: Emerging Disciplines in Colonial Bengal*, ed. Partha Chatterjee. Minneapolis: University of Minnesota Press, 1995, pp. 1–29.

Das Gupta, Chidananda. *The Painted Face: Studies in India's Popular Cinema.* New Delhi: Roli Books, 1991.

Fabian, Johannes. *Moments of Freedom: Anthropology and Popular Culture.* Charlottesville: University Press of Virginia, 1998.

Ghosh, Anjan. "Durga Puja: A Consuming Passion," *Seminar* 559 (March 2006): 31–34.

Gramsci, Antonio. *Selections from the Prison Notebooks*, trans. Quintin Hoare and Geoffrey Nowell-Smith. New York: International Publishers, 1971.

Guha-Thakurta, Tapati. "From Spectacle to 'Art,'" *Art India* 9, no. 3 (2004): 34–56.

——. *Aesthetics of the Popular Print: Lithographs and Oleographs from 19th and 20th Century India.* Kolkata: Birla Academy of Art and Culture, 2006, pp. 3–9.

Gutman, Judith Mara. *Through Indian Eyes: Nineteenth and Early Twentieth Century Photography from India.* New York: Oxford University Press, 1982.

Hall, Stuart. "Cultural Studies and Its Theoretical Legacies," in *Cultural Studies*, ed. Lawrence Grossberg, Cary Nelson, and Paula Treichler. London: Routledge, 1992, pp. 277–94.

Jain, Kajri. "More Than Meets the Eye: The Circulation of Images and the Embodiment of Value," in *Beyond Appearances? Visual Practices and Ideologies in Modern India*, ed. Sumathi Ramaswamy. New Delhi: Sage, 2003, pp. 33–70.

Kapur, Geeta. "Revelation and Doubt in Sant Tukaram and Devi," in Kapur, *When Was Modernism: Essays on Contemporary Cultural Practice in India.* New Delhi: Tulika, 2000.

Nandy, Ashis. "The Intelligent Film Critic's Guide to Indian Cinema," in Nandy, *The Savage Freud and Other Essays on Possible and Retrievable Selves.* Delhi: Oxford University Press, 1995.

——. "Introduction: Indian Popular Cinema as a Slum's Eye View of Politics," in *The Secret Politics of Our Desires: Innocence, Culpability and Indian Popular Cinema*, ed. Ashis Nandy. Delhi: Oxford University Press, 1998.

Pinney, Christopher. *Camera Indica: The Social Life of Indian Photographs*. Chicago: University of Chicago Press, 1997.

——. *Photos of the Gods: The Printed Image and Political Struggle in India*. Delhi: Oxford University Press, 2004.

Subramanian, Lakshmi. *From the Tanjore Court to the Madras Music Academy: A Social History of Music in South India*. Delhi: Oxford University Press, 2006.

Vasudevan, Ravi S. "Introduction," in *Making Meaning in Indian Cinema*, ed. Ravi S. Vasudevan. Delhi: Oxford University Press, 2000, pp. 1–36.

Weidman, Amanda J. *Singing the Classical, Voicing the Modern: The Postcolonial Politics of Music in South India*. Durham, N.C.: Duke University Press, 2006.

6

On *Mumbai Police* and *Drishyam*

Reading Desire into Two New Wave Crime Thrillers in Malayalam

Jenson Joseph

The contemporary as a historical moment, abounding with contradictions and ironies, makes the task of doing aesthetic theory or cultural criticism simultaneously challenging, genuinely fun, as well as a matter of political urgency. Even as knowledges about social relations, conditions of life and their ideological fabric tend to become increasingly demotic, the apparatuses of power begin to show a capacity to evolve dynamically in response and consolidate even more effectively. Consciousness raising and knowledge production are no longer the exclusive domains of counter cultural practices, parallel cinema and experimental art. Yet, such a scenario has led only to a routinisation of political devices in aesthetic practices, leading to an explosion in cultural expression as well as critique, which the institutions of power and the culture industry are often able to respond to with enthusiasm and absorb. Against such a context, the cultural critic as well as academic disciplines invested in the domain of aesthetic theory must reassess their tasks. One meaningful intervention would be to update and sharpen the tools of ideological critique—rather than abandoning it as a worn method—by paying attention to the new equations between permeating cultural expressions and present-day forms of power.

In this paper, I take up two recent Malayalam crime thriller films—*Mumbai Police* (Rosshan Andrrews) and *Drishyam* (Jeethu Joseph), both released in 2013—to identify two frames within which popular culture in Kerala attempts to grasp, and formulate an aesthetic response to the historicity of the contemporary times. I intend to do so by first analysing the modes in which these films undertake a charting of the present, mainly through their attempts at representing what has changed about conditions of existence today. I then identify two distinct, yet related, desires that figure centrally in these films—desires which I hope to illustrate as key to understanding the new relations emerging between contemporary shifts in cultural expression and how power takes its form today. I interpret *Mumbai Police* as a film that explores de-subjectivation as the desirable path towards (paradoxically) an ideal subjectivity, analysing this desire against the context of a growing general awareness about ideology and its operations. I try to show how the film attempts to imagine 'an ideology-free subject' through the means of de-subjectivation, which in turn is arrived at through the idea of sex-neutrality. Later in the paper, I propose that the desire for a moral framework evident in *Drishyam* must be approached from the point of view of the hysteric subject of contemporary media cultures. I argue that there is a counter-intuitive reification of the image in the film, despite its tagline 'visuals can be deceiving', which must be understood against the context of today's dominant media forms—typified by the Internet, New Media, smartphones and computers—privileging categories and values like data and immediacy in order to gain legitimacy as more transparent truth-revealing devices. In other words, the paper uses these two films to generate a commentary about the political implications of the contradictions, desires and anxieties that constitute the contemporary as a historical juncture.

I take two phenomena from popular media cultures in the region during the last decade as evidence of a recent, renewed aesthetic interest in the thematic of the modern subject/subjectivation and the symbolic order, specifically as a way of contemplating the contemporary. The first is the emergence of the debate about 'New Generation Cinema'—a genre title that critics and commentators endowed on a new breed of films in Malayalam during the last decade which they identified as having effected a break from the past conventions in terms of their making, the stories they told and the worlds they represented. I use this discourse as a framing device for my discussion of *Mumbai Police* as a film that was responding to a recent optimism about the prospects of achieving a 'subjective perfection', an optimism identifiable as central to the commentaries on New Generation Cinema. The second is the revival of a sort of cinephilia on the Internet, resulting from the digital media cultures in the region redeploying captured stills, snippets, punchy dialogues and scenes from films in order to make memes and to troll. This peculiar dependence of popular Internet cultures on the region's cinema as a repertoire of collective consciousness becomes the backdrop to my discussion of *Drishyam*, a film about cinephilia as such.

Early during the last decade, with the release of *Traffic* (Rajesh Pillai, 2011), *Chappa Kurishu* ('Head or Tails'; Sameer Thahir, 2011), *Salt N' Pepper* (Ashiq Abu, 2011), *Ustad Hotel* (Anwar Rasheed), and *22 Female Kottayam* (Ashiq Abu, 2012), critics and industry observers announced the arrival of a new breed of films in Malayalam called 'New Generation Cinema', signifying a coming of age for the institution of cinema in the region. Endorsed as a positive development, critics considered this new wave of films as the sign of mainstream Malayalam cinema adopting certain reform measures in order to synchronise its practices with what was perceived as the coming into existence of a historical condition in which there is a general progressive improvement in subjective formation among film viewers, and in society at large. In other words, 'New Generation Cinema' was taken to be the result of a modern reformist section in the film industry investing in realigning mainstream cinema's spectatorial address to make it correspond positively to the perceived refinement in subjective formation, leading to a not-so-far-away scenario of everyone graduating to an ideal or proper subjectivity. It is this condition that the 'generational shift' implied in the invented generic title primarily alludes to. Often, films would identify and name the Internet as one of the key agents of this historical change, along with the general exposure to the post-modern global media cultures facilitated by the neoliberal economic-cultural regime.[1] It is also not uncommon for contemporary popular culture to make references to the broadening reach of cultural criticism as effecting an attitudinal shift among people towards art and cultural products, making them sharper and more critical.[2]

The first part of this paper takes up this optimism about achieving subjective perfection as its main thematic, proposing that upon closer analysis, this optimism can reveal an interesting contradiction: de-subjectivation is identified as the route to achieving an ideal, progressive subjectivity. Thus, a paradoxical desire for de-subjectivation exists alongside the contemporary optimism about reaching a subjective perfection, the former becoming the condition for the realisation of the latter. Sexuality often becomes the nodal point around which the contradictory pulls of these desires are explored and resolved narratively. The crime thriller *Mumbai Police* is useful to explore the shades of this thematic.

Mumbai Police tells the story of Antony Moses (Prithviraj), Assistant Commissioner of Police, who loses his memory in an accident moments after he solves a murder case, presenting him with the challenge of having to regain his memory as swiftly as possible so as to reconstruct the narrative he had assembled to solve the murder mystery. What is most fascinating about the film is that the accident, which causes a total memory loss for the protagonist, is shown as causing a fatal impairment to the protagonist *and* also resulting in a rather desirable condition in which he can reinvent himself as de-subjectivated, which endows him with a highly valuable objectivity. Antony Moses loses his identity—his subjectivity—even though the accident has not impaired his other senses, his muscle memory, physical functions and capabilities, the combat skills he had acquired from police training, and more importantly his ability to think logically and systematically like an effective investigator must. This has the interesting effect of the subject being split into two: Subject A, who is the integrated subject before the accident, and Subject B, which is an abstraction of the subject minus the subjectivity. This condition is stated precisely in these terms in a scene in the film showing the protagonist talking about his dilemma as that of Antony Moses B struggling to figure out who Antony Moses A was.

The film is unique in the way it dramatises this condition and its consequence. To reveal the film's structure, it is important that we first take the sexual element out of the equation, only to put it back into the scheme of things later in order to delineate the proper function it serves in the narrative. Once we do this, the story can be summed up as follows: Antony Moses A—that is, the protagonist before the accident—was in fact a manipulative police officer who not only killed his own colleague and his best friend, but also tried covering up the crime under the guise of leading the investigation into the murder. Yet, just before the fateful accident, a crucial subjective-transformative experience makes him realise that it was a silly misunderstanding on his part about his friend's intentions that eventually led him to plot the murder. This realisation prompts a guilt-ridden Antony Moses A to confess to the murder by calling the Police Commissioner on the phone, moments before the accident. However, just as he begins to explain the circumstances that led to him killing his own friend, the accident happens, erasing his memory—and his subjectivity, by extension. The investigation in the film begins when the Police Commissioner Farhan Aman (played by the actor Rahman) decides to get Antony Moses B to reconstruct the case diary brick by brick, turning him against Antony Moses A, realising that the protagonist's condition can be converted into an advantage in the reinvestigation, now that the subject/subjectivity shrouding the truth has been eliminated from the equation, making available the investigator in his pure form with only his desirable faculties, devoid of anything subjective that might taint them.

This is when the film enters untrodden territory. Antony Moses B's loss/lack of subjectivity, though it disorients him socially, proves to be his best ally in solving the case: he is able to look at things objectively and re-analyse Antony Moses A's life and activities from a distance that becomes crucial. In other words, if Antony Moses A's social-sexual subjectivity had made him a morally corrupt police officer and a murderer, then losing the same subjectivity provides Antony Moses B with a priceless clarity, enabling him to see things clearly and objectively. Thus, what we began by considering as a handicap—the protagonist's loss of memory, which the narrative presents as having the ultimate effect of him losing his subjectivity—turns out to be one's biggest asset, as it takes one closer to the possibility of realising oneself as an ideal or proper subject, effectively presenting subjectivity as a baggage of excesses that hinders one from realising oneself fully.

Thus, on the one hand, the film ends on a dark note rendering subjectivation as such as suspect—as something that essentially corrupts and shrouds one's perspective. Nevertheless, this darkness is accompanied by an ecstasy in the film about the progressive possibilities that de-subjectivation affords, especially as the path towards achieving subjective perfection. In other words, the accident de-subjectivates the protagonist because it has the ultimate effect of him not knowing who he is any longer; yet, this problem–which normally should make the protagonist impaired and dysfunctional–turns out rather to be a boon, as de-subjectivation allows him to function ideally. On the other hand, the de-subjectivated Antony Moses B, in pursuit of the truth, is shown as being on the brink of despair as he tries reconstructing the case diary like a puzzle, because he is unable to derive a sense of totality out of the evidences he pieces together meticulously. Assembling the facts by seeing the web of lies that his former self had spun around the murder to conceal his own guilt is not a difficult task for him. It doesn't take long for him to realise that he himself had killed his colleague-friend, and that he kept sabotaging the investigation into the murder; he also figures out that he had eventually confessed to the crime to his superior officer. However, two crucial questions remain, without resolving which a closure seems unattainable: what was Antony Moses A's motive, and why the eventual confession. The film exploits this impasse to the maximum so as to to prolong the suspense as well as to make the audience also share the protagonist's despair. It teases us with the trope of the final piece of evidence that would solve the puzzle. It turns out that Antony Moses A, in his attempt to eliminate the last shred of evidence that could have implicated him, had come across a phone video clip. Realising that seeing this video clip had helped his former self to solve the case, Antony Moses B goes in search of it too, convinced that the vital clue to the mystery lies in it. This search, however, ends in vain as the video clip only mystifies the case further, merely adding to the pile of data that has emerged during the reinvestigation.

In order to push the narrative towards a closure, the film must now plug the protagonist back into the domain of the social by endowing him with the subjective faculties so that he may begin to see the facts in relation, within the field of the social. Unsurprisingly, it is also the time for the pivotal ingredient of sexuality—the hitherto suppressed element—to burst into the film dramatically. Here is a brief account of the events that unfold in the film from this point onwards, thrusting Antony Moses B into the domains of the subjective and the sexual at once, causing him trauma and relief equally: In the most controversial scene in the film, Antony Moses's sexual partner—a male flight attendant—turns up at the door unaware of his lover's memory loss. It then strikes our protagonist that Antony Moses A was a closeted gay; he had kept his sexuality a secret in order to protect his masculine image within the police force; when his friend chances upon this closely guarded secret, his paranoia drives him to committing murder, suspecting that he might have fallen in his heterosexual friend's eyes, and that the latter was planning to make his sexuality public; he plots an elaborate plan to kill the former by making sure that no evidence is left behind, and ties up loose ends under the guise of leading the investigation into the murder.

Antony Moses must now reconcile with his re-discovery about his 'deviant' sexuality he had lost consciousness of due to the accident. Yet, this (re)sexuation puts an end to his earlier despair, as he regains his subjective faculties, enabling him to make a series of quick imaginative leaps which also bring a closure to the case. First of all, he is able to gain the faculty of identification. He can now think from the perspective of his former self. He realises that Antony Moses A's paranoia about his sexuality being made public must have become the motive for him to plot to kill his own colleague-friend. He is also able to make instant sense of why Antony Moses A confessed to killing his colleague after watching the mobile phone video clip. The clip only proves that his colleague-friend had no plans to humiliate him after all; rather, the video clip turns out to be a testimony about their intimate friendship. Watching the video clip had made Antony Moses A realise that he had terribly misunderstood his friend's intentions whom he ended up killing eventually for no reason, prompting him to turn himself in as an act of repentance. Once again, it is nothing in the clip per se, but the ability to imagine and identify with the subjective-transformative impact that Antony Moses A must have undergone while watching the clip, that helps the protagonist to derive a conclusion and close the case. In other words, when Antony Moses B is able to make sense of the case through a purely subjective experience of identifying with Antony Moses A and his repentance, the subjective reasserts itself as the precondition for interpretation and sense-making, leading to a narrative closure, as things finally begin to fall in place. This is the paradox in the film: it wants to privilege de-subjectivation as liberating; yet it eventually has to depend on the subjective to effect a narrative closure.

But how does the introduction of the sexual bring about a narrative closure?

Subjectivation as Sexual; Sexual as Signifying Closure

At first look, the gay protagonist's closeted-ness and his homophobia directed against himself—constituting his subjectivity as one rooted in toxic masculinity and self-denial—become stand-ins for subjectivation as such and its excesses. After all, his closeted-ness as well as the compulsion to put up an alpha male appearance in order to conceal his gayness are presented as the subjective traits one acquires in the process of negotiating one's sexual orientation with the society.[3] It is the same subjectivity that eventually makes him an unethical police officer and a cold-blooded murderer. Here, subjectivity is connoted negatively because it attaches to us from the outside rather than being an expression of our selves. The sexual—and by extension, the subjective—figures here as a taint or a hindrance to proper self-realisation. De-subjectivation, in this framework, is signified as the process of shedding the baggage of excesses that the social attaches to us from the outside. In addition to the precious objectivity in perspective that it is supposed to offer us (like in the case of Antony Moses B), de-subjectivation is presented as the escape route from manipulative ideological influences, which figure in the film in the form of heteronormative imagination and homophobia. Taking these two dimensions together, we can see that there is an interesting conflation of sexuality with subjectivity in the film.

There is a scene early in the film which illustrates this conflation quite dramatically and effectively. It comes soon after the opening sequence showing the accident and the title credits that follow. We see the Police Commissioner Farhan taking Antony Moses back from the hospital to drop him at his apartment. We realise that Antony Moses is struggling to recollect anything about his past life, as we see that Farhan has to remind him that they are close friends as well as related by marriage. As Farhan is about to leave after dropping him, an anxious Antony Moses stops him and asks: 'Is there anyone in my apartment? Do I live with somebody?' When Farhan says 'No', it is a relief for Antony Moses. The trajectory of the rest of the narrative depends entirely on the answer to this question: because to de-subjectivate Antony Moses is to devoid him of his sexuality as such—not because sexuality is a part of subjectivity; rather, to be subjectivated and to be sexualised (possessed by others' desires) are the same. Antony Moses B, presented as the bare essence of Antony Moses A, cannot be sexual because he, having been subtracted from the domains of the social and the symbolic, cannot access (others') desire, and is instead thrown into the disorienting sphere of proliferating data, evidences and facts.

The film cleverly disguises the protagonist's homosexual orientation as a source of suspense, by taking advantage of the contiguity between the absence of sexuality in a de-subjectivated state of being and the erasure/suppression of the sexual within the heteronormative imaginary—the latter often taken to be the default normality. The de-subjectivated condition that Antony Moses B is in, subtracted from the field of the social, automatically evacuates sexuality from his domains (quite like the genre conventions in classical detective stories which stipulate that the domain of the male investigator be made devoid of the woman/sexual so that he can represent and occupy the realms of the symbolic and desire—as opposed to the domains of the real and the drive).[4] We don't expect to deal with the sexual in our protagonist's domain precisely because he is presented as devoid of a social subjectivity, just like he—after the assurance that he doesn't live with anybody—can forget about the sexual and the subjective, so as to dedicate his attention entirely on finding and reassembling evidence that can help reconstruct the narrative that had solved the murder mystery. But towards the end, when the film breaks the above mentioned stricture in detective stories in order to introduce the sexual abruptly into the protagonist's domain, it (naturally) traumatises the protagonist and shocks the viewer, who is caught off guard, too.

We must understand the film's choice to break the genre convention by introducing the sexual abruptly into the scheme as necessitated by its need to provide the de-subjectivated protagonist an entry back into the field of the social from which he has so far been subtracted, so that he regains a shred of the subjective faculties of identification and empathy which become crucial in enabling him to make the final imaginative leap, bringing the narrative to a closure. In doing so, the film acknowledges the limitations of its own political project that proposes the idea of subjective perfection by subtracting oneself from the fields of the social and the ideological. In fact, subjectivity—which until then was considered an impurity that shrouds one's perspective—now becomes the condition that makes interpretation, and thus the narrative closure, possible. In other words, sexuality is brought into the narrative precisely at the moment when the subjective needs to be invoked in order to compensate for the evacuation of the social and the ideological from the protagonist's (Antony Moses B's) domains, which instills in him a lasting paranoia (See the screen grabs from the film, given below).

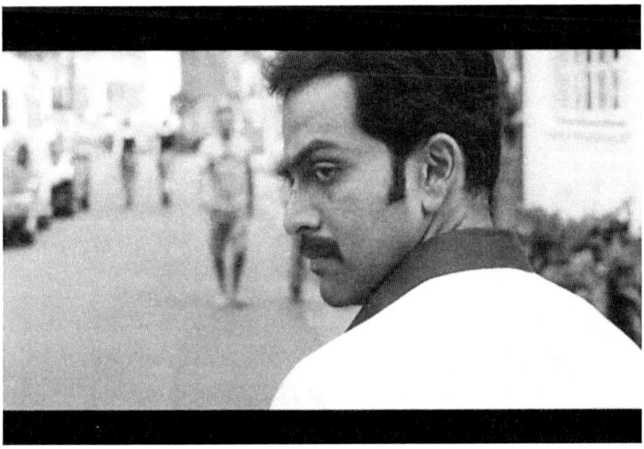

Image 6.1: Screengrabs from *Mumbai Police* (Rosshan Andrrews, 2013; Courtesy: Nisad Haneefa Productions/Central Pictures)

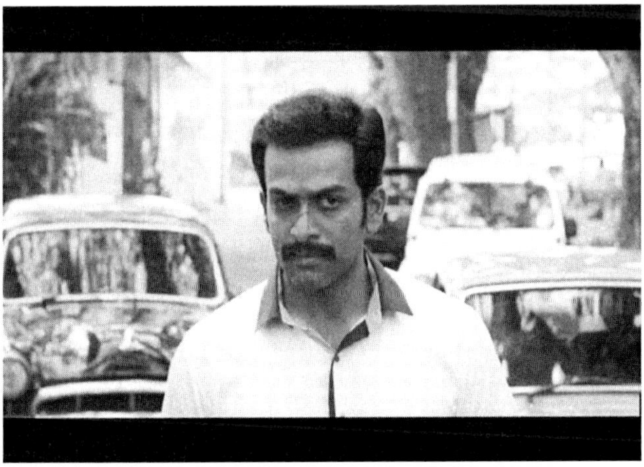

Image 6.2: Screengrabs from *Mumbai Police* (Rosshan Andrrews, 2013; Courtesy: Nisad Haneefa Productions/Central Pictures)

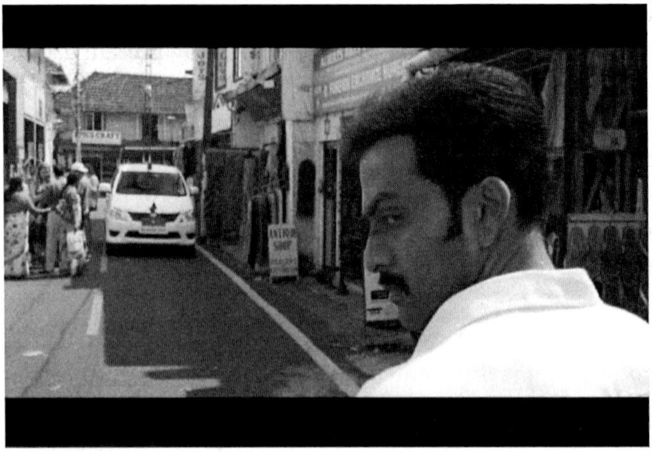

Image 6.3: Screengrabs from *Mumbai Police* (Rosshan Andrrews, 2013; Courtesy: Nisad Haneefa Productions/Central Pictures)

But by making this argument about the introduction of the sexual as providing a way back into the social and the subjective, am I not contradicting myself, because I had also argued a few sentences earlier that it is the absence of the woman and the sexual from the domains of the male detective in classical detective stories that allows the detective to operate within the limits of the symbolic and thus desire? In other words, how can the absence of the sexual from the domains of the male detective (in the classical detective genre) as well as the abrupt introduction of the sexual into the world of the protagonist in *Mumbai Police* both have the same effect of situating the protagonist within the social, the subjective and the symbolic? I shall demonstrate that this contradiction can be resolved by resorting to Joan Copjec (1994), who shows us in her analysis of the film noir world, that 'sex is the structural incompleteness of language' (206)—meaning that sex does not signify something positive, but it stands for the impossibility of unending signification, or the limitation of language as a structure which will inevitably fail in achieving total signification. Invoking sex, thus, acknowledges this inadequacy of language, and thus *opens up the possibility of a closure*. In the case of the classical detective genre, the sexual as the limit of the signifying system has already been acknowledged and thus becomes the ground on which the detective world is represented—as devoid of the woman and the sexual. The classical detective never gets drawn to the world of unending signification by pursuing more and more evidences hiding the truth beneath them. (This is the domain of the drive, jouissance, the real, in psychoanalytic terms, which the classical detective is smart enough to ignore). Rather, the absence of the woman and the sexual puts him in the domain of desire, orienting him to read others' desires in the clues left behind. He is driven by desire, the desire for interpretation. In *Mumbai Police,* the figuration of the sexual as the limit of signification must be staged in the narrative, rather than taking that as its beginning point. The de-subjectivated protagonist, who is disoriented after his pursuit for the final piece of evidence also turns futile, must acknowledge that evidences can only take us so far, and that one must turn to the subjective and the domain of interpretation in order to attain a closure.

Mumbai Police, in wanting to convert the shock effect of the sudden introduction of the sexual into a matter of declaring political solidarity with sexual minorities, is able to exploit the contiguity between the invisibilisation/suppression of the sexual in the heteronormative status-quo and the evacuation of the sexual that accompanies the aesthetic project of de-subjectivation. The film—quite ambitious of the prospects of being received as a groundbreaking attempt in popular cinema that problematises the heteronormativity of the dominant imaginary—manages to conceal the evacuation of the sexual (that naturally follows its intention to present Antony Moses B as subtracted from the field of the social) by aligning it with the invisibilised status of the sexual that is key to the normative heterosexuality—that is, the limiting of the sexual into binaries and closing off the sexual domain as not open to further elaboration *precisely because the sexual is the limit of signification.* And when the film introduces the sexual abruptly into the scheme for shock effect—by breaking both the narrative contract until then as well as the conventions of representing the male detective in classical crime films—it succeeds, however, in revealing the heteronormative structure because we are forced to encounter the element of the sexual which remained suppressed as part of the narrative contract, though we all know it has never been totally erased or adequately signified/represented.

Cinephilia Online: A *Drishyam* Hypothesis

If *Mumbai Police* engages primarily with the desire for de-subjectivation only to eventually illustrate its impossibility, we can identify the desire for the symbolic order as driving much of contemporary media cultures. In the following section, I will take up Jeethu Joseph's superhit film *Drishyam*, another Malayalam crime thriller from 2013, as a useful text that will help us make theoretical sense of the deployment of images and clips from cinema in popular Internet cultures in the region. The present peaking of the informatic media regime, catalysed by the ubiquitous use of the Internet, smartphones and social media, has brought about a revival of a sort of cinephilia among Malayalis—though phenomena similar to the one I describe here could very well be found elsewhere too.[5] Malayali users of the Internet and social media have turned massively to the public archive of Malayalam cinema for a range of communicative and sense-making practices: their memes and stickers are predominantly made out of extracted images from Malayalam films; they use film clips to satirise contemporary politics by establishing a correlation between the clip and an unfolding political scandal or a controversy; they borrow catchphrases from films to bring clarity to a scenario or to effect a closure to an ongoing debate. In fact, sampling and riffing from cinema constitute a major part of online cultural production among Malayalis today.

What makes Internet cultures turn to cinema so often, and what purpose does the redeployment of these film clips and imageries serve in general? We could begin with the tentative argument that referencing film imagery in this way invokes a community feeling by riding on the general familiarity of the invoked images, a familiarity made possible by cinema's status as one of the foremost public-cultural institutions in the region until now. This memory of the collective that the film imageries are able to invoke in online cultures seems to be crucial for both the Internet users as well as for the digital media. For Internet users, it compensates for certain de-humanising (or alienating) tendencies of the computer for which the world is a resource of computable data, emptied out of the values previously attributed to it. It thus helps the Internet user to *orient* oneself socially and culturally because these images function as the antidote to the dry computational codes and commands that make up the language of the personalised New Media. In the case of the digital media, the dependence on borrowed images from cinema is one way in which it leverages the 'spectacle society' that we still continue to be, because we haven't entirely come out of our dependence on images, imageries and spectacles in our social-cultural-political practices despite our growing fascination with the computer and its language of codes which seem to be capable of mediating the world better for us. Seen in this way, we can understand the Internet's present dependence on film images as indicating the transitional stage in which the digital media, which looks to colonise our world and lives through codes, computational language and software, is still in negotiation with the old impulses of an image-centric society.

Yet, there is no reason to begin by presuming that collective affect is alien to the Internet and computer cultures, or that 'being online' is essentially an alienating experience. We know that New Media can often materialise mobs, swarms and collectives of various types, even when it fetishises the ideas of individual customisation and personalisation to make advancements into all spheres of contemporary life. Thus, we know that collective energies are not extrinsic to digital media cultures such that they would need to be imported from outside. Collective affect of different sorts saturate the Internet. In fact, it is with the popularity of the Internet that various coinages signifying mob behaviour—like 'herd mentality', 'going viral' (which implies promiscuity rather than isolation), cyber bullying, sharing, and trolling—started becoming so commonplace in our everyday conversations. But we also know that the collectives that the Internet and digital media cultures materialise are qualitatively different from the familiar formations of communities around a central unifying object—like the nation, the linguistic community, the tribe, or the fan club. To take into account this distinction, let us work with the following hypothesis: The collectives in varied forms that manifest in New Media cultures are the ones that the Internet constantly assembles, dissolves and reassembles around mostly transient objects, by re-channelising and re-accommodating communitarian energies within its economy, while the earlier familiar models of communities have begun disintegrating following the decline in the ideological efficacy of centralised structures and institutions.[6]

The proposition above can be rephrased as the historical shift away from societies organised structurally, towards a new order of self-regulation and control. The latter takes its own 'post-structural state' or 'structureless-ness' as the ground from which protocols of organisation, production, value extraction and management are constantly derived, which are then codified and updated, only to be broken and reformulated again. If we agree that this shift can be made the framework to understand transformations in contemporary life and culture, then the question of the symbolic order comes up as crucial. The symbolic order *structures*: it structures our desire and a given social form. Under conditions of modernity, the place of the state and art were central to the production and sustenance of the symbolic order as well as to resistances against the dominant symbolic order. Over the last few decades, we have seen indications of both the state and enterprises of art facing critiques, assaults and disavowal from quarters which are ideologically-politically incompatible—ranging from various post structural academic traditions to the right-wing political consolidations. Considering this, we could argue that perhaps what animates contemporary media cultures are the twin processes of:

(a) the exhilarations about the structure and the symbolic order falling apart as the result of our (sometimes legitimate/political, sometimes clearly anarchic/reactionary) collective desires, and as the logical outcome of the political-intellectual labour that has sought the disintegration of the systems and structures, so that we can set ourselves and our desires free, on the one hand, and
(b) on the other hand, the persistent yearning to fill the vacuum left by the collapse of the old symbolic order with a given framework—a moral/symbolic order—so that the world would still cohere.

If we think of New Media cultures' dependence on cinema by keeping this context in mind, we can see that cinema here signifies a collective institution that was central to the sustenance of the symbolic order hitherto. Approaching the theme from this angle, we can understand the redeployment of cinematic images online as allusions to the institution of cinema which has come to provide moral frameworks to relate to the world and cohere it, irrespective of whether the moral worldviews that cinema used to propagate were regressive or progressive. Interestingly, thus, the online cultures seem to endow cinema with a value which perhaps cinema has always struggled to claim for itself: cinema figures online as the cultural institution that has come to host the collective consciousness.[7] The recurring references to cinema in online cultures thus signifies the longing for a symbolic order, emanating from a present in which the world, after being freed from ideologies, given commandments, manifestos and constitutions, has been rendered into an *object world* composed of molecules and data which the computer can now recombine and calculate so as to attribute them with value afresh. It is true that the digital world has its own priests who attempt to compensate for the lack of the old symbolic order with new ideologies that reify data and code, or even hippies and anarchists of the digital world who sustain subcultures of free software, cults of hacktivism and so on. Yet, the nostalgia for the image—and by extension, cinema—seems to persist in digital cultures.

Thus, if these online invocations of cinema, and images from cinema, indeed function as the longing for a symbolic order, how does such a yearning help us think afresh about the image, cinema and data, and their relation to consciousness and the symbolic? The 2013 Malayalam super-hit suspense thriller *Drishyam*, which thematises this yearning for a symbolic order by compellingly linking this longing as having something to do with the image and cinema, is a very insightful cultural text to explore this theme. The film's plot has many striking similarities with the globally popular 2005 novel by the Japanese writer Keigo Higashino, titled *The Devotion of Suspect X*, though director Jeethu Joseph has denied that the film is based on the novel, responding to widespread discussions online about the similarities and the assumption that the novel must have inspired the film.

The film tells the story of Georgekutty, a family man, who succeeds in protecting his minor daughter and his wife from arrest after he comes to know they have murdered the only son of a high ranking police official. The latter was blackmailing them for sexual favours by threatening to leak a nude video of the daughter that he made on his mobile phone during a school trip. Georgekutty manages this by cleverly manipulating people and getting them to inadvertently testify to the false alibi that he has provided to the police, claiming that he and his family were away on the day when the murder took place. The cunning way in which Georgekutty succeeds in doing this becomes the high point of the film. Moreover, the clue to understanding the reification of the image and cinema in the film also lies in this aspect.

Georgekutty is played by Mohanlal, one of the twin superstars of Malayalam film industry, whose popular appeal is channelised towards the symbolic elevation of the cinematic image, which in turn represents, as I already suggested, a desire for the symbolic order—a desire that must be understood within its historicity. Georgekutty is an uneducated common-man from the village, yet he is extremely intelligent—a faculty he has acquired from his compulsive habit of watching films; he is thus a cinephile whose big dream is to buy and revive an ailing cinema theatre in his village. Georgekutty's passion for cinema makes him a cable television service provider, which is another way for the film to link Mohanlal's stardom to cinema itself, as this effectively makes his character a trader-distributor of cinema through television.[8] His own cinephilia has taught Georgekutty that consciousness works like the moving image, or like cinema as such;[9] taking cues from how his own mind is so captured or absorbed by the cinematic image, he decides to manipulate people's minds by providing them with vivid images of events that actually didn't take place.[10] The film's promotions used the tagline 'Visuals Can Be Deceiving' in order to play up this dimension to the story. At first look, the tagline might sound as if it is a warning against the deceptive quality of the image and cinema. Yet, there is a counter-intuitive reification of the image in the film—which is after all titled *Drishyam*, meaning 'the image'. Things begin to make sense if we expand the tagline to say, 'visuals can be deceiving, because they work all too well with our minds (and we like/miss being deceived by them)'. Seen in this way, the tagline in fact becomes a eulogy for the image and cinema, and by extension, for ideology and the symbolic order that work with the faculties of 'deception and manipulation' so as to put in place a given frame that will help us cohere the world. In other words, the film also allows us to contemplate on the nature of ideology as the economy of the image. The image can orient us by giving us a perspective by putting things in relation to each other, precisely by placing them within a given frame. And this cognitive operation seems to be at the centre of how ideology works too, by prompting us to imagine relations between variables in life, and to take those relations as given or as natural. Thus, there seems to be a contiguity between the economy of the image and how ideology or the symbolic order works.

This dimension also makes *Drishyam* an anomalous film carrying at its heart a desire for the symbolic order, at a time when the contemporary new wave cinema in Malayalam derives most of its creative energies from the critical deconstructionist discursive traditions that privilege seeking gratifications for our desires by exposing the fallacy of the symbolic order. The fact that *Drishyam* was a widely accepted film in the region, even amidst different strands of new wave films in Malayalam, including the commercially successful 'New Generation Cinema', which have begun to exert a cultural hegemony in the region as well as across the country, indicates that both these desires—for the symbolic order as well as for gratifying our desires by defying the symbolic order—persists simultaneously within us, in contest with each other. The contemporary New Media culture takes this tension between these two desires as the ground to promote its own ideology and infrastructure which can cater to both these desires, that is, to see the computer code taking over as the preferred mode of processing the world given over to us as composed of bare data and molecules, as well as the persisting purchase of the image and the spectacle, the deceptive powers of which we want to surrender to.

But how do I proceed from identifying the reification of the image in *Drishyam* to arguing that it signifies a desire for the symbolic order? The film's pitting of the common man against a tyrannical state rationality becomes significant for me in this regard. Riding again on Mohanlal's star appeal, the film treads the difficult path of securing the moral victory of the protagonist who in fact covers up a murder, that too by manipulating a whole lot of well-meaning people in the village and in the town in the process. To achieve this, the film has to first suggest what we could call the postmodern historical condition in its own way, against which it then constructs a compelling moral frame which will then justify the protagonist's actions. In the film, the condition of postmodernity is signified by two elements. The trope of the taboo act is one indication: the murdered boy's lust first towards the minor daughter and then towards her mother makes him deserve death beyond redemption, while also using this character to symbolise contemporary moral anarchy—a suggestion made stronger by showing the boy as a spoilt, typical millennial youth and as someone given over to the lures of new media technologies like the smartphone.

The second trope that the film uses to make references to the postmodern condition is through its critique of the state machinery—represented by the police department—and the purposes it serves today. The story begins in the milieu of the police station in the village being renovated as part of the community policing project of the Kerala Police called 'Janamaithri Policing' ('People Friendly Policing'). Georgekutty is deeply suspicious of such projects, as he thinks this won't change the corrupt nature of the police force in any fundamental way. This suspicion accommodates the critical pessimism that the ideology of decentralisation could be turned against people and the community in the hands of the state machinery, which often applies the spirit of decentralisation merely to extend its reach even into areas and geographies which were previously considered out of its bounds. And his suspicions soon come true: the film shows us that the police force will eventually operate according to an instrumental rationality that cannot ensure justice.[11] To signify this as what is absurd about today's historical condition when the spirit of decentralisation is turned against its own grain to further expand the reach of instrumental rationality, the film uses the Dalit body (of the actor Kalabhavan Shajohn) and the figure of the woman (played by Asha Sarath) as representative figures of the police force, presenting us also with an interesting internal dynamic between the positions they represent within the force. The Inspector General, whom Asha Sarath portrays, combines the traditional masculine repressive brutality of the police with a new feminine shrewdness; she can think like the common man Georgekutty, making the contest between the two into a mind-game of 'equals' despite the asymmetry in their positions in terms of power. Her cunning also helps her to identify and exploit the rivalry between Constable Sahadevan, played by Shajohn, and Georgekutty, as she delegates the former to unleash conventional methods of torture on the family, including women and children, while she stays away from directly getting implicated in administering such brutality and repression. The absurdity of this scenario—when the feminine has become an added modality of repressive power—is foregrounded in these scenes through the mediating figure of the IG's husband (played by Siddique) who is stunned at seeing the extent to which his wife is able to use her position to push the boundaries of protocol, a shock that the film expects the audience to feel as well. The redeployment of Asha Sarath's own stardom, which derived from the lead female characters she played in television serials popular among women viewers in the region, adds to this effect (See also screen grabs from the relevant part in the film below).

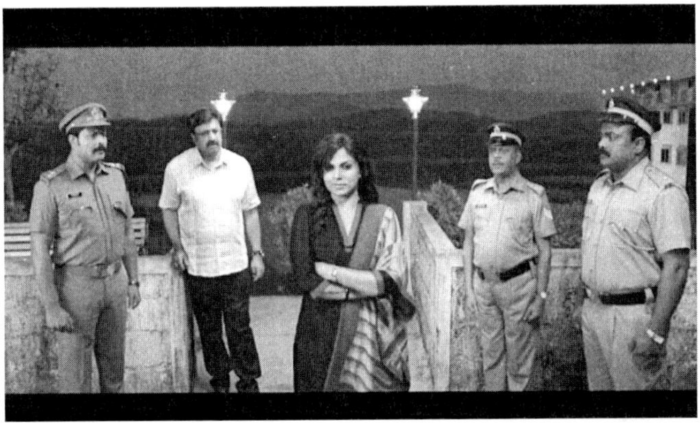

Image 6.4: Screengrabs from *Drishyam* (Jeethu Joseph, 2013; Courtesy: Aashirwad Cinemas)

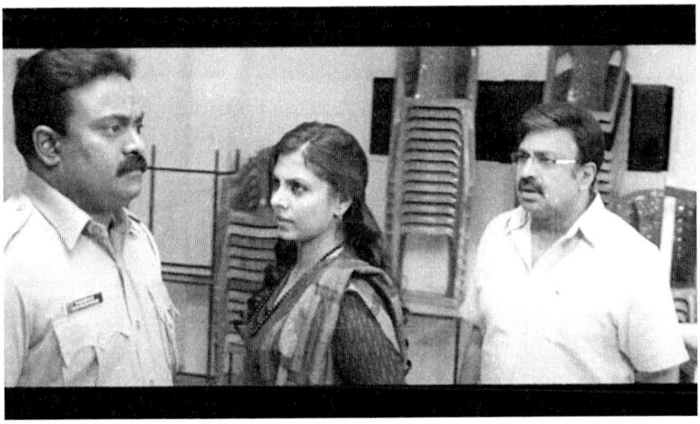

Image 6.5: Screengrabs from *Drishyam* (Jeethu Joseph, 2013; Courtesy: Aashirwad Cinemas)

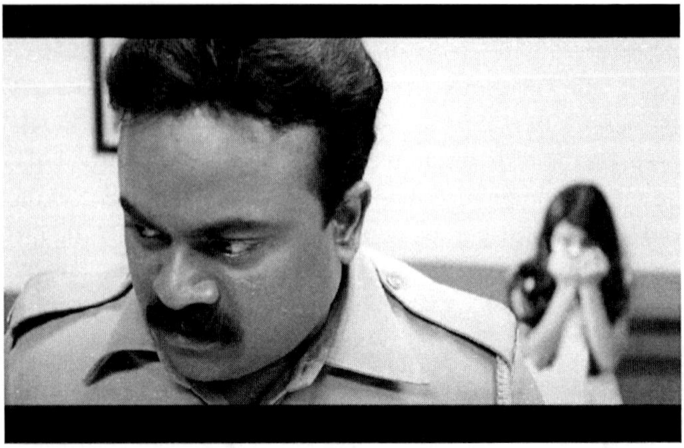

Image 6.6: Screengrabs from *Drishyam* (Jeethu Joseph, 2013; Courtesy: Aashirwad Cinemas)

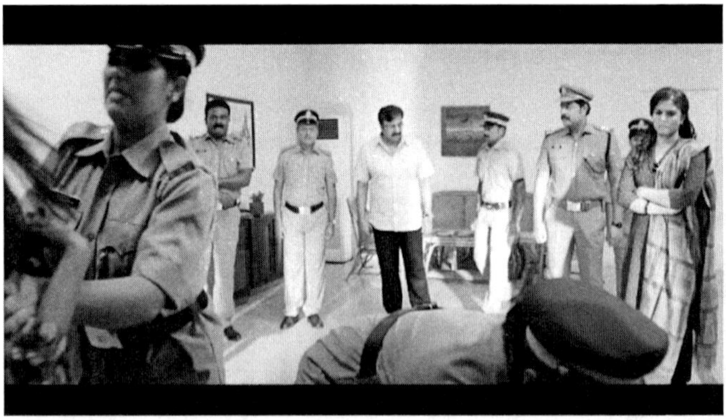

Image 6.7: Screengrabs from *Drishyam* (Jeethu Joseph, 2013; Courtesy: Aashirwad Cinemas)

It is against this mapping of the historicity of the present that the film compels the audience to take a moral stance in judging Georgekutty: can he be pardoned for all that he has done by first covering up the murder, and then manipulating people into corroborating the false alibi? Is the objective truth to be privileged, in which case, Georgekutty and his family must face legal consequences for what they did irrespective of the circumstances? Or, will the moral framework ultimately triumph, in disallowing a family from suffering for accidentally murdering someone who was evil anyway? In the final revelation, as we realise that Georgekutty has disposed of the dead body by burying it beneath the police station under construction, there is a suggestion that real justice prevails now as the police has been made to function as the guardian of general welfare, which should be its actual *moral* duty rather than serving a clinical frigid rationality. If *Drishyam* has an anti-realist core, it is in its privileging of the moral order over empirical truth, or image over data. In contrast, Georgekutty eventually continues to *represent* the common man even though he had cleverly deceived everyone in trying to protect his family, as being deceived in representation is precisely what desiring a moral frame or the symbolic order entails.

To conclude, the privileging of the moral frame in *Drishyam*, which I have argued as signifying the desire for the symbolic order, needs to be understood within the historicisation that the film itself seems to have undertaken, outside of which the film as well as its popular acceptance will come across as an a-historical conservative reaction against a rapidly advancing technological modernity. The popular enthusiasm about contemporary modernity, especially towards New Media forms and the various possibilities of promiscuity and liberation they offer, far outweighs the anxieties about them—even when many such anxieties about the prying of New Media into our lives are quite legitimate concerns. Of late, the region's cinema audience has been polarised into those who like and patronise the contemporary new wave that looks to break away from conventional cinema, its representational registers and its icons on the one hand and a more traditional audience segment whom the dominant industry and its star system still count on, on the other. Capitalising on Mohanlal's stardom as a bridge, *Drishyam* was indeed a singular film, whose acceptance managed to cut across this divide. My attempt was to offer an explanation for the film's universal acceptance by suggesting that its privileging of the moral order must be seen as a response to the specific historical condition we inhabit today—no matter what name we choose to call it—rather than essentially as regressive simply *because* of the moral ingredient in it.

To approach *Drishyam* as a cultural text that helps us map the present by using the text's own properties, however, need not entail absolving the film of various conservative values that one can hold it responsible for upholding explicitly. For example, the moral order that the film privileges eventually institutes the patriarch at its centre, whose figuration has not undergone much reform vis-à-vis the familiar traditional patriarchal figure, other than that he is portrayed as sexually liberal in comparison—in an attempt to present him as relevant in today's context when traditional patriarchal moralities are under public scrutiny (see also Mokkil 2019). Similarly, the portrayal of Georgekutty as the common man is disappointingly a reinvention of the old conventions of construing the upper castes' life experiences as synonymous with the life and the struggles of 'the average citizen'. The protagonist's Christian-ness and his orphan status do not take this characterisation significantly away from the conventional registers of signifying the common man in Malayalam cinema whose default identity has been that of the Hindu upper caste man. Above all, the villainy of constable Sahadevan, an evidently lower caste character, is presented with no historicity: he is simply evil, foreclosing all possibilities of this character gaining an interiority. As a result, much of the narrative becomes a restaging of the post-1990s thematic of the Hindu secular citizen's disillusionment with the secular state machinery—a drama in which the subaltern figures either as the obstacle in the path to modernity who needs to be eliminated or reformed, or as merely the victim on whose behalf modernity is disavowed altogether and the aristocratic order re-legitimised. In other words, despite the impulse in *Drishyam* to privilege the symbolic order—an impulse that I see as against the general cultural grain today—the film fails to propose a moral order that is significantly different from the familiar moral registers, suggesting perhaps that this is precisely the challenge before us: having desired the disintegration of the prevailing structure for good reasons, how do we reimagine ourselves as a moral collective, or a society that works with certain principles about what we ought to be?

Acknowledgements: I have found theoretical base for my arguments in the works of a set of scholars who engage with the ongoing transformations in media cultures. My understanding of the ideology and structure of the Internet and new media is borrowed from the works of Alexander Galloway, especially his two books, *The Interface Effect* (2012) and *Protocol: How Control Exists After Decentralisation* (2006). The idea that consciousness works analogous to the cinematic image is elaborated in Bernard Steigler's *Technics and Time 3: Cinematic Time and the Question of Malaise* (2010). Vilem Flusser's book *Into the Universe of*

Technical Images (2011) has helped me think about the image in relation to concepts like data and abstraction. I got introduced to this body of work during the one year I spent at the Department of Humanities and Social Sciences, IIT Bombay (2016–17). I am indebted to the department, its English cluster and especially the research scholar Anand Karthikeyan, whose work-in-progress presentations led me into discovering the theoretical orientation implicit in the works cited above. I also thank Samhita Sunya for her suggestions. I am also indebted immensely to the Alexander von Humboldt Foundation, Germany, for a generous fellowship tenure during which I wrote this piece.

Note on the use of film visuals: For film stills, I have used screen grabs through available technology. I take the position that such use falls within the purview of fair use as stated in Sec. 52 of the Indian Copyright Act, 1957, as the proposed draft amendments initiated in 2006 make amply clear. Further, such use, intended for research, criticism and review, also clearly falls within Article 13 of the Agreement on Trade-Related Aspects of Intellectual Property Rights (TRIPS), which invokes what has come to be known as the Berne Three Step Test in permitting fair use in special cases which do not conflict with a normal exploitation of the work and do not unreasonably prejudice the legitimate interests of the rights-holder. This test, originating in Article 9(2) of the Berne Convention for the Protection of Literary and Artistic Works, 1967, has also been extended to the WIPO Copyright Treaty and the EU Copyright Directive (1996). Additionally, such frame reproductions in an academic book are protected by Section 107 of the Copyright Law of the United States of America (Limitations on exclusive rights: Fair use) as coming under the domain of 'criticism, comment, scholarship, or research', 'for nonprofit educational purposes', in the fact that such stills are an insubstantial part of the film as a whole; and lastly, in that this activity in no way damages the 'potential market for or value of the copyrighted work'. Such research is also protected by Britain's 1988 Copyright, Designs and Patent Act (Chapter III, Section 28–29).

Notes

1. For example, the 2012 film *Bachelor Party*, directed by Amal Neerad—a key figure in the contemporary new wave in Malayalam—has a scene in which one of the protagonists played by the young actor Indrajit deflates the villain's conventional threat with the following retort: 'Nowadays, even small kids download films and watch. They will boo at you. [Why don't you try something new?]'
2. The 2010 film *Best Actor* (Martin Prakkat) includes a scene in which a toddy tapper in the village dismisses the aura about popular cinema by terming it as 'a savarna-fascist enterprise'—a common phrase used in critical discourse in the region to refer to cultural products with conservative ideological content.

3. The bizarreness of the film also lies here. It is not easy for the film to absolve itself of the criticism that it presents homophobia and heteronormativity as first/also problems for the homosexual to grow out of, thus effectively inverting the well-established queer studies critique that puts the onus on the heteronormative status-quo for pushing non-normative sexual beings into the margins of social-political existence. This inversion makes the critique of normative sexuality as a matter of attitudinal adjustments at the individual level, or as an issue of subjective refinements, by ignoring the operations of power in producing sexual marginalities. In short, the problem with the mode of critiquing heteronormativity that the film proposes is linked directly to its proposition of de-subjectivation as a political solution to ideologies that create marginalities and discriminatory structures. Acquiring ideal subjectivities through de-subjectivation—that is, through a retrieval of our essential selves by shedding the subjective excesses that the negotiations with the social will attach to us—is the political project proposed here.
4. See Chapter 7, "Locked Room/Lonely Room: Private Space in Film Noir", in Copjec 1994.
5. For example, see Al-Ghassi (2018) for a discussion of Syrian Internet cultures redeploying clips from the Arabic-dubbed Japanese anime broadcast on Arab government TV in the 1980s.
6. The *popularity* of the Internet, which takes the distributed network as its functional model (as opposed to the more familiar centralised or a de-centralised organisation), itself must be taken as the proof of the decline of the old structures and their appeal. Making this claim, however, raises the question: how do we argue that the Internet signifies the waning of the centralised/decentralised structures, considering that, for example, Hindutva groups or jingoistic nationalist groups thrive online too? Doesn't the persistence of such ideologies across these (pre-digital as well as digital) historical periods suggest that the older familiar structures and modes of community formation still hold forth? I propose that such continuities at the level of content must not distract our attention from the fundamental shift at the structural level. The communities that the Internet materialises have the nature of swarms which form spontaneously around contingent and unpredictable themes and objects, operating according to protocols that they evolve internally in real time (as opposed to the communities bound together by a given hard-set tenet/constitution), and so on. The model of the distributed network produces, sustains, dissolves and reassembles such communities. It is true that the Internet as distributed network can be redeployed in the service of familiar ideologies like religious fanaticism, nationalism or misogyny. This presents us with the challenge of understanding what the above-mentioned shift—away from the reign of centralised and decentralised social structures to the hegemony of distributed networks today—means for ideologies

like religious fundamentalism, nationalist euphoria, male chauvinism, and so on.

7. See also my discussion of the 2019 Malayalam film *Jallikkattu* directed by Lijo Jose Pellissery, one of the leading figures of contemporary new wave cinema in the region: 'Just A Buffalo or Not: What to See In *Jallikkattu* If You Can't See a Good Film', *Film Companion*, 20 November, 2019; available at https://www.filmcompanion.in/features/malayalam-features/just-a-buffalo-or-not-a-nuanced-take-on-lijo-jose-pellisserys-jallikattu/
8. The dependence of private television services and channels on cinema from the late 1990s onwards can be identified as the precursor to the contemporary media cultures redeploying cinema. For example, one of the solutions that Asianet, the first private television channel in Malayalam, found for generating program content when it launched its transmission during the mid-1990s was to acquire the rights of old and new Malayalam films and assigning Diana Silvester, who later became a legendary TV producer, with the task of producing program segments by combining scenes from across films. One of the flagship programs of Asianet, produced by Diana Silvester, was called 'Cinemala', meaning 'garland made out of film scenes'.
9. Bernard Steigler (2011) explains the power of cinema as lying in the fact cinematic images are temporal objects, a quality which he argues, makes the former analogous to human consciousness which also functions temporally. This affinity between cinema and consciousness makes it easy for the consciousness to be absorbed by the cinematic image. To Steigler, media forms are exteriorisations of human consciousness which can then be adopted by another consciousness, which is central to the production of collective consciousness.
10. The same can be said about the novel as well, though it does not develop it into an argument about images and consciousness: its protagonist also manipulates people's memories by offering them vivid images of events that never took place in order to protect his love interest and her daughter by helping them construct false alibis.
11. Here, we should remember that the desire to see this (instrumental) rationality prevailing was once a progressive modernist impulse, as Madhava Prasad (1998) has shown in his analysis of the 1958 Hindi crime film *Kala Pani* (Raj Khosla), which privileges the historic "shift from the [feudal] morality of sinning by association to the legality of guilt by commission". In the film, the hero investigates a 15-year old murder of a courtesan which took place in a brothel, for which his father was wrongly convicted. For the hero, the dilemma is that the father's immorality is beyond question, *which he should set aside to seek the truth*: even if he did not kill the courtesan, he frequented the brothel. Prasad illustrates, thus, that there is a historicity to the fact that the 'truth' that the hero of *Kala Pani* seeks is a legal truth, based on the legal

discourse's emphasis on precision of language, which signifies a desire for escape from the moral categories of shame and sinfulness. He identifies this as the anti-aristocratic thrust in *Kala Pani*, which he contrasts with the ideology of the dominant feudal family romances of the 1950s and 60s which always secured the feudal moral order over legality (See the section 'Feudal Family Romance'; pp. 64–72).

Works Cited

Al-Ghassi, Omar. "Grendizer Leaves for Sweden: Japanese Anime Nostalgia on Syrian Social Media". *Middle East Journal of Culture and Communication*, 2018, pp. 52–71.

Copjec, Joan. *Read My Desire: Lacan against the Historicists*. Cambridge: MIT Press, 1994.

Joseph, Jenson. "Just a Buffalo or Not? What to See in *Jallikkattu* if You can't see a Good Film in it." *Film Companion*, 20 November, 2019; https://www.filmcompanion.in/features/malayalam-features/just-a-buffalo-or-not-a-nuanced-take-on-lijo-jose-pellisserys-jallikattu/

Mokkil, Navaneetha. "Anxieties of Seeing: The Sensational World of Cinema, Digital Media and Politics." *BioScope: South Asian Screen Studies*, 9(2), 2019, pp. 1–19.

Prasad, Madhava. *Ideology of the Hindi Film: A Historical Construction*. New Delhi: OUP, 1998.

Steigler, Bernard. *Technics and Time 3: Cinematic Time and the Question of Malaise*. Stanford, California: Stanford University Press, 2011.

7

Of Pain and Other Tragic Emotions

A Study of Divinity in Kaṟisial Kādu

Swathi Sudhakaran and *Milind Brahme*

The fierce goddesses, club-bearing Karuppan, brightly-coloured Aiyyannar, and the terracotta horses for him and Munis to ride out are ubiquitous presences that dot the Tamil countryside. Mines observes that 'in any village and neighborhood in Tamil Nadu where Hindus reside, there too reside gods. But in no two places do the very same gods live' (17). These divinities of blood and power—categorised as *amman* or goddess and *virās,* the masculine figures—partake of all the passions and uncontained generative forces of human experiences (Bayly 27–30). Not limited to a cosmic heaven above, these deities, specific to their territory, infiltrate the earth below as a perceptible presence in the lives of the people.

These folk deities, however, are said to merge with the scriptural deities and sometimes are seen as their lesser forms. Fuller calls this phenomenon in the Hindu tradition of many deities becoming one and one deity being many as the polytheistic logic of fluid continuity. For him, the relationship among the Hindu deities is continuous although hierarchical (30). Despite the continuity, the experience of divinity associated with folk deities and scriptural deities is not the same. This divergence is evident in the emotions embodied in them: Bhairava, the lower form of Shiva, for instance, is more ferocious than the higher form. A study of emotions would hence be useful in understanding the nature of divinity associated with these deities.

Emotions have been viewed as both undesirable, as things to be controlled or avoided, and as desirable, as embodying the divine, in various traditions of Hinduism. Detailed discussion on emotions begins in the Vedanta tradition with texts such as the Upanishads that come after the Vedas. While there is scarce reference to emotions in Vedic Hinduism, emotions have been viewed as negative in both the Vedanta and yogic traditions (McDaniel 177–178).[1] However, Bhakti or devotional Hinduism, even while worshiping the deities Vishnu, Shiva, and the Goddess, sees emotion as central to the experience of the divine. The personal and loving devotion, *bhakti*, and not *njāna* (knowledge) or *karmā* (action), is the path that brings a person closest to the divine here (Roberts 57–60).[2] The insistence on emotion and not *njāna* or *karmā* as the path to the divine in devotionalism is subversive, as it challenges the knowledge monopolised by Brahmins and priesthood, by proclaiming devotion as the means to attain divinity (Fuller 157). Emotion, hence, is an important aspect of the experience of the divine and has the potential to maintain or challenge societal hierarchies and morality.

Emotion in folk Hinduism, however, is yet to receive sufficient scholarly attention. McDaniel says there are no elaborate studies on self or emotions in folk Hinduism although a distinction between soul and the body or different levels of the soul is made many a time (117). This paper investigates this lesser-explored terrain of emotions embodied in the folk deities and the experience of divinity that gets formulated by it.

Despite their expressive visuality, the realm of the folk deities is predominantly textual, in the sense that the living environment of folk deities is sacred myths and mundane stories that describe the intervention of the supernatural in the lives of the people (Ülo and Lourdusamy 4). Hence a close analysis of the folktales collected by Ki Rajanarayanan from Kaṟisial Kādu, the dry zone to the extreme south of Tamil Nadu, has been taken up for study.

Kaṟisial Kādu covers few taluks of Tuticorin, and Virudhunagar districts and some parts of Tirunelveli and Ramanathapuram districts (Venkatachalapathy 205). Belonging to the dry zone, the Kaṟisial region—unlike the wet zone that tends to focus on Sanskritic religion—regards the fierce *amman* (female guardian deity), *pey* (a spirit both benevolent and malevolent) and male divinities as beings who embody divine force (Bayly 27).[3] Oral tales have been a significant part of constituting religious and social ideas and activities in the region. The stories collected from the common people of Kaṟisial Kādu are reflective and constitutive of the religion they practice.

Folk Emotions in Stories from Kaṟisial Kādu

The folktales collected by Ki Rajanarayanan with their narrative universe of talking animals, wish-granting gods and goddesses are similar to fables and parables. However, what marks these tales out from parables or fables is the lack of a moral universe in them. The tales that don't adhere to any universal codes of right and wrong are outside the logic of *dharmā*.[4] Many a time, it is shrewdness that triumphs rather than principle unlike in fables or parables. People cheat, trick the other, and get away with shrewdness and the stories say that 'they lived happily ever after'. These folktales don't teach a moral, or for that matter instruct the reader/listener to abide by righteous action. Despite this, Ki Rajanarayanan says:

> If a person masters a hundred folktales, his knowledge about the world in general increases. As we grow up, there are certain things taught to us at school and at home—but isn't there a whole other world of knowledge that is not spoken of? Perhaps that's the purpose of these tales: to act as our friendly tutor on these matters. (1)

The wisdom entailed in these tales that Ki Rajanarayanan talks about then is different from universal principles of right and wrong. The logic of the folktales doesn't work in the paradigm of *karma* (action) either. Ramanujan defines *karmā* as:

1. Causality: Any human (or other) action is non-random; it is motivated and explained by previous actions of the actors themselves.
2. Ethics: Acts are divided into 'good', 'virtuous' and 'bad', 'sinful'; the former accrue *punya* ('merit'), the latter *pāpa* (sin, demerit).
3. Rebirth or re-death (*punarjanmā* or *punarmrtyu*): souls transmigrate and have many lives in which to clear their ethical accounts. Past lives contain motives and explanations for the present, and the present initiates the future (430).

Ramanujan says that while *karmā* is almost synonymous with Indian or Hindu belief systems, the hundreds of Kannada folktales he had collected had no reference to it. The logic of these tales is not governed by self-determinism; instead, it is determined by *talaividi*[5] (destiny) (37–38). Man has little control over *talaividi*, fortune is random and the ways of life inexplicable. Fortune doesn't favour the righteous man; being virtuous doesn't accrue *punya* or sinful *pāpa*. While *karmā* is referred to as an iron chain of cause and effect, *talaividi* is about arbitrariness. The following close analysis of the story the 'Stone Pillar Son-in-Law' from Ki Rajanarayanan's *Nattupura Kathai Kalanjiyam,* translated by Pritham K. Chakravarthy as *Where Are You Going, You Monkeys?* is an exploration of this unique distinction. The story is premised on the idea of god writing the immutable destiny of his daughter on her forehead post creation; the scene described in the following terms almost portrays god as a quasi-mortal and offers a conception of fate that is both simple and nuanced at the same time.

> Every time God created human life, he would make her stand with her head facing him, while he wrote her destiny on her forehead. While doing this, he would never look at the person's face. Actually, even while he was writing, he would never know what he was going to write. For some, the scripted fate might be very good, while for others, it might be horrible. Whatever it was, he would never erase it or rewrite it. (Rajanarayanan 31)

Although god wants his daughter to have a happy life, he is shocked to see what he has written on her forehead: the destiny on the forehead of the daughter declared widowhood. It is interesting to note that even god is incapable of changing what he has written on his daughter's forehead—the idea of divine omniscience is casually unsettled. To save her from the misfortune, god arranges her marriage to a stone pillar thinking that a stone husband would be beyond death. He, however, is utterly helpless to see the stone pillar reduced to rubble after a thunderstorm. The story says, 'it was then that God understood: not even he could change destiny!' (ibid). God in this story is a male, unlike fate being popularly imagined as a woman in folktales. Ramanujan says fate, referred to as *Vidhiyammā* in south Kannada or *śeṭivi tāyi* in North Kannada and Marathi, writes a person's destiny on his forehead at the time of his birth (434). Also, unlike most folk deities, the god in the story doesn't seem to have a non-divine origin nor is he depicted as being ferocious. The story type thus varies from the violation-death-deification-revenge pattern prominent in *villupāte* (bow-song tradition), a folk tradition prominent in southern districts of Tamil

Nadu (Blackburn 171).[6] The story seems closer to the pan-Indian mythology in being neither historic nor specific to a territory.

The story, however, lacks the auspiciousness seen in pan-Indian mythology as god is depicted as terrorised and helpless in the face of destiny. The story says that god was so terrified that he stays indoors even when the thunderstorm strikes. Terror experienced by god in the story is an uncommon emotion associated with gods in pan-Indian mythology. Classical Sanskrit drama, which deals chiefly with *vīra* (heroic), *śṛṅgāra* (erotic), and *karuṇa* (pathos) *rasās* or emotions, also does not prefer emotions like *raudra* (anger) and *bhayānaka* (terror) central to the tragic (Ramanujan 72). The story although not historic is tragic like the violation-death-deification-revenge story type.

The predominant emotion associated with god in the story is terror. God seems terrified not just at the recognition of his inability to alter *talaividi* when confronted with the destiny of his daughter but also at his vulnerability during the heavy thunderstorm. God seems vulnerable to the precariousness of nature that he needs the protection of his house to keep him safe. Terror, however, is not the predominant emotion associated with folk deities. Deities have been categorised as *metuvana* (gentle) and *ukkiramāna* (fierce) based on the emotions embodied in them, with the scriptural deities belonging to the former and folk deities[7] to the latter. The distinction also corresponds to cool to hot, orderly to chaotic, and stable to unstable (Mines 17). Although god in the story corresponds to chaotic and unstable signified by the category *ukkiramāna*, it manifests as terror and not ferociousness here. The emotion terror associated with god in the story seems not to be fully explained by the emotion *ukkiramāna* as conceptualised by Mines. The emotion, terror, embodied by god hence requires closer attention.

The *bhayānaka rasa*, with fear as the *sthāyibhāva*[8] seems to be the closest to the emotional state of terror associated with god in the story. *Nāṭyaśāstra* describes *bhayānaka rasa* as follows: 'That is *bhayānaka* which is produced by fear (1) of seeing or hearing weird persons or sounds, (2) of getting into fights, forests, and uninhabited dwellings, and (3) of having wronged elders or the king' (Rangacharya 61).

Bhayānaka rasa according to the *Nāṭyaśāstra* is the fear of encountering the unfamiliar in points 1 and 2. The third point also indicates the fear of authority or the failure to abide by the accepted

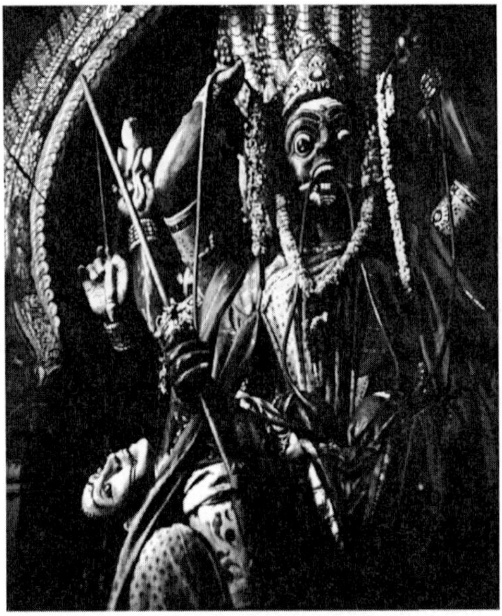

Periyachi *amman*, a fierce goddess in southern Tamil Nadu
(Reproduced with permission from Yannick Cormier)

moral code of conduct in a given society. Both these ideas imply a departure from the normal or a prescribed mode of behavior as producing *bhayānaka rasa.* While the terror in god when faced with the thunderstorm can be explained by point 1 of the definition of *bhayānaka* rasa, it falls short in explaining the terror that emanates from his helplessness when faced with *talaividi. Talaividi* is irreplaceable and central to the folk world-view, unlike the unfamiliar that produces *bhayānaka rasa* which is a mere aberration from the normal. Terror associated with *talaividi* is a more powerful emotion in the story and more at odds with the established notions of terror and fate in classical aesthetics.

Terror is notably linked to pain by Burke in *A Philosophical Enquiry into the Origin of our Ideas of the Sublime and Beautiful.* 'No passion so effectively robs the mind of all its powers of acting and reasoning as fear. Fear being an apprehension of pain or death, it operates in a manner that resembles actual pain' (Burke 96). It will be useful to explore this relationship between terror and pain to better understand the emotional state associated with god in the story. The recognition of the futility of *karmā* or action in the story is the recognition that pain is central to existence. *Talaividi* then is an idea based on pain, and terror associated with god in the story is a manifestation of it.

The object of terror is sublime and can't be considered trifling or contemptible (Burke 96). *Talaividi* that renders god helpless is not a source of small terror. Burke sees pain as the 'strongest emotion which the mind is capable of feeling' and sees 'ideas of pain' as more powerful than that of pleasure (58). The terror that has its roots in pain is the only emotion that enables god to break his indifference in order to realise the vision the story offers. It is then important to see terror as something beyond a mere negative emotion in the story. It is powerful enough to break open established ways of seeing, thus aiding in the richness of perception.

Pain is not merely a sensation here, nor is it a feeling that corresponds to bodily damage. The experience of pain involves the attribution of meaning in our lived experience and the association between different negative feelings. While it might seem self-evident, the recognition of it requires an association between different sensations and feeling states (Ahmed 23). Although pain is intrinsic to the idea of *talaividi*, god himself seems not to perceive it. It is through the particular experience of the crumbling of the stone-pillar son-in-law, making his daughter a widow, and the feeling of terror that emanates from the precariousness of fate that god recognises pain as central to existence. Pain then is a complex emotion and not a simple self-evident sensation here.

The pain central to *talaividi* is not something that the storyline attempts to eliminate. God or divinity is, in fact, incapable of replacing pain with pleasure. Pain is not necessarily annexed with evil as against the pleasure annexed to the idea of good in the folk religious worldview. Hence, in folk religion, as Locke conceptualises it, the text does not strive to replace pain with pleasure. Instead, what constitutes divinity is the response to pain inherent in life. Ramanujan quotes a Kannada proverb '*nāri munidare māri*' meaning a woman, when furious, is a goddess' (56). Fury as a response to pain, far from being a negative emotion that is sought to be eliminated, is an emotion central to folk religion as it is constitutive of divinity.

Pain from which tragedy takes its roots is an emotion that is central to the ancient Greeks as well. According to Nietzsche, pain in the Greek context is not seen as a sign of decay; it instead stems from overwhelming fullness. He sees Socratic optimism[9] as the outcome of weakness in Greeks (42–50). *Talaividi*, the idea based on pain, in the folk world view, however, doesn't seem to be born out of prosperity as the tragic in Greek society. Fuller observes that *talaividi* is majorly invoked by people of the lower strata of society and that large sections of the society including women and the lower castes don't call upon *karmā* to explain their misfortune (250).[10] Pain in the Kaṟisial world view is hence born out of vulnerability and poverty, not fullness.

Pain—including fury and terror emanating from it—although central to the economically and socially vulnerable, is not an undesirable emotion. Many a time, it is an empowering emotion in a non-egalitarian society. Sherinian says:

> In Tamil village religions, empowerment occurs through transphysical rituals of possession by the sami (deity). The village deity possessing or "coming upon" a villager allows even the weakest member of the community to gain power both physically and emotionally. Emotions such as anger and fear are not pacified but rather channelled into action. (92)

Pain is thus more than a private, subjective feeling or sensation in folk Hinduism. It transcends the particularity of individual experience to become a generalised affect. Terror in god is produced by the events leading to the crumbling of the stone-pillar son-in-law, by one particular incident; his recognition of pain, however, transcends the particularity of the incident. Shared pain that transcends particularity is a major aspect of the formation of folk religious cults. Even in the violation-death-deification-revenge story type seen in southern Tamil Nadu, shared pain which transcends particularity is the basis of the formation of religious cults. Therefore, pain rather than terror or fury is the emotion that more precisely differentiates folk deities and religion in Kaṟisial Kādu and the concept of pain that emerges from these stories offers a more variegated version of itself compared to the idea of pain and fury one finds in classical tragedy.

Conclusion

The defining emotion in the experience of the divine in folk religion and deities in Kaṟisial Kādu is pain. Although fury has been discussed as the predominant emotion associated with folk deities—Mines' category of *ukkiramana* deities, for instance—such tragic emotions stem from pain. While in the story 'Stone-Pillar Son-in-Law' pain manifests as terror, in the religious cults based on the story type violation-death-deification-revenge, it manifests as fury. Pain is, hence, at the base of the tragic emotions terror and fury which characterise folk deities.

Emotions—pain and tragic emotions such as fury and terror—not *karmā* or action become the means to partake of divinity in folk Hinduism. In the Kaṟisial worldview, where action or *karmā* doesn't determine merit, a culture of compensation—where all forms of injury are assumed to be related to innocence and guilt and where it is assumed that responsibility for injury can be ascribed to an individual or collective (Ahmed 32)—is absent. Pain is thus a major aspect in determining the nature of divinity and ethics of social activity in Kaṟisial Kādu.

These oral tales that people tell in Kaṟisial Kādu help the community organise their worldview. The story 'Stone-Pillar Son-in-Law', for instance, helps the listener/reader recognise pain as central to the religious realm, determining both the religious and societal activities of the community. This probably is the wisdom that Ki Rajanarayanan says is to be gained from these stories—a recognition of the inevitability of pain.

Notes

1. Emotion, according to these dualistic and ascetic traditions that emphasise the spiritual world over the physical world, is a disturbance in attaining the tranquil state of consciousness.
2. In the Gaudiya Vaishnava tradition, loving devotion, or *bhakti*, is manifested as *vatsalya bhakti rasa* (paternal love), *priti* or *dasya bhakti rasa* (service), *santa bhakti rasa* (peace), *sakhya* or *preyo bhakti rasa* (friendship), and *madhurya bhakti rasa* (erotic love) for Krishna. The highest form of devotion, however, is embodied in erotic love, the relationship between Krishna and Radha (Roberts 57–60, McDaniel 183–186). The erotic love, *madhurya bhakti rasa*, apart from

challenging the hierarchy of the priestly class, also subverts the very idea of the experience of divine and morality within Hinduism.

3. South of India can be seen as a land of two contrasting natural environments; the fertile river valley and deltas that constitute the wet south and the fringe areas called the dry zone. The caste grouping in the wet zone consisted of the Vellalars of Tamil Nadu and Nayars of Kerala who adopted hierarchical social conventions from the priestly Brahmin partnership to reinforce their power over subordinate agrarian labourers that consisted of Pallars, Vanniyars, Parayans, and Chakkalaiyars in Tamil Nadu and Cherumas and Pulayas in Kerala. The dry zone, an unsettled territory, outside the favoured deltas and river valleys, inhabited largely by Maravas, Kallars, and Akamutaiyars worshipped the divinities of blood and power. The Telugu-speaking northerners such as the Kammas and Reddis, who settled in the dry zone in the fourteenth century CE and brought the land under cultivation for the first time, also belonged to segmentary clans and tribal groupings. Their gods and conventions were distinct from the Sanskritic valley people (Bayly 20–27).
4. The moral code of good and evil by which actions are evaluated in Hindu philosophy
5. Several expressions are used to refer to the notion of fate as pre-ordained and immutable for each person. In Tamil, *talaividi* and *talaiyeluttu* literally mean inscribed on one's forehead; in Kannada *haneli barediddu* and *hanebareha* or 'the writing on one's forehead'; in Sanskrit and Sanskritised dialects of various Indian languages, *phālalikitha* or what is written on the forehead' and *brahmalipi* or Brahma, the Creator's script. Sometimes these phrases are used as interjections and exclamations when misfortune strikes (Ramanujan 434–435).
6. Blackburn says a lot of religious cults are based on the violation-death-deification-revenge story pattern in the folk tradition. A tragic narrative, it's a biography centered on the undeserved death of the main character. Divided into two segments, the first part describes the birth and youth of a certain character. Some kind of violation happens then which leads to the undeserved death of the main character. The second segment describes the deification of the murdered character. The deity later returns to earth to seek revenge on those responsible for the bad death (169–170).
7. Mines talks of three categories, *piramanka tevarkal* (brahmanical gods), *ur ammankal* (village goddesses), and *matan* or *pey* translated as ghosts (fierce gods) in Yanaimangalam (17). Mines distinguishes between *ur ammankal* and *matan* or *pey* among the folk deities and it is only *matan* and *pey* that are called fierce.
8. It is the predominant emotion that produces the *rasa*. There are eight *sthāyibhāva*, love, laughter, grief, anger, energy or vigour, fear, disgust and wonder producing the eight rasas *śṛṅgāra, hasya, karuṇa, raudra, vīra, bhayānaka, bibhasta* and *adbhuta* respectively (Rangacharya 65–66).

9. Nietzsche sees "the Socratism of morality, the dialectics, modesty and cheerfulness of theoretical man", which brought about the death of tragedy, as a sign of decline and fear of pessimism (43).
10. Fuller says there are important sociological factors that decide this choice of principles and belief systems. He says the *karma* principle is some ethical justification for the comfortably settled class as it gives some explanation for the privileges they enjoy. To be vulnerable to personified agencies would indicate a weakness in an individual and so explaining the misfortune that has befallen one to *karma* and not the personified agencies would only assert the mental strength of an individual thereby helping them maintain the social superiority they enjoy (ibid).

Works Cited

Ahmed, Sara. "The Contingency of Pain". *The Cultural Politics of Emotion.* Edinburgh: Edinburgh UP, 2014. 20–42. Print.

Bayly, Susan. *Saints, Goddesses, and Kings: Muslims and Christians in South Indian Society 1700–1900.* Cambridge: Cambridge UP, 1992. Print.

Blackburn, H. Stuart. "Performance Markers in an Indian Story-Type". *Another Harmony: New Essays on the Folklore of India.* Eds. Stuart H. Blackburn and A.K. Ramanujan. Berkeley: U of California P, 1986. 167–195. Print.

Burke, Edmund. *A Philosophical Enquiry into the Origin of Our Ideas of the Sublime and Beautiful.* Michigan: Gale Research, Inc., 2018.

Fuller, C.J. *The Camphor Flame: Popular Hinduism and Society in India.* New Jersey: Princeton UP, 2004. Print.

Locke, John. *An Essay Concerning Human Understanding.* Ed. Kenneth P. Indianapolis: Winkler. Hackett, 1996. Web. 24 June 2020.

McDaniel, June. "Hinduism." *The Oxford Handbook of Religion and Emotion.* Ed. John Corrigan. New York: Oxford UP, 2007. 176–200.

Mines, P. Diane. *Fierce Gods: Inequality, Ritual, and the Politics of Dignity in a South Indian Village.* Bloomington: Indiana UP, 2005. Print.

Nietzsche, Friedrich. *Birth of Tragedy: Out of the Spirit of Music.* Trans. Shaun Whiteside and Ed. Michael Tanner. New Delhi: Penguin, 2003. Print.

Rajanarayanan, Ki. "Stone-Pillar Son-in-Law". *Where are you Going, you Monkeys?* Ed. and Trans. Pritham. K. Chakravarthy. Chennai: Blaft, 2008. 31. Print.

Ramanujan, A.K. "Is There an Indian Way of Thinking? An Informal Essay". *The Collected Essays of A.K. Ramanujan.* Ed. Vinay Dharwadker. New Delhi: Oxford UP, 1999. 34–52. Print.

———. "Towards a Counter-system: Women's Tales". *The Collected Essays of A.K. Ramanujan,* Ed. Vinay Dharwadker. New Delhi: Oxford UP, 1999. 429–448. Print.

——. "Two Realms of Kannada Folktales". *Another Harmony: New Essays on the Folklore of India*. Eds. Stuart H. Blackburn and A.K. Ramanujan. Berkeley: U of California P, 1986. 41–76. Print.

Rangacharya, Adya. *The Nāṭyaśāstra: English Translation with Critical Notes*. New Delhi: Munshiram Manoharlal, 1984. Print.

Roberts, Michelle Voss. *Tastes of the Divine: Hindu and Christian Theologies of Emotion*. New York: Fordham UP, 2014. Print.

Sherinian, C. Zoe. *Tamil Folk Music as Dalit Liberation Theology*. Bloomington: Indiana UP, 2014. Print.

Valk, Ülo, and S. Lourdusamy. "Village Deities of Tamil Nadu in Myths and Legends: The Narrated Experience". *Asian Folklore Studies* 66 (2007): 179–199. Web. 28 June 2019.

Venkatachalapathy, A.R. "Cho. Dharman: Peacock on Black Cotton Soil". *Tamil Characters: Personalities, Politics, Culture*. New Delhi: Pan Macmillan, 2018. 205–220. Print.

8

From Dialectics to Dialects

A Reading of O.V. Vijayan's *The Legends of Khasak*

E.V. Ramakrishnan

It was fifty years ago that Ravi got down at the bus-stop in Koomankavu, on his way to Khasak, a land-locked village in the shade of the Chetali mountain, lost in the remote rural plains of Palghat in Kerala, bordering on Tamil Nadu. That is how the novel *Khasakkinte Ithihasam* (The Legends of Khasak, 1968) by O.V. Vijayan (1930–2005) opens. The novel was serialised in a literary weekly in 1968, and was published in book form in 1969. Vijayan was a reputed cartoonist, columnist and commentator besides being one of the pioneering Malayalam novelists of the 'modernist' generation of the 1960s. *The Legends of Khasak,* which went on to become a modern Malayalam classic, still marks the highest point scaled by any Malayalam novelist in terms of intensity of vision and inventiveness of language. It narrates how Ravi, deputed by the District Board to start a school in Khasak, is gradually sucked into its archaic charm, unending tales and vibrant ways of life, trapped as he is in his own personal dilemmas. As Kerala reels under the after-effects of the unprecedented deluges of 2018 and 2019, the people still struggling to recover from the trauma of devastation that will take years to heal, revisiting an iconic text that voiced fundamental doubts about our received notions of modernity may help us comprehend the text from a new perspective.

The sixties in India were a watershed that produced some of the enduring works of twentieth century Indian fiction: *Kosla* by Bhalchandra Nemade (1963), *Samskara* by U.R. Ananthamurthy (1965), *Aadha Gaon* by Rahi Masoom Raza (1966) and *Khasakkinte Ithihasam* by O.V. Vijayan (1969). All of them shared a dissenting, critical voice, reclaiming the fundamental role of the novel as a counter-narrative that questioned official versions of reality. Their authors had suffered a loss of faith; bereft of the safety net of ideologies, they plumbed the depths of their inner resources by exploring the limits of language. In shoring up the fragments of their spiritual and mental lives, they reinvented the form of the novel for a new generation, investing it with the burden of intractable questions of ethics that exceeded the formalist concerns of aesthetics.

Vijayan went beyond these issues of ideology to address an epistemological problem that still haunts us: he had serious misgivings about the way modernity produced and legitimated knowledge that met with uncritical acceptance. Modernity was as much content as form, and one could not step outside it, without surrendering one's speaking voice. What happens to forms of knowledge that lie outside its institutional spaces? *The Legends of Khasak* was about the imaginative apprehension of an order of reality that lay beyond language. Ecologists like Eduardo Kohn (author of *How Forests Think)* have argued that we need to go beyond language to see how the environment thinks through us. Vijayan's narrative, replete with resonant images informed by the echoes of other worlds that reach out to us, transcends the templates of linear time that novels embody, to invoke a vast eco-system of interconnectedness across the living and the non-living. This is how the novel resists the impulse to classify and conquer that pervades the Cartesian logic of modernity. Vijayan's was a dissenting note on the Euro-centric epistemology with its will to power.

In his 'An Afterword' to the English self-translation, *The Legends of Khasak,* Vijayan described how he lost his faith in communism: 'It was then that tragedy from afar shattered the carnival of liberation. In Hungary, they tricked and shot Imre Nagy. It blew my mind. I turned away, I began my unchartered journey' (205). Vijayan's insights came as much from his disillusionment with dialectics as from his intense imaginative engagements with the dialects around him. His great discovery was that language as dialect in its rudimentary and radical mould was a life form that gave access to a society's conceptual cosmology. The epiphanies of Vijayan's novel were made possible by the subliminal layers of an oral subculture that animated Khasak with its mythopoesis. In bringing this orality into a dialogic relation with the standard idiom of the written and conventions of formal knowledge, he demonstrated that the subaltern could speak to the centre, and that the novel as a grand narrative cannot embody the marginal voices. Allapitcha Mollacka, Nizamali, Kuppuvachan, Maimuna, Tithibi, Kunjamina, Chukru Ravuthar, Aliyar, Kuttadan, Kuttappu, Appukkili, Kali, Neeli—these characters and many more, sculpted in sensuous local idioms with their rhythms and rhymes, become a presence which has a poetic significance of its own, that cannot be grasped by the standard syntax of modern Malayalam. That Vijayan calibrated a tone that could convey the nuances of their voices problematised the ideology of the novelistic form. He deviated from the narrative orientations of mimesis to defy the hegemonic conventions of social realism. Khasak was myth and memory, rituals and customs, sacred groves and dragonflies, laughter and melancholy performed through the tales that do not make a distinction between the sacred and the profane. The fabulist nomads of Khasak who travel in and out of it, and the stunted Appukkili, who moves between religions and wears a gown with the emblems of many faiths, belong to a world without closure, where multiple possibilities of identities co-exist with no rigid boundaries. The author says, 'What obtained in Thasarack (the original village which became a model for the fictional Khasack) was a playful interface between being and beyond being' (207). The sense of play holds the key to the carnivalised sense of space and time rooted in polysemy. Vijayan's fictional text was more like a musical score that conjured up a kinetic field of life-force, liberating us from our habitual ways of seeing.

Vijayan brought into the purview of the novel the collective and the communitarian through the semiotics of the local. But the early reception of the novel viewed it through the prism of individualism. The middleclass Malayali readers, including the informed critics, persisted in their belief for decades that *Khasak* was an existential tract on Ravi's guilt-ridden alienation and his quest for metaphysical illumination. In this reading, the village of Khasak became an anthropological museum peopled with curious figures from an insubstantial world. This shows an inability to relate to the voice of the collective in the narrative. To be more precise, Vijayan's use of the proliferating discourses of Khasak, signifying a polyphonic vision that can hold contradictions without incorporating them into a singular belief system, was reduced to an exotic spectacle with no inherent meaning. Two of the recurring phrases heard in Khasak are 'truth; (*sathiyam, unma*) and 'myth/fiction' (*poi*). That the village community could think through their crises and interpret the world with sophistication was never accepted by the majority of readers. Vijayan's craft created a liminal world where the boundary between the real and the surreal was blurred. His metaphorical flourishes altered the optics of perception, bringing the visionary within the familiar. For instance, the sight of the parrots flying into distance against the setting sun becomes a stunning visual metaphor of 'the latched bows of the palm parrots receding in the sky against fading light'. On the macro level, the novel's narrative, as a whole, resists the process of disenchantment, the progressive erasure of the world of magic and mystery, to provide a critique of the sanitised world of instrumental rationality we inhabit.

The modern novel, for all its championing of social justice and freedom, cannot escape its complicity with capital and imperialism. And hence, for an Indian novelist, any attempt to decolonise the form of the novel will have to begin with a self-reflexive reflection on what is it that the novel does as a literary form in her language? It is this self-reflexivity that distinguishes Vijayan from other novelists in Malayalam. Invoking the magical to assert the primacy of the sacred becomes a way of re-enchanting the world, looking beyond the narrow humanist ideals of the welfare state, moving beyond the moral order defined and sanctified by anthropocentric views of man and development. Commenting on the other-worldly time of Khasak, Vijayan says: 'In that sense, *The Legends of Khasak* is a ballad of re-enchantment' (208). In the chapter titled 'The First Lessons', Ravi tells the children the story of two sisters. They were two spores (*jeeva bindu* or specks of life) to begin with. The elder one stayed behind in the green valley, while the younger one moved on to explore the world beyond. The elder one asked the younger one if she would forget her. 'Never,' replied the younger one. Ages later, a girl with silver anklets and black eyes came to pluck flowers from a champak tree in Chetali's valley. As she plucked the flower holding down a twig which broke, the champak tree said, 'My little sister, you have forgotten me!' This story reverberates through the pages of *Khasak* because it looks beyond the human, re-ordering our narrow sense of humanism and ethics. It does not matter if Ravi lives or dies in the fictional scheme of things Vijayan has created because the novel is located on a moral plane that transcends the individual. The middleclass readers were agitated over the snake-bite that Ravi invites at the end. But decay, disease, death, divinity and desire are embedded in the Khasak ways of living, life triumphing at each stage despite the relapse of ruinous forces. Khasak distils calamities into folk-wisdom and preserves it in the surplus value of their tales, proverbs and a comic sense that can accommodate contradictions without containing them.

Vijayan's own English translation miserably failed to put across the vibrancy of his original narrative by succumbing to the linearity of a stilted, normative, and often archaic English prose with none of the fluency of the original. The visual metaphor of the parrots' flight mentioned above is translated by Vijayan in this matter-of-fact way: 'The last flight of parrots receded over the horizon' (85). There were more violations of the polyphonic, syncretic vision that pervaded the original. When the villagers discuss various view-points regarding the new school, they finally conclude: 'Truths are many'. However, in Vijayan's self-translation, this becomes: 'Many truths make the big truth' (36). In the original, there are only Ravuthars and Ezhavas, the local castes, but they become in English translation, 'the Muslims and the Hindus' (11). Obviously, the creative turbulence of self-doubts and scepticism that produced *Khasak* was replaced by a dogmatic faith in worn-out clichés of social divisions and sectarian spirituality by the time he came to translate the novel. Vijayan's own complex intellectual development demands a separate, detailed study. Once Vijayan had the answers, the novelist in him turned into a seer, as some of the later novels, with the exception of *Thalamurakal* (Generations, 1996), testify.

In 2016, Deepan Sivaraman, the well-known theatre director, produced a stage version of *Khasak*. It was a subversive translation, which succeeded in recovering the communitarian elements of the novel. Deepan employed spectacle on a scale that eclipsed the individual actor's interpretation of his or her role. This is pardonable in an experimental production that assimilates many elements of *theyyam*, a ritualistic performance in honour of ancestors, practised in north Kerala with its own elaborate forms of dance, music and spectacular visual imagery. In this production, Ravi becomes a marginal figure who has nowhere to go and a lot to learn. What the dramatic version testified to was the essential multivocal nature of the text which could not be grasped in terms of linear modes of thinking. The play begins with the *asaan* (call to prayer) of the muezzin that punctuates the play, adding an otherworldly ambiance that is enhanced throughout the play by the ebb and flow of the background music. The use of the folk version of Islam that carries the imprint of the local, communicates a poetics of the place that cannot be separated from Khasak's legendary compassion, immortalised in the myth of Syed Mian Sheikh whose army halted there to nurse a dying horse. The play succeeded in translating the communitarian ethos of the novel into visual images.

Paraphrasing Benjamin's comments in 'The Concept of History', one may say that *Khasak* becomes recognisable as a contemporary text only when 'it is seized as an image' that 'flashes up in a moment of danger'. *Khasak* speaks to us through its carnivalised sense of community that affirms the collective will to endure against all odds. *Khasak* is inhabited by voices that contextualise the moral economy of the local, where dialects, myths and memories constitute a rich cultural capital that sustains communities and enables them to survive. What belongs to the community as a whole is common, and in that sense, the fund of stories that instils the capacity for compassion and the memories that go back to Syed Mian Sheikh and the goddess on the tamarind tree, binding people into a community, create a common repository of cultural capital. In times of climate change, isolated individuals perish, while the poor and the abandoned whose organic bonds are still strong, survive because of their ability to endure, share and reach out to each other.

The above discussion may lead us to a reconsideration of certain aspects of 'Indian aesthetics'. The high modernist moment in the Indian literatures, in the post-1960s period, was concerned with the assertion of extreme states of individualism. In his discussion of existential aestheticism in the Hindi novel, Jaidev has observed that 'both High Modernism and existentialism favour a self that is solitary, asocial or anti-social and subjective' (25). Jaidev has shown how Hindi novelists such as Nirmal Varma, Mridula Garg and Krishna Baldev Vaid borrow Western cultural codes, but 'distort their characters and socio-cultural contexts to fit the contours of High Modernism and existentialism' (183). They fail to engage the West in a 'significant, purposive dialogue'.

The failure to integrate the cultural codes borrowed from elsewhere with our experiential worlds results in the creation of 'pastiche' (36). Similar trends can be seen in most of Indian literatures. This is where Vijayan's novel differs from the mainstream 'high modernist' tradition. He subjects the epistemic ideological world-view, derived from colonial modernity, to a critique by engaging with the Western codes of representation. Ravi as an outsider, trained in Western modes of knowing and making sense of the world, encounters in Khasak another order of reality, which cannot be grasped in terms of the categories he has internalised. The two worlds are mutually incommensurable. This is where we have the glimpse of a new aesthetic. The novelist does not view Khasak through the eyes of the alienated outsider, but portrays it as a legitimate world in its own right. The narrative allows the social landscape of the people of Khasak to come alive in their everyday world, with all their contradictions and conflicts. This is where the dialects used in the novel become a mode of critical evaluation. Its inflections evaluate the standardised idiom of modernity and deny it primacy. The individualistic and the subjective are brought into a critical relation with the collective and the social.

This is where a performative element becomes central to the 'aesthetic' vision of Khasak. By denying primacy to the individualistic as well as the collective, the novel stages the unfinished, the contingent and the ongoing. The fact that this novel has been rewritten several times, through the stage version I mentioned above, and also through many of the short stories written about the characters in the novel, suggests how the novel resists closure. By viewing/embodying the world in its act of becoming, Vijayan invests the act of representation with an ethical dimension. There is an aesthetic vision here which brings to mind the famous song by Kabir, who says that his body is like a blanket (*jheeni jheeni beeni chadariya*) woven with the five elements of the world and the three essences of life: 'That blanket covers both gods and wise men/ They wrap it around and the blanket gets dirty/Kabir has covered himself with care/He keeps his blanket as good as new' (Agrawal 46). Kabir, as a weaver, knew that every thread has to be carefully integrated into the larger pattern to create a blanket. In using this metaphor, there is the hint of an aesthetic that is rooted in everyday life, manual work, ethical living. Vijayan's attention to the dying dialects of a rural community recovered entire ways of life, multiple modes of knowing and articulated a worldview that does not celebrate the narcissistic and the alienated. In foregrounding the pluralistic and the polyphonic, he recovered a realm that is beyond the sacred and the profane, which points to art as self-criticism and aesthetics as ethics.

Works Cited

Agrawal, Purushottam. *Kabir, Kabir: The life and work of the early modern poet-philosopher.* Chennai: Westland Books, 2021.

Benjamin, Walter, "On the Concept of History". http://folk.uib.no/hlils/TBLR-B/Benjamin-History.pdf. Accessed 25 Aug. 2018.

Jaidev. *The Culture of Pastiche: Existential Aestheticism in the Contemporary Hindi Novel.* Shimla: Indian Institute of Advanced Study, 1993

Vijayan, O.V. *Khasakkinte Ithihasam,* Kottayam: D.C. Books, 2001.

——. Trans. *The Legends of Khasak.* New Delhi: Penguin Books, 1994.

Section Three

The Scattered Present of Aesthetics

9

The Critical Scene

Towards an Alternative Aesthetics?

K. Satchidanandan

I

Traditional Indian poetics is in a crisis today. Its categories are proving clearly insufficient to explain several of the modern genres, forms, and movements in Indian literature. This often-unacknowledged crisis had already begun with the maturing of Indian languages, which declared their independence from Sanskrit centuries ago, even while retaining many of its aspects that they found useful to their flowering and growth. These languages had their own literary traditions, mostly oral, that informed their new developments. Some of them, like Tamil, had different poetics altogether. Their canons were formed not only with examples from Sanskrit literature, (many of which were translated or adapted) but from Western, especially English, classics as well, which were either translated or followed as models.

The inadequacy of the existing paradigms became acute in the 19th century when, mostly under the Western influence, new prose genres like the novel, the short story, and even modern prose drama began to develop in Indian languages. Criticism for some time continued to fight shy of these genres and to confine itself to poetry and verse drama since it hardly had any tools to explain and interpret the new forms.

The crisis began to affect even traditional forms like poetry with the advent of new genres like the sonnet, the pastoral, the elegy, the new lyric or the sequence poem and new movements like modernism that replaced the simile and the metaphor with the symbol and the image and experimented with free verse and prose as the vehicles of poetic imagination. Imagination itself had grown unconventional with new modes such as symbolism, surrealism, anti-poetry, and the like. Then came the new movements like Dalit writing, women's writing, tribal writing, nativism, ecocentric writings, and modern folk writing, not to speak of the Indian variants of postmodernism, all of which sprang from new social awakenings and carried a new intellectual and verbal energy that could hardly be explained by traditional poetics. In addition, now there are concrete poetry, blog-poetry, hyperlink, and multimedia forms that are trying to go beyond the limits of language with the additional use of visual images, both still and moving, as well as sound.

Behind all these were the radical changes happening in Indian life itself—the complexification of life brought about by the changing environment; the new textures of urban living with its contradictory aspects of penury and luxury made possible by new technologies; the intensification of the alienation among the intelligentsia; the angst of the new awareness of space and time; the growing consumer instinct; the loss of traditional values and the growth of the new post-industrial ethos; the continued intervention of the modern state in every aspect of the lives of its subjects; the revolutionary awakenings of the marginalised and oppressed sections of the people against discrimination based on caste, class, race, religion, and gender; the threats of war, poverty and terrorism; the search for new identities; and the new structures of feeling generated by these transformed environments of existence. The canons were being constantly transformed, the institution of literature itself was under threat, the status-quo concepts were being challenged and the paradigms proved hopelessly inadequate to meet the needs of literary criticism. The history of Indian criticism in the past few decades has been the history of the varied responses to these challenges and the attempts to arrive at some critical canon that might help unlock and explain contemporary Indian texts.

II

One response, call it a form of enlightened revivalism, has been an attempt to extend, develop and reinterpret traditional poetics in order to apply its concepts to modern texts and genres, at times incorporating the concepts of Western poetics in the process. Indian poetics has often been identified with Sanskrit poetics though there is a whole parallel tradition in Tamil and Urdu, derived from the Persian tradition, not to speak of individual texts, like *Kavirajāmārga* in Kannada, available in the languages and the poetics implied in our oral literary practices. Critics like (the late) Krishna Rayan read Sanskrit poetics in the light of the new theories from the West and came up with extended and flexible interpretations of the central concepts of Sanskrit poetics like *dhvani* (suggestion), *rasa* (basic emotion), *vakrokti* (indirect speech) and *anumāna* (theory of reception) along with their peripheral concepts.

In his book *Text and Sub-text* (1987), Krishna Rayan looked at the theory of suggestion and tried to establish that suggestion—the production of unstated, subsurface, indirect, multiple, emotive meaning—was what distinguished modern literature from the literature of earlier periods. Rayan examined texts like Alfred Tennyson's *Becket* alongside T.S. Eliot's *Murder in the Cathedral*, Christopher Fry's *Curtmantle*, and Jean Anouilh's *Becket ou L'Honneur de Dieu*. Four of Thomas Hardy's novels exploring the notion of a return to the roots were analysed in relation to novels by Margaret Drabble that pursue a similar theme. The book also looks at the practice of suggestion and evocation in Milton's *Paradise Lost* and the poetry of W.B. Yeats and the minimalist, micro-suggestive, poetic practice of the *Review* poets. The critic quoted critical passages from Western theorists to relate the theory of suggestion to symbolist practice as well as to the Sanskrit concept of *rasa-dhvani*. He also considered the binary oppositions like emotive/referential meaning (I.A. Richards), oblique/direct (E.M.W. Tillyard), local texture/logical structure (J.C. Ransom), and intensive/extensive meaning (Allen Tate) to be the renamings of the suggestion/statement distinction found in Eastern as well as Western poetics.

In *Burning Bush: Suggestion in Indian Literature* (1988), Krishna Rayan extended the *rasa-dhvani* concept to modern subcontinental texts in various languages by authors like Nirmal Verma, Kiran Nagarkar, Lokenath Bhattacharya, Rajinder Singh Bedi (fiction); P. Lankesh, Kumaran Asan, Jayanta Mahapatra, Nissim Ezekiel, Dina Nath Nadim and Soubhagya Kumar Mishra (poetry); and others besides some older texts from classical Tamil and Sindhi in order to demonstrate the applicability of the theory to different languages, genres and periods.

In *Sahitya: A Theory for Indian Critical Practice*, Rayan produced an eclectic theory for Indian critical practice by bringing together Sanskrit, Tamil, and Western concepts with plenty of examples and quotations.

Nāṭyaṣāstra and *Tolkkāppiyam* were referred to as two basic texts. Here, he also established parallels between the *rasas* of *Nāṭyaṣāstra* and the *meypadus* of *Tolkkāppiyam*. The critic looked at the diverse aspects of literature like literariness, image, narrative, character, style, rhythm, landscape, and evaluation. In the chapter on the landscape, he introduced the *tiṇai* concept of *Tolkkāppiyam*. The landscape here was the signifier, and the bond that held it to the signified was arbitrary and fixed by conventions that were sustained for several generations during the Sangam period. Ayyappa Paniker tried to apply the *tiṇai* theory to Thakazhi Sivasankara Pillai's novel *Kayar*, while V.J. Sebastian did it to a series of contemporary poems. S. Carlos (Tamilavan) also tried to extend and apply the theory to modern texts in Tamil.

While these are interesting experiments, the method can work fully only in a stable static culture with a lot of received assumptions and capable of a large number of shared responses. The theory of *rasas* is also too limited and rigid to make it critically effective when applied to modern texts where the boundaries of emotions are blurred, the moods are in flux and the responses more complex. Behind these theories are a whole static world view and a fixed view of literature and literariness. They also tend to look at literature, especially poetry, as a craft detached from its time and society. Both classical Sanskrit and Tamil poetics, therefore, fail to historicise their texts. So, they need to be historicised to be understood. Concepts like *dhvani* and *aucitya* (propriety) and the linguistic injunctions against *aślīla* (obscene), *grāmya* (rustic) and *chyutasamskāra* (uncouth) can hardly be isolated from the class that generated them and hence do not apply to several subaltern forms and movements, both ancient and modern.

The traditional concepts of *pratibha* or genius, *sahṛdaya* or the competent reader, the *sahitatva* or the fixed togetherness of the word and the meaning—compared to the bond of Pārvatī and Parameśvara, meaning as something deposited in the work by the author and the authorial institution itself emerge from an idealist philosophical premise. The concept of the reader as the producer of meaning, of the text as a flux, and the absence of the eternal "deferance"— deferring—of a "final meaning", literariness itself as the effect of reading, and the historical and ideological determinations of the text are alien to this aesthetic ideology.

While the concepts of *dhvani* and *anumāna* do take the reader into account, it is an abstract reader outside real history. It is seldom bothered with the question of the historical construction of subjectivity and hence fails to answer several questions about writing, reading, and authorship. This also applies to Persian poetics, which deals exclusively with forms available in classical Persian or Arabic from which Urdu has adopted them like *masnavi, nazm, ghazal, rubai, qavvali, manaqib, nama, qasida, qit'a* (or *muqatta'at*), their prosody, rhyme patterns, rules of composition, style, and evocation of moods and feelings. The tradition is still alive in the criticism of traditional poetry, but while discussing new poetry and fiction, critics often depend on modern Western theories as can be seen in the practices of Shamsur Rahman Faruqi, Shamim Hanfi, and Gopichand Narang.

III

Quite a few critics, in English as well as in other languages, have been employing Western theoretical tools to analyse Indian texts, both old and new. The influence of Western criticism was evident from the very beginning of modern criticism in India, which emerged along with the new genres like the short story, the novel, and the modern prose-play. Only the credos and fashions have changed with changes in Western theory. If initially, it was only English criticism that influenced Indian critics, later Russian, French, and German schools also began to have their impact. This began chiefly with the emergence of Marxist and Freudian analytical models. The early Marxist models were often reductive as the critics were not yet familiar with the works of Antonio Gramsci, the Frankfurt School—like those of Adorno, Habermas or Horkheimer, or even of Michael Bakhtin, Ernst Fischer, Ernst Bloch, Walter Benjamin, and Raymond Williams—and the later theorists—like Louis Althusser, Pierre Macherey, Fredric Jameson, Roland Barthes—not to speak of the post-structuralists like Slavoj Zizek, Giorgio Agamben or Jacques Ranciere who were yet to emerge.

In that circumstance, the models were chiefly from the Soviet Union and eastern Europe: Zhadanov, Lunacharsky, Plekhanov, Lukacs, and others. No wonder the critics equated modernism with decadence, upheld socialist realism as the sacred model for committed writers to follow. It is also significant to note that they often pursued a narrow class-reductionist approach. One of the reasons for the fall of the Progressive Literary Movement was this exclusionist approach. They did not try to read literary works using modern tools to grasp their progressive implications or to interpret commitment in a larger context where it could also involve social concerns of various kinds other than purely class concerns. The Progressives would not have committed this mistake if they had carefully read even Marx or Lenin. Marx was a great admirer of the Greeks and Shakespeare and in many of his analyses exposed the contradictions in the self-proclaimed committed writing (for example, in his detailed critique of Eugene Sue's *The Mysteries of Paris* in *The Holy Family*, he brings out the contrast between the authorial claims to radicalism and the reactionary implications of the text itself), while upholding certain other forms of writing that did not make any claim to commitment. Macherey looked closely at Lenin's symptomatic reading and appreciation of Tolstoy as the "mirror of the Russian revolution" as against Plekahanov's accusation that Tolstoy was a reactionary as he was a Catholic and an aristocrat by birth. Here, Lenin goes beyond the empirical biographical facts to the truth of the text itself, which transcends the author's class origins and proclaimed opinions.

A similar hermeneutic conflict can also be seen in the well-known argument over Kafka between Lukacs on one side and Benjamin and Bloch on the other. To Lukacs, Kafka represented decadence and morbidity, but Benjamin and Bloch read Kafka politically and saw in his works a sharp critique of bureaucracy, an expression of the solitude of the individual cut off from the community and the premonitions of the Nazi nightmare. The exclusivist approach of the early Progressives blurred the distinction between party literature and literature *itself*.

While their method could partly explain "Progressive" literary works as they understood them, it was incapable of understanding more complex works of literature that contained many voices and grappled with multiple contradictions. The result was that some of the better writers of the period, whose multiple articulations did great justice to the society of the times, were kept out of the Marxist canon. In Kerala, for example, fiction writers like D.M. Pottekkat and poets like Kedamangalam Pappukutty were hailed as revolutionaries, while fiction writers like Basheer, Uroob and poets like Edassery and Vailoppilli who captured the deeper contradictions of their society remained outside the canon.

Only recently have some unorthodox Marxist and Marxisant critics begun to develop a more open approach to literature, taking into account the postcolonial and post-structuralist insights into the working of language, the unconscious, and society. Early Freudian criticism too suffered from reductionist attitudes that analysed the characters as though they were living beings and attributed their motifs to their author. It was only after Lacan, Deleuze and Guattari, that Freud was understood in all his complexity, as also his concept of the unconscious, which is structured like a language.

Sydney and Arnold had held sway for some time in liberal Indian criticism; later they were replaced by Eliot and I.A. Richards. This happened especially during the emergence of modern poetry, which came to be associated with Eliot's modes and mores. Eliot did have an influence on early modernist poets like Mardhekar, Muktibodh, Bishnu Dey, Navkant Barua, Gopal Krishna Adiga, Kaa. Naa. Subramanyam, Ayyappa Paniker and others. But they chiefly imbibed Eliot's iconoclasm in terms of form, while their poetry was by no means a "pastiche". It was sufficiently indigenous and their formal innovations sprang from the inner need of their literary histories. They were no more "Elioteans" than the new novelists like Nirmal Verma, Krishna Baldev Vaid, and U.R. Ananthamurthy were "Joyceans".

The new critical tools were patently inadequate to understand the new writing in Indian languages as they also had their deeper social roots in the urbanisation of the country, the alienation of the intellectuals, and the disillusionment with the system and the values it stood for. Semantics and semiotics would have helped one grasp the verbal plays and the deployment of symbols and metaphors in the new writing, but not their socio-spiritual environment. Existentialist and phenomenological tendencies dominated the critical scene in the 1960s when literature was conceived as the apotheosis of solitude and the articulation of metaphysical angst and alienation. Northrop Frye's archetypal patterns were at times contextualised and put to effective use, especially in the study of poetry.

Another interesting development was the developing dialogue between Marxist and post-structuralist approaches to writing. Roland Barthes' political semiology and his concept of the death of the author and the distinctions he drew between the "work" and the "text", Jacques Lacan's theory of the unconscious as the "discourse of the other" and the mode of symptomatic reading that derives from it as illustrated by Althusser and Macherey, Jacques Derrida's strategies of deconstruction meant to subvert the hegemonic discourses and institutions by reading them from the margins and bowing them up by developing their contradiction, and Michel Foucault's theories of the power-knowledge nexus and the construction of subjectivity combined with Bakhtin's concept of ideology "inscribed" in the linguistic sign, of dialogic imagination and the "carnivalesque", Gramsci's concept of the "popular", Ranciere's concept of "the political"—all these can liberate Marxist criticism from the sociological reductionism and the mechanical application of class theory that had characterised its earlier phases.

In fact, this is happening in a big way in languages like Malayalam and Bengali, where, as Octavio Paz said of Latin America, Marxist concepts and terms have become natural components of social and literary discourse. This is chiefly being pursued by young academics seeking an escape from the empiricist-positivist or idealist-iconic models offered by conventional English criticism, thus de-Anglicising and indirectly decolonising the critical discourse.

Re-readings of canonical texts, side by side with the discovery of buried and forgotten texts, have certainly unleashed a lot of radical energy in the realm of criticism. Critics like B. Rajeevan, V.C. Sreejan, S.S. Sreekumar, E.V. Ramakrishnan, P. Udayakumar, V. Sanil, S. Saradakutty, J. Devika, Dileep Menon, M.T. Ansari, and others have been consistently rereading texts from various, mostly subaltern, points of view. They have been trying to expose the ideological determinations that underlie representations, especially of Dalits, Muslims, Adivasis and women in the texts they choose to re-read. The new reading of Sreenarayana Guru and C.V. Raman Pillai by Udayakumar, the reading of Pothery Kunhambu's *Saraswativijayam*, a Dalit novel, by Dileep Menon, the readings of some texts of Kumaran Asan by S. Saradakutty and V. Sanil illustrate this trend. P. Udayakumar, for example, has looked at the evolution of the concept of the body in Sreenarayana Guru, as he moves from works like *Mananateetam*, *Siva Satakam*, and *Indriya Vairagyam* to *Atmopadesa Satakam*, *Advaita Jeevitam*, and *Suddhipanchakam*. Sreenarayana denies ontological status to the body, but gives it epistemological status and discovers a subtle body (*Sookshmasareeram*) within the gross body (*sthoolasareera*). The body can attain purity once it is liberated from the gross body. Then it will be capable of spiritual bliss. This is the moment where community enters Sreenarayana's system, for the reforms within the communities—in education, economy, health, etc. –enable society to attain this bliss, as the material and spiritual arrangements need to be co-coordinated like the organs of the body to lead to enlightenment, to recall his statement in *Advaitajeevitam*. Here he reminds us of Tirumular, the Tamil Saivite Saint, as well as Basava, the Kannada Saivite reformer, both of whom accepted the interdependence of the body and the soul. It is the body that bears the organic marks of distinction in man; the caste marks and caste titles are an aberration that hides these organic markers. So there are only two castes among the humans—men and women. Sreenarayana thus views caste as a false distinction, religion as nothing more than a matter of opinion, and the community as the locus of concrete action. In 1916, Narayana declared that he does not belong to any caste or religion. The human community, he said, will be born only when false distinctions and hierarchies disappear. This was the basic principle of the Renaissance that was soon to transform the society in Kerala.

Dileep Menon's reading of *Saraswativijayam*, a novel by Potheri Kunhambu, published in 1892, looks at Kunhambu's project closely to discover that initially he too had thought of reforming the Hindu Society, but later abandoned it as impossible. The author, an *ezhava*, who was often called Pulayan Kunhambu for his concern for the Pulaya community, found that tradition is impervious to modernity. The novel is an example of the spatial delineation of the issues of power, hierarchy, and inequality, as the characters travers different territories of freedom and knowledge. Travel becomes a metaphor of individual redemption here, as the cruel landlord Kuberan Namboodiri travels to Kasi; Marathan, the Pulaya protagonist travels to Madras and Subhadra, the Namboodiri's daughter, falsely accused of extramarital relations and banished from her caste, travels to Kannoor to escape from the enclosed space of historical memory. Kuberan has a change of heart, Marathan converts to Christianity, studies law, and becomes a judge. Subhadra too converts and becomes a teacher and gets reunited with her husband who also converts to Christianity. Christianity is the mediator of modernity in the text. Kunhambu did share the creative tension between the possibility of an internal critic of Hinduism and the pragmatic and robust alternative of empowerment through colonial education, though finally, he found that liberation is unattainable in the Hindu fold, a fact that Ambedkar too was to discover later, though his choice was not Christianity, but Buddhism. *Saraswativijayam* is not a revenge novel, nor a conversion tract; conversion here is a metaphor for the new possibilities opened by colonialism and modernity. It may be noted that while elite thinkers like Ramakrishna, Vivekananda, and Dayanand Saraswati championed an internal critique of Hinduism and found habitation within reformed religion, most of the subaltern thinkers found a solution to caste inequality only in conversion. Sreenarayana was an exception, as, through a philosophical inversion, he could free himself from all religions.

Romila Thapar has reread Kālidasa's *Abhijñānaśākuntalam* from a historical point of view to reveal the Orientalist determinations behind its reception. She has shown how Kālidasa's Śakuntala is delicate, shy, meek, faithful and unquestioning in her obedience, returning with tears from Duṣyanta' s court when he disowns her, as different from the Śakuntala of *Ādiparva* in the *Mahābhārata.* where she is strong and independent, and boldly interrogates Duṣyanta' s sense of justice and decorum. She puts certain conditions even before she enters into a *gāndharva* relationship with the king. Kālidasa's description fits in very much with the romantic concept of the innocent forest virgin embarrassed by the awakening of desire. In fact, there is a whole romantic opposition at work here between the simple, picturesque ashram in the woods that represents rusticity and innocence and the splendid palace of the king that stands for the urban with its accent on power and cunning. Kālidasa's Śakuntala was the kind of ideal heroine that the romantics were looking for. Goethe describes her as 'a rustic girl', a 'child of nature' with elegant limbs and graceful undulating gait. Popularized in the West through Monier Williams' English translation, from which the German translation was done by

Georg Forster in 1791, *Abhijñānaśākuntalam* fitted very well with the Orientalist project of romanticizing the East, reflected equally well in colonial photography and the Company paintings. The Germans also exulted in the racial bonds between the ancient Indians and Europeans, whom they considered 'Aryans', whatever that term stands for. For French Indologists, like Sylvane Levy, and Russian Indologists like Oldenberg, Śakuntala was part of their fantasy about India. She was the ideal Hindoo woman also for the Indian middle-class Nationalists, who like the Orientalists bemoaned the 'fall' of the ideal Indian womanhood.

Rabindranath Tagore also upheld Śakuntala, combining in his approach the British Orientalist attitudes of the 19th century, the nascent nationalist sentiment, and Victorian moralism. Romila Thapar upholds Shantaram's portrayal of Śakuntala in his film *Stree* as being faithful to her portrayal in the *Mahabhārata,* as also the contemporary interpretation one comes across in Nachiket Patwardhan 's *Anantyatra,* which brings Śakuntala to modern Bombay where Duśyanta is a business executive. The film hints that any appreciation of the naive and frail Śakuntala today can only be an escape from today's oppressive patriarchal urban reality.

Post-colonial readings, especially informed by Edward Said's theoretical insights have helped unearth the colonial prejudices behind a lot of work on India—not literature alone, but also photographs and paintings. These interrogations, while at times reductive or eclectic, have helped make writers and readers conscious of the dangers of (mis) representation.

At the same time, post-colonial theory makes certain assumptions that need to be re-examined. Arun P. Mukherjee has summed them up like this[1]: (a) The theory claims that the major theme of works of literature from post-colonial societies is discursive resistance to the now absent coloniser. (b) It unproblematically assumes that the writers who write back to the center are representing the people of their society authentically. (c) The theory downplays the difference between the settler-colonial and those colonized in their home territories using the term 'colonized' for both of them. It trivializes the experience of those who suffered genocide and pauperization under colonial rule, not to mention cultural deprivation. (d) In its use of terminology like 'the oppressed', 'the colonized peoples' and 'the indigenous' to describe post-colonial societies, the theory suppresses internal hierarchies and divisions in these societies. It does a great disservice to the minorities in these societies by deflecting attention away from their oppression by using a unitary vocabulary that confers a 'subaltern' status on the entire post-colonial world, disregarding the fact that it is ridden with hierarchies. This last erasure is particularly dangerous as it glosses over the distinctions of class, caste, race, and religion in these societies. I also feel that the post-colonialists often assume that history begins with colonialism, which is exactly what the colonialists want us to believe. The paradigm has also been used by the rightwing to promote their agenda of a revival of pre-colonial practices and justify hierarchies like the *varna* system and even superstitious practices like astrology, *sati* (eg. Ashis Nandy), and nude worship (e.g. U.R. Ananthamurthy).

Another strange fact about its application is that only Indian writing in English is considered to be postcolonial by the academics. It may be true about some works like those of Mulk Raj Anand *(Untouchable, Coolie)*, Khushwant Singh (*Train to Pakistan*), Salman Rushdie (*Midnight's Children, Shame*) or Kiran Nagarkar *(The Little Soldier)*, while post-colonial reality is expressed with greater authenticity in language texts like *Kayar* (Thakazhi Shivasankara Pillai), *Dharmapuranam* (O.V. Vijayan), *Abhayarthikal, Marubhoomikal Undakunnathu* (Anand), *Bharathipura* (Ananthamurthy), *Kusumabale* (Devanoor Mahadeva). *Malapally* (U. Lakshmi Narayana), *Karukku* and *Sangati* (Bama), *Kosla* (Bhalchandra Nemade), *Uchalya* (Laxman Gaikwad), *Upara* (Laxman Mane), *Akkarmashee* (Sharan Kumar Limbale), *Angaliyat* (Joseph Macwan), *Aranyer Adhikar, Agnigarbha* (Mahasweta Devi), *Parasa* (Gurdial Singh), *Maila Anchal* (Phaneeswar Nath Renu), *Tamas, Madhavi* (Bhisham Sahni), *Zindaginama* (Krishna Sobti), *Kitne Pakistan* (Kamaleswar), *lyaru Ingam* (Birendrakumar Bhattacharya) and *Aag ka Dariya* (Qurratulain Hyder), just to take a few random samples from the novel alone. The post-colonialists also do not see the distinct ways in which the elite and the downtrodden reacted to colonialism—like Ambedkar and Sreenarayana Guru welcoming the reformative and egalitarian aspects of the colonial rule. They also fail to see the neocolonial forces seeking hegemony in the post-colonial India, now masquerading as globalization.

Said's formulations in *Orientalism* have also been challenged by a host of theoreticians. Aijaz Ahmad[2] has shown how Said is silent about the modes by which the colonial subjects received, challenged, changed, or rejected the Western conceptualizations about them. Patrick Williams and Laura Chrisman[3] have also pointed to Said's neglect of the colonial subject's power of resistance. Sara Mills[4] is rightly critical of Said's neglect of gender: did the Western woman share the Western man's fantasies about the Oriental woman, as the passive subject of desire? There are other objections too: historians feel that colonial discourse analysis tends to make large generalizations based on a limited number of largely literary texts. It also dehistoricizes and treats all texts as synchronic, as if they existed in an ahistorical, unchanging textual continuum. The textualism and idealism of colonial discourse analysis occur at the expense of materialist historical inquiry and politicized understanding.

IV

Feminist critics have also responded to the crisis by using gender as the organizing principle of writing as well as reading. Feminist scholarship has retrieved a lot of forgotten or suppressed writing in the Indian languages done by women in the past, the most famous example being *Radhikasantwanam,* Muddupalani's Telugu text of the 18th century, proscribed by the British Raj and willed into oblivion by indigenous patriarchy, including the nationalists as a frank, and hence threatening, expression of female desire. The patriarchal canons are being interrogated, myths re-visioned, texts decoded and literary history revised. Susie Tharu and K. Lalita have traced in their introduction to the anthology *Women Writing in India, Sixth Century B.C. to the Present,* the evolution of women's writing in India across centuries. Uma Chakravarty, Vijaya Dabbe, Sonal Shukla, Madhu Kishwar, Leela Mullati, Parita Mukta, Vijaya Ramaswamy and others have explored the poetry of women saints like Lal Ded, Akka Mahadevi, Satyakka, Kadire Rammavve, Aydakki Lakkamma, Muktayakka, Andal, Karaikkal Ammaiyar, Meerabai, Gangasati, Janabai and Bahinabai to show how Bhakti was to them a tool to escape gender distinction, patriarchal oppression, and domestic confinement, just as it was to the Buddhist nuns like Mutta, Ubbiri or Sumangala Mata of the sixth-century. God becomes a way of dissolving an otherwise impossible situation in these saints. Their worldly marriages, actual as well as potential, represent both the lure and the bondage of the world, while their relationship to God represents a renunciation of the world and the woman's traditional roles in it. Tharu finds the lyrics of *Terigatha* to be epiphanic experiences in which the painful constructions of secular life fall away and the torment of feelings subsides, as the peace and freedom of *nirvana* are attained. While they exult in their new life transformed by Bhakti, they also contrast it to the painful worlds they have left behind. These poets created an alternative family, resisted the oppressive social role imposed upon them by the male-dominated society, and simultaneously created a parallel language of experience and emotion.

A lot of scholars and academics like Nabaneeta Dev Sen, Malashree Lal, Vrinda Nabbar, Brinda Bose, Ruth Vanita, Gayatri Chakravarty Spivak, J. Devika, Anita Devasia, A.K. Jayasree, and S.Saradakkutty have also done considerable research in women's discourses and the representation of women in literary texts by men. The complexity of gender construction in India is a challenge to the students of gender as it is overdetermined by other formations like class, caste, religion, regional cultures and languages, specific traditions, taboos, laws of marriage, sexual kinship and inheritance, and the contradictions between the country and the city and the feudal moral codes and the new roles popularized by the indigenous and the Western media.

Feminist inquiry in literary historiography means discovering the past from the women's angle, questioning the existing modes of periodization, examining past texts for feminine inscriptions, unburying the marginalized, relating literature to the differential articulation of the various levels of the superstructure, and defining and explaining the breaks and continuities in the history of women's writing in the country. In literary theory, it means challenging the patriarchal canon, deconstructing the phallocentric creative and critical discourse, defining the feminine literary texts in the Indian context, unearthing the ideological determinations that lay behind the reception and rejection of literary texts in the different periods, relating their formal constituents to the specific environment and regional traditions, thus developing an indigenous semiotics that connects signs to their specific space and lineage, decoding gender as an organizing principle of experience and relating forms of feminine articulation to the changing social, racial and conceptual permutations in our history—for example, the employment of dialects and images of domesticity in the quest for deliverance in the Bhakti period, the tactical redeployment of hegemonic discourses to constitute a new enlightened middle class female subject in the colonial-reformist period, the creation of new enunciative modalities and rhetorical strategies to articulate the gender-class nexus in the Progressivist writing and the caste-gender nexus in Dalit writing, or the use of body-imagery, emphasis on female bonding and open defiance of the set norms and structures of writing in more recent, openly feminist,. writing. While the Western feminist critical theories—right from Virginia Woolf, Simone de Beauvoir, Elaine Showalter, Kate Millet, and Sandra Gilbert and Susan Gubar to Helene Cixous, Annette Kolodny, Ellen Moers, Mary Ellman, Gayle Greene, Coppelia Kahn, Jane Flax, Julia Kristeva, and Barbara Smith—will certainly be of use, and have been used, in Indian feminist criticism, we should also come across some areas of resistance to Western theories in Indian literary practice. While the Bhakti poets provide a fine example of such resistance, contemporary texts, say of Ismat Chughtai, Kamala Das, Sara Joseph, Bama, Amrita Pritam, Mahasweta Devi, Krishna Sobti, Alka Saraogi, Arundhati Roy, etc., (again to take some fiction writers) also have a lot that is specifically Indian or regional about them that call for different critical strategies.

Eco-criticism is another response to the existing theories that focuses entirely on the text without looking at its organic relationship with nature and the larger universe. Even though it was William Rueckert (*Literature and Ecology: An Experiment in Eco-Criticism,* 1978) who introduced the term, it was Joseph Meeker's *The Comedy of Survival: Studies in Literary Ecology* (1974) that first defined the subject. According to Meeker, literary ecology was concerned with the biological themes appearing in literature. Its aim was also to discover the role of literature in human ecology. Literary works, he said, often reveal man's beliefs about the truth of natural processes and the cultural ideologies that have brought the human race to the modem environmental crisis. Cheryll Glotfelty who edited the first eco-criticism reader (1996) describes eco-criticism as an attempt to unravel the exchanges between nature and culture. It has one leg in literature and the other on earth: as theoretical discourse, it connects equally with human beings and non-human ones. The writers' world is not only the social world but the ecosphere itself. Earth, she says, is at the center of eco-criticism, just as gender is at the center of feminist criticism and class at that of Marxist criticism. Eco-Criticism, according to Lawrence Buel, brings space into the critical agenda that has so far been confined to theme, plot, and characters. He sees it as an umbrella term that embraces various modes and approaches. It has also been called 'ego-criticism' (Sven Birkerts, *Only God can Make a Tree: Theology: The Joys and Sorrows of Eco-Criticism*) as it tries to discover what literature has to say about man's egocentrism, greed, and craze for wealth and power. Some eco-critics also draw strength from Engels' *Dialectics of Nature,* Raymond Williams' insights into the city-country contradictions, and the works of Adorno, Walter Benjamin, and other new Marxist thinkers. The anthology *Haritaniroopanam Malayalathil* (*Green Criticism in Malayalam*) edited by G. Madhusoodanan carries different samples of what can be broadly called eco-criticism in Malayalam along with 16 theoretical pieces that began to grow with the environmental awareness generated by the struggle against the proposed dam in the rainforests of the Silent Valley. The book carries applications of the concepts of eco-Marxism, eco-Feminism, eco-Ethics, and eco-Spirituality in literary criticism.

The emergence of strong Dalit writing in Marathi, Gujarati, Hindi, Punjabi, Telugu, and Tamil has given rise to a Dalit poetics that, though not fully defined, finds its expression in the works of D.R. Nagaraj, Daya Pawar, Arjun Dangle, Saran Kumar Limbale, Chandrakant Patil, Mulk Raj Anand, M.S.S. Pandyan, Cho. Dharman, G.Lakshmi, Narasiah, Malay Dewanji, Arun. P.Mukherjee, S.P. Punalekar, A. Satyanarayana, Jyotsna Macwan, Kalpana Rentala, Eleanor Zelliot, K.K. Kochu, K.K. Baburaj and others. It was perhaps Sharad Patil's book in Marathi, *Abrahmani Sahityache Saundaryasastra* that first launched an attack on Brahmin aesthetics and spoke of the need for a counter-poetics. Sharan Kumar Limbale in his book, *Towards an Aesthetics of Dalit Literature* has attempted a critique of status-quoist Marathi aesthetics as well as a negative criticism of Dalit literature by the *savarna* critics. He points out that Dalit literature is not meant to entertain the readers, but to provoke them into rethinking their society and its ethics and aesthetics.

It is impossible to investigate the Dalit writing with its rebellion, rejection and commitment, using the established critical tools meant for the literature of acquiescence and consent. He does not agree with critics like Yadunath Thatte who want to enlarge the *rasa* theory to include revolt and cry as the tenth and eleventh *rasa*. What is needed is a new aesthetics that takes into account the differentness of Dalit writing in content as well as form. Aestheticist criticism cannot digest the non-traditional stance of Dalit literature.

For that, freedom will have to be recognized as an aesthetic value. The intensity of experience, the way the experience is socialized, its power to cross the boundaries of time and space—are the standards Limbale proposes for the evaluation of Dalit literature. D.R. Nagaraj in his book, *The Flaming Feet: A Study of the Dalit Movement in India,* has gone deeper into the specifics of the Dalit sensibility and Dalit imagination and the problem of cultural memory in the context of the cosmologies of caste and the realism in Kannada fiction. He traces the cultural memory of the Dalits to the subaltern, radical, traditions, folk cosmologies, rural myths, and oral narratives which are getting lost in the oppressive process of Sanskritization pursued by the Hindu revivalists. He looks at the cults of Madeswara and Manteswamy in Southern Karnataka as examples. He points out how the cultural paradigm of the nationalists had no place for the Dalit cultural traditions and practices. The monolithic cultural model erected based on Vedanta by the Hindu Right also precludes all the philosophic and cultural expressions of the Dalits. Nagaraj makes a very insightful comparison between U.R. Ananthamurthy's *Samskara* and Devanoor Mahadeva's *Kusumabale* showing how caste has been an important factor in determining their modes of representation and imagination. *Samskara* gives the readers an insight into the self-image of the Brahmin by allowing them to see the world through the eyes of Pranesacharya, whose attempts to break the system miserably fail, as, against that of Naranappa, his alter ego, who completely breaks free of tradition and its taboos. This is also the failure of the novel as it cannot establish the sexual contact between the Brahmin and the non-Brahmin as a possible way to break free of the oppressive caste society. Reality frustrates the novel's radical ambitions. But *Kusumabale* rejects the notion of verifiable reality at the very outset and follows a folk narrative form.

While *Samskara* ignores the socio-economic power structures, thus turning its concern more metaphysical, *Kusumabale* counterposes the personal and the political realms of the caste structure and finds that sexual contact like the one in *Samskara* can only lead to violence within the existing power structure. Devanoor Mahadeva revives the Dalit mode of imagination as when a cot tells a story and a lamp turns into a woman who comments on the events of the day. The narrative is open and works at multiple levels while *Samskara* is highly centered and has an ending that closes the narrative.

Dalit literature has created a new poetics by redrawing the map of literature, discovering and exploring a whole new continent of experience that had so far been left to darkness and silence, by helping literature overcome stagnation through a cleansing renewal, by disturbing the sterile complacency of the dominant social groups, by challenging their set modes of looking at reality and their stale habits of ordering knowledge, beauty and power and their established literary canons, bringing to focus marginalized or suppressed aspects of experience, vision, language and reality and forcing the community to refashion its tools and observe itself critically from a fresh and different angle. Dalit writing has thrown overboard classical virtues like propriety, balance, restraint, and understatement, using a deliberately subversive diction that celebrates Dalit values and challenges the middle-class notions of linguistic decency. It has renewed literary language by bringing in fresh words, usages, and modes of imagination kept out by the so-called mainstream literature. The new tribal literature emerging in languages like Santali, Bodo, Bhili, Tenyidie, Angami, Ao, Gondi, Mundari, and others, also share many of these characteristics while celebrating the tribal vision of the world and nature, demanding an alternative poetics.

There are also independent attempts like Bhalchandra Nemade's *Teeka Swayamvar* that uses a methodology drawn from Marathi literary history itself to describe the evolution of the Marathi novel, Namwar Singh's *Doosari Parampara* that speaks of the second tradition in Indian thought and literature, E.V. Ramakrishnan's *Making It New,* a comparative study of modern poetry in Hindi, Marathi, Malayalam and Gujarati, Sisir Kumar Das's *History of Indian Literature* that tries to develop a history of Indian literature without ignoring the regional and linguistic differences and Ayyappa Paniker's *Indian Narratology* that seeks to found a theory of Indian narrative practices.

I am in the process of exploring an alternative democratic poetics that I have temporarily called *sramanic* as against the dominant brahmanic poetics, which alone can explain the second tradition in Indian literature that includes the tribal, oral, and folk literature, the literature of Bhakti and Sufi movements, Buddhist and Jain literary practices, anti-colonial literature, and contemporary subaltern writing done by women, tribals, Dalits, socialist radicals and other dissenters to the system. Let me conclude with a statement made by Terry Eagleton in his *Significance of Theory* that seems relevant to our discussion:

> Theory on a dramatic level happens when it is both possible and necessary for it to do so when the traditional rationales, which have silently underpinned our daily practices stand in danger of being discredited, and need either to be revised or discarded. This may come about for reasons internal to those practices, because of a certain external pressure, or, more typically, because of a combination of both. Theory is just a practice forced into a new form of self-reflectiveness is an account of certain grievous problems it has encountered.[5]

Notes

1. Mukherjee, Arun P. "Postcolonialism: Some Uneasy conjunctures." *Interrogating Post-Colonialism: Theory, Text and Context.* Eds.Trivedi, Harish and Mukherjee, Meenakshi. IIAS Shimla, 1996, 13–22.
2. Ahmad, Aijaz. *In Theory, Classes, Nations, Literature.* Oxford University Press, 1992.
3. Chrisman, Laura. "The Imperial Unconscious? Representations of Imperial Discourse." *Colonial/Discourse and Post-colonial Theory: A Reader.* Eds. Williams, Patrick and Chrisman, Laura. Columbia University Press, 1994, 498–516.
4. Mills, Sara. *Discourses of Difference: An Analysis of Women's Travel Writing and Colonialism.* Routledge, 1991.
5. Eagleton. Terry. *Significance of Theory.* John Wiley and Sons Ltd, 1993.

10

Labour, Service, Performance

Towards a Global Shudrafication of Aesthetics and Politics

Soumyabrata Choudhury

An Introduction to the Labour-Service Conundrum in Marx

In his 1857 notebooks (published as *Grundrisse* or groundwork) towards the several volumes of the *Capital,* Karl Marx presents the following conundrum. While the time the piano maker spends in labouring to construct a piano is justified only by the fact that the piano player will one day play the same, the piano maker's labour can be *valued* as productive and the piano player's 'art' or 'performance' must only be consigned to the category of an unproductive *service.* This could also be termed an ontological conundrum because the being-performed of the piano while obviously its fundamental reason of existence is, nevertheless, powerless in the sphere of economic valourisation to dignify the art of the pianist with measurable value. We will not explain the economic reasoning within the logic of capital that produces this conundrum and which Marx himself wrestles with in different places in the *Grundrisse* and elsewhere. In fact, towards the later part of his notebooks, Marx can be heard adopting a brutal tone towards 'services' when he dismisses all providers of service, from the Pope to the prostitute, as having very little significance for the real object of the analysis of modern economic value as produced, exchanged and circulated by capitalist logic (*Grundisse* 272). The question that, however, remains is with regard to what might lead someone like Marx, who pioneers this analysis in the history of thought, to become so impatient with the inescapable persistence of 'services' in an otherwise self-contained and consistent regime of labour, production of values and the capitalisation and circulation of these values.

A possible reason for Marx's apparent scientific impatience even in the face of his ontological recognition of the perpetual pre-existence of service to the regime of values, is that the real interest motivating the Marxian project is political. Only upon the quantitative valorisation of productive labour and its qualitative manifestation in subjective alienation within the conditions of capitalism that the worker experiences—which involves the extraction of the surplus value from the process of this valorisation—can the collective project of a working class politics commence. In other words, the articulation between an objective exploitation and subjective alienation can produce the necessary conditions for a certain 'class consciousness'. Ontologically though, primary (or to borrow the well-known adjective from Marx's coinage primitive accumulation, 'primitive') service eludes the subsequent forms of political consciousness that the imperative of Marxist strategy towards organised politics requires. So, it seems that while the provider of 'services', whether a doctor or a pianist, lives in the same alienated society that the productive wage worker does, she cannot somehow be sufficiently grasped in an objective form. In that sense, the provider of services remains alien to the very logic of alienation that Marx makes so powerfully intelligible in his analysis of labour and capital. The labour-service conundrum could then also be paraphrased as the alienated-alien conundrum of human subjectivity in capitalist society.

We will not further explore the political ground of the hierarchy that Marx responds to with his paradoxical attitude of both ontologically recognising and methodologically deprioritising service. We will have occasion to come back to this. Let it be noted here that there is an obvious historical reason for the ambiguity in Marx's attitude since the pioneering critical thinker of capitalism is responding to the increasingly consolidated industrial form of nineteenth century Europe. This form dictated a particular set of collective formal and spatial prescriptions that the anonymous and fragmented agents and providers of service could not possibly fulfil. It was neither possible to politically organise a workers' collective form of representation such as that of a 'union' with respect to the individual provider of service nor could the ontological pre-existence of service and serving 'bodies' be recuperated as a collective experience in the way that industrial alienation could be for the purposes of the subjective organisation of a workers' politics. The latter could also be called an intensive or aesthetic deficit in the conditions necessary for collective political articulation in the era of industrial consolidation.

What is remarkable, however, is that in his *German Ideology,* Marx actually proposes a vision for a communist society where this ontological conundrum would dissolve, not merely in terms of the earlier strategic hierarchy between labour and service but also in terms of the measure of value itself. The very ground of the conundrum lay in the ontological yet alien pre-existence of 'service' as something immeasurable in so far as it was entirely saturated and spent in the being of the human act—the pianist's aesthetic service entirely saturated and disappeared into the ephemeral act of *performance*—for the thought of communism became, for Marx, the basis for all human actions and experiences. Marx visualised the human being as a polymorphous creature who worked during the day, went fishing in the afternoon and was a critic of the arts during the evening (*German Ideology* 53). This everyday nomadism could not be disaggregated into objective labour and subjective services. To that extent, the time of life could not be divided between value and enjoyment. At the same time, according to this vision, enjoyment that runs through the very encounter between the act of service, the nature of the service, and the experience of being served was all of a piece, all of a social value without this value being quantitatively measured. That is to say, communism was not imagined merely as a society of polymorphous continuous enjoyment but was actually thought of as a society which was capable of recognising the value of enjoyment itself. More precisely, the vision brought together the production of so-called utilities and objects of leisure in a generalised space of enjoyment, which means a space of generalised aesthetic materiality. This very space was proposed to be an opening for the generic capacity of all humanity to realise itself—and yet which could not and need not be countable as a set of 'productive' or 'unproductive' activities in any historical present.

In this sense, Marx's vision in the *The German Ideology* was not a vision for any historical society. For Marx, the question was one of exacerbating and intensifying the communist *politics* in his own historical present: how to orient this present to such an intense and organised extent that not only would it critically expose the alienating conditions of capitalist society but also make possible the impossible proposition—to make thinkable the unthinkable thought that humanity is generically capable of both enjoying and valuing, without one being the degradation of the other. Thus, a communist politics was revolutionary insofar as it was practically able to push existing historical conditions to the limit and open up an impossible thought for any known history. This thought was indeed communist insofar as it dissolved the very terms that made all hitherto historical societies intelligible: power, value and enjoyment as distinct terms through which societies were routed and governed.

Yet, it was Marx who—in the existing historical conditions of capitalism at the time when he was writing—recoiled in an almost brutal reaction to the very *idea* of service as something both lacking and redundant with respect to the needs of organised politics. Therefore, we must now enquire into the destiny of the labour-service conundrum in its relationship to the history of capitalism as the latter moved through the stage of industrial capitalism to newer conjunctures in the twentieth century and the twenty-first. Does the conundrum still frustrate the systematic critique of capitalism and its political prescription or does it actually release, in changed conditions, a new political hypothesis?

An Autonomist Hypothesis on Performance and its Ontological Hopes

In an interesting and important article 'Virtuosity and Revolution: The Political Theory of Exodus', the Italian thinker Paolo Virno offers an 'autonomist' hypothesis on the relationship between labour, performance, and politics (189–212). The hypothesis is meant to extract a certain ontological possibility which consequently would also entail new political possibilities in an age of capitalist production which no longer conforms to the industrial paradigm usually encapsulated as the Fordist and Taylorist modes of organising production. In the industrial paradigm, as we noted earlier, what was crucial for a political imagination towards both critique and revolution was the organised subjectivation of the alienated industrial workers as a class subject, but the rousing name that is usually attached to this subject—the 'proletariat'—does not really stand for a class. Rather, it stands for that limit point (indicated above in our reference to Marx) which both separates and puts into contact the most extreme negative experience of alienated labouring lives and the *thought* of another life, a 'communist' one—a thought that arises with the political reorientation of the limit experience into a kind of revolutionary 'consciousness'. Marx and Engels, in their own times, stood firm to this project of organised reorientation of industrial experience into 'politics' and when almost entirely isolated from the extant historical movements of their times in their eventual retreat (during the Paris Commune, for example), the two thinkers were willing to orient or convert their own isolation into the form of a granular but rigorous political 'party'. One could mark this minimal revolutionary party as the subject of politics to hold the maximal historical optimism one could imagine at that time.

Meanwhile, Virno's hypothesis implies an exit or in his own words 'exodus' from the earlier form of political optimism. A logical question arises here: does Virno's diagnosis and prescription for his own times represent a political pessimism, or does it actually signal a new optimism—an optimism that is based, not simply on the force of the proletariat negativity produced by the history of industrial exploitation nor on the strategic recuperation of this negativity by a proletariat 'party', but rather on something which could be called an *ontological* optimism? This second reading, which finds an unexpected ontological hope in the very capitalist conjuncture of our present, is indeed the interest of Virno's 'autonomist' thesis.

To begin with, the diagnosis of present-day capitalism actually looks even more overwhelming and damning than Marx's thesis on industrial alienation. Following Antonio Negri, Virno (among several other Italian thinkers) actually mobilises Marx's own category of the real subsumption of labour to capital in order to produce this present-day diagnostic. Under such conditions, real subsumption means not just the formal extraction of surplus value from the labour process, but also the *direct* appropriation of the labouring worker as a 'life'. What does this mean? Though the latest inspiration for this diagnosis comes from the biopolitical style of analysis along with the original philosophical reconfiguration of our 'control society' by Gilles Deleuze, the seeds of the analysis are already present in Marx.

When Marx notes that in the larger circuits of exchange of commodities, an open-ended circulation with no intrinsic limits takes place (hence already globalising in a virtual sense), the only common 'substance' that supports such an endless movement of exchange values is what he calls 'abstract labour'. Abstract labour is a purely empty, universal, de-substantified substance that is totally cut off from the specific labouring reality that produces utilities and use values. Yet, this virtually global circuit of capitalist expansion seems to already depend on a paradoxical ontological optimism that the human being has, in some undefined potential sense, the capacity to stand in or even manifest the total possibility of satisfying human needs—needs which in themselves can only be specific and can be only produced through specific labouring activities. This is the extreme self-glorification of the human species as radiating a direct ontology of satisfaction or enjoyment, and at the same time, this glorious ontology is historically realised in at least two hundred years of exploitation and degradation of the larger part of the population of this very species.

Virno in no way diminishes the history of this paradoxical experience up to the present. What he does, to use a figure of expression of his own discourse, is 'virtuosic'. His political argument, created on an ontological ground that in the present threshold of capitalism, a new form of collective being is implicated in the very mode of capitalist exploitation, virtuosically converts this implicated being into a kind of auto-poetic or self-organised subject of history. In this sense, Virno's hypothesis exits the party form of a so-called political consciousness and thus it is crucially an 'autonomist' hypothesis. However, we must enquire into at least two things to verify this hypothesis. Firstly, what is the empirical content of this post-Taylorist stage of capitalism? Secondly, how does this so-called present-day reality of capitalism *perform* its double virtuosic acts: that of exiting the capitalist structure of production and of affirming a revolutionary politics that is capable of producing the truly autonomous task—freeing a thought of generic humanity from all structures of historical implication, including the so-called revolutionary one?

To the first line of enquiry, Virno, instead of pursuing the analysis of abstract labour as either a pure quantity or pure metaphysics, goes to another section of Marx's 1857 *Grundrisse*. If the latest experience of capitalism is one of the direct appropriation of the very living substance of the labouring individual, then this substance is neither an entirely abstract and empty universal to be realised as exchange value in the vertiginous circuits of capitalism, nor is it some kind of energetic or muscular potentiality of the human animal to accomplish the passage from biological metabolism to social metabolism. Rather, it is something which Marx calls the 'General Intellect' (Virno 199). In Virno's interpretation, this enigmatic and evocative phrase is intrinsically ontological. It does not imply a specific quality, skill or branch of production but the very capacity for conceiving the web of relations that we consider to be the basis of all social production. In that sense, General Intellect can mean an ontological capacity for human cooperation that is not immediately readable as a project, a party, or a corporation. In this interpretation, the capacity for associativity pre-exists any individual historical association. But here, Virno's empirical diagnosis quickly mutates into a politico-ontological horizon for the hope, particular to this conjuncture of capitalism, of reaching a post-capitalist world.

The main feature of this empirical portrait of present-day capitalism is that it stages the human being not on the floors of the assembly line in the industrial factory, but in the front-office of all economic units, insofar as the front-office signals something like the 'hospitalitisation' of all industry including manufacture and services. The direct appropriation of the so-called living substance of the worker is carried out most evidently and paradigmatically in not this service industry or that, but in the belief that all industry, including manufacture, *is* service. All industry is now the direct plugging into what Marx calls the 'system of needs' of a society instead of being unfolded through the labour process which traverses the entire sequence from specific expenditure of labour time to the production, exchange, consumption and capitalisation of commodities. In this sense, 'service' is the very command to satisfy the system of needs of a society and this command must be fulfilled here and now in absolute simultaneity with the imperious demand for such satisfaction. As labour becomes more and more akin to the space of productive service in the capitalist process of surplus extraction, the ideology of service becomes more and more magical and virtuosic. As the system of organising capitalist production moves towards the permanent presence of the worker in her virtuality, that is, simply on a computer, thus scrambling the initial distinction between leisure and labour time as well as the division of labour between discreet skills and departments, this very virtual presence of the worker is now commanded to be present at hand, in readiness to permanently serve the system of command itself. This strange permanent presence of the worker to 'others'—the ones she is ready to serve—is a kind of permanent virtuality, whether empirically situated next to a computer or not. Thus, exactly when Virno discovers great political and ontological hopes in the structure of present-day capitalist implicature, we are also confronted with the diagnosis of a *commanded* ontology.

Now that we look at the second line of enquiry as to how the empirical transformation in historical capitalism can incite new forms of political organisation, we are met with a very interesting aesthetic challenge: in the very moment that one diagnoses a virtuosic appropriation of labour as performance in capitalist production, and the polymorphous and nomadic image of performance as the other pole of an empty and abstract labouring substance uniting the world of commodities, we are also asked to imagine this virtuosically extracted virtuosity as a generic human capacity at a collective level. Several questions arise with this solicitation. First, what makes us so sure that the empirical course of capitalist formations is irreversible? Isn't it possible that this particular threshold of the paradigmatic appropriation of 'life' by a 'capitalism of services' is only a particular node in the cyclical destiny of capitalism? There is enough evidence to show that the empirical destiny of global capitalism is not globalising in one direction even while there is an essential globalising virtuality in capitalism as Marx definitively shows. In the same way, the 'hospitalitisation' of capitalism might well reveal an essential structural power of capture that capitalism possesses without it being an irreversible historical form. Secondly, one has to ask whether the diagnosis of capitalism, now having reached the ontological stage of species-capture of the human being so as to make possible the overwhelming of that very power of capture by an ontological excess of collective capacity, isn't a simple case of magical thinking or—which is to say the same thing—philosophical opportunism?

Finally, one must make a sustained aesthetic investigation into the very register or metaphor of virtuosity which harkens to the language of theatre. On the one hand, Paolo Virno's beautiful evocation of performance and its intrinsic world of virtuality and variation gladdens our sensibility, which is always in need to be attuned to the greater networks of human creativity than those employed by the sights of capitalist work within those very sights. Indeed, the collective imaginary of a subversive creative network of capitalist workers, engaged in immaterial acts of 'anti-work' while at work is a tribute to the auto-poetic hopes underlying Virno's autonomist thinking. It is also true that nothing exemplifies better this excess of virtuosity and variation than the world of artistic performance that even within the most disciplined structures always manages to overrun the structure, or move imperceptibly through its interstices to reach the most hidden sources of human enjoyment at a generic level. Virno's own reference to Glenn Gould's lifelong performances of Bach in all their variations testifies to this generic possibility (Virno 190).

Even at a more practical level, we can correlate the world of theatre with a passion for cooperation and collective creation. To this extent, theatre exhibits both dimensions of collective creation, of being present to others in a living precarious way such that this precarity lies in the flux of constant new appearances rather than being conserved in any metaphysical or ideological essence. All theatre is appearing and all appearing, as Hannah Arendt pointed out, is a proto-political presence to others beyond traditional anthropological structures of society and economy (Virno 192). Theatre as an assembly of real human beings in their bodily life and intellectual animation is indeed a kind of proto-space for political action which also involves bodies, intellects and sensibilities beyond their repetitive reflexes anchored in biology and society. To this extent, Virno's virtuosic evocation is a persuasive appeal to a new imagination of anti-capitalist and anti-workerist politics.

Having noted this range of optimistic possibilities flowing between an aesthetics and a politics, one must still ask whether the history of capitalism has not in its very forms of mutation and transformation, subjected art including the art of theatre to a certain capitalisation. For Marx, it was evidently a relative waste of time to envisage the production of art as a principal object of either the analysis of capitalist value or the construction of a revolutionary politics. In the greater sense, art could well be a retrospective and transfigurative depiction of social contradictions and in the propagandist sense, it could aesthetically vitalise the existent but relatively dry political programs. But it would not be either the site or the paradigm of a politics which, in Marx's time, was both observing the passing away of the traditional centrality of the arts in more organic and communitarian social forms as well as judging the artistic sphere to be somewhat lagging behind the practical exigencies of the present needs for political intervention. In contrast to this mediated relationship to art for someone in Marx's place, the twentieth century already saw from its very beginning a more direct and even violent presence of the arts, including the art of theatre in the insurrectionary or revolutionary movements taking place in different parts of the world, beginning with Europe, as the main stage of the transition from industrial to late capitalism. So it is an extraordinary but not surprising movement within the extension of capitalist appropriation between the twentieth and twenty-first centuries that these very explosive artistic movements become both grist to the culture mills of capitalism and eventually crystallise into the very model for the analysis of capitalist relations including labour, value and extraction of surplus.

To this extent, the ontological, political and linguistic hopes that Virno and the autonomist thinkers place in the idiom of virtuosity might already be partly compromised by the institutional normalisation of this very language in the sphere of capitalist discourse, particularly the discourse of the modern university. What is called 'performance studies' in the modern Anglo-Saxon and post-colonial universities, while indicating several interesting analytic turns in the empirical and ethnographic studies of forms of culture, does not necessarily add up to a discourse of revolutionary politics. This is not to disqualify a philosopher from completely reinventing the language of performance for the sake of new political thought but it is definitely to incite such a philosopher to both conduct a consistent critique of her own choice of discourse in the very institutional context that she directs that discourse at, as well as to ask the fundamental question of whether the aesthetic/performative/theatrical analogy actually enables the enunciation of a new and generic *thought* of politics at all. Before we return to this fundamental and, in a provisional way, conclusive question, let us see if we can find another genealogy or context for the discourse of service and human subjectivity than the capitalist one—a language and a context which we can reinsert into the experience of modern command and subjection which will enable us to understand this experience better.

Shudrafication as a Commanded Ontology of Service

It has to be admitted that Paulo Virno's explicit ontological optimism with regard to labour as performance or virtuosity confers a certain weight on the being of the worker in the mode of an aesthetic producer of immaterial values. These immaterial values are those of service and indeed, service is capitalised and appropriated for profits, but the autonomist hypothesis puts its ontological and political hopes on a certain irreducibility of the being of the human producer of these values in excess of the production itself. In the 'hospitalitised' conjuncture of capitalism, both things happen at once: the being of human existence is expropriated as a capitalizable force of 'life' and life reveals its inappropriable ontological and existential excess. In Marx's relegation of service to something secondary and unproductive, while admitting the conundrum that without the rationality of a certain 'serviceability' the specific labouring activity would be gratuitous and unjustified, we are confronted with a conundrum which is implicitly ontological without the creator of this conundrum positing it as such. This changes with Virno's autonomist diagnoses of a capitalism of services in which the ontological stakes are revealed both in principle and in practice. This conferral of an explicit ontological weight of labour as productive service can be illustrated briefly through the initial example from Marx of the piano-maker and the piano-player.

Clearly, in Marx's analysis, the playing of the piano is an aesthetic or cultural performance that must be thought of at an empirical level. The piano-player performs for an audience and makes possible a certain aesthetic enjoyment which the audience both feels and dissolves into. The entire ontological difficulty of grasping an ephemeral, disappearing act culminates in the aesthetic effect of a performance which itself is a disappearing experience. However, at an empirical level, the artistic and cultural distinction of the performer and the spectator is clearly presupposed in the structure of 'service' that the performer is meant to provide to the spectator. The problem is one of analysis and measurement in the context of the other distinction which is between use value and exchange value within the capitalist commodity. The ontological and existential dimensions of the subjectivity of the piano player is hardly of any consequence for the Marxian analysis of economic value.

With Virno's reconfiguration of the problem, we see that the new 'service provider' as the paradigm of labour is entirely capitalisable as a human subject. The very materiality of the human subject is now conceivable as a materiality of dispositions, emotions, and intensities. If labour in the sense of the new 'knowledge worker' is a continuous graph of improvisation and variation—the analogous image being that of the virtuosic piano player—then the corresponding aesthetic (or hospitalatising) side of generalised service is not simply to provide enjoyment to the consumer but to project a kind of permanent auto-enjoyment, the analogous experience being that of the audience for the piano performance with the proviso that the performer now traverses the entire field of subjective positions from performing to enjoying. It is to Virno's virtuosic credit that he converts this ontological auto-affectivity or auto-enjoyment into a political potentiality for auto-poesis and auto-organisation. From Marx's common-sense invocation of the piano as materially justified only by its aesthetic performance bringing together the player and the audience as two empirically separate categories, we are now transported to a zone of generalised virtuosity in which not only does the performer provide the consumer with a certain 'enjoyment' but also the performer is herself constituted aesthetically. This is not a redundant expression because the image of the purely professional performer remains locked in a kind of neutral subjectivity while the new subjective or performative service provider is not imagined anymore as someone necessarily 'skilled' as playing a piano or any other instrument but as offering her 'human material' or 'life' as exchangeable subjective capacity at the most generic level which is indifferent to the hierarchy between being skilled or unskilled. Virno's hypothesis on the political theory of exodus is communistic in the most 'common' sense of the human potentiality in so far as we are all subjectively available for auto-affectivity, self-transformation and we subject ourselves to a continuous virtuosity of 'living life' both below and beyond the professional form of technical or skilled work. This is the availability of a kind of generic amateurism which later-day capitalism would appropriate as part of its structure of real subsumption.

Finally, Virno's political hopes lie in being able to exit the structure of subsumption through the very force of the generic amateur potentiality for the self-transformation of common humanity towards a new communistic society. So the question to be asked simply is whether the thought of politics for Virno means a new creation of subjectivity at all or whether it simply follows from the logic of transformation that a certain drastic threshold of forms of capitalist work would create the conditions for the collective exit from these very conditions. Before we arrive at the question of the new political subject in the next concluding section, let us briefly enquire into the paradox of generic subjective availability for capitalist work in our times through a textual source somewhat removed from this historical context.

In the ancient Indian text of customary Hindu law, *Manusmriti,* a text with very little jurisprudence but possessing the consistent force of command or ordinance, we are addressed with a four-part division of duties and services for the four *varnas*/classes in Hindu society. The structure of these divisions is particularly striking because, for the three higher classes, it is ordained that their duties correspond to a certain horizon of ontological obligation as well as transformation through the performance of these duties or services. So, if the Brahmin is meant to perform sacrifices and pursue knowledge, then it is prescribed that these services are part of both a kind of ontological debt that the Brahmin must pay because of being born into this varna but also that the fulfilment of this ontological obligation promises the Brahmin a certain incorporeal or immaterial and subjective transformation of status. The Brahmin is purified. Similarly, the Kshatriya is glorified and the Vaishya, in a strange way, civilised into civic virtue. If purification corresponds to the performance of sacrifices and the ritual enunciation of holy texts, then glorification includes some of the Brahminical elements (for instance performing sacrifices) of subjectivation but also modifies them towards the performance of martial obligations.

The civic virtue promised to the Vaishya is again not entirely divorced from the subjective horizons for the other two higher varnas but actually forms a network of power and value that promises a certain social 'enjoyment' which is clearly both pre-capitalist in the general series of the different modes of production with their corresponding 'enjoyments' and peculiarly casteist to the extent that the enjoyment of caste privilege cannot be quite reconciled with the logic of transitions, whether from pre-feudal to feudal society or from feudal to capitalist society.

For the fourth varna called the *Shudra* (literally meaning the smallest or the most minor), the injunction is somewhat asymmetrical. In the old Sanskrit text of *Manusmriti*, the word used in relation to the Shudras' obligations is *Anusuya*. In the different English translations, this conjoined Sanskrit word has been rendered differently: the Shudra is commanded or ordained to serve 'without complaining' or as Wendy Doniger renders it, 'without resentment' (54). This negative style of translating the Sanskrit word is interesting because it clearly addresses the social class called the Shudra in such a way that a whole range of tasks, labours, services, are piled upon it to the extent that it is impossible to specify the exact nature of the work that the Shudra is meant to perform. It is possible to read *Manusmriti*'s general classification for the four varnas with B.R. Ambedkar's enumeration of the duties of the *Balai* untouchable caste in the central provinces during the early twentieth century as part of *Annihilation of Caste* (Ambedkar 39). In Ambedkar's enumeration, we find that *Balai* men are obliged to perform a whole set of tasks with various degrees of skills and physical expenditure of labour. For example, performing songs and dances in village rituals including marriage or serving as messengers for the upper classes to deliver news of birth and death in these families to their relatives in far off villages, and the *Balai* women are asked to serve as midwives at childbirth in upper caste households—all of these lists of tasks showing that, irrespective of the skill or intensity of labour required, the *Balai* community is meant to be *available* in all of their being at any time for society. This is a kind of polymorphous virtuosic requirement of a people at their most basic and irreducible level of daily existence. In this sense, somewhat conflating the example from Ambedkar with *Manusmriti*'s ordinance of Shudra, we can conclude that the Shudra is not simply the servant of this class or that but is the Shudra of society itself. That is to say, the Shudra's ontological debt to social being is of a second order or rather an nth order debt to an already encoded structure of higher varna debts that the Brahmin, the Kshatriya and the Vaishya enjoy.

The Shudra then embodies a peculiar structure of obligation towards debt payment which enables the debt of other powerful classes who are incentivised with singular subjective rewards upon such payment. However, no such incentive is provided to the Shudra and there is no horizon of subjective transformation promised for the Shudra's sub-ontological servicing of higher ontological debts. The *Manusmriti* is entirely silent on the Shudra's subjective transformation in the very performance of her services and to this extent, the negative style of translating *Anasuya* deafeningly echoes this silence.

Yet, we cannot miss the subjective force of the enunciation that the Shudra must serve 'without resentment'. This very negative injunction indicates that the Shudra's position and repertoire in society's distinction of labour and services implicates her in a structure of subjective degradation and its corresponding affect, one of which is clearly resentment. We will not go into the possible association of this particular word 'resentment' with the great Nietzschean diagnosis of *Ressentiment* in Christian slave morality, but it is enough to note that it is exactly when the possibility of a certain collective antipathy—if not anathema—arises with the nature of one's social degradation that a monumental law text without jurisprudence forbids any such negative affect. But the only way to normalise and sustain a forbidding command is to remain silent about the entire structure of subjectivity for the Shudra, not just for one type of reactive emotion or another. In other words, we are forbidden to either ask or know what the Shudra feels as she lives her life at every moment available in her ontological serviceability for society; that is to say that the Shudra is asked to serve but forbidden to exist. This is not an accidental prohibition because it is only from blocking the Shudra's individual existence that one can also foreclose her articulation with any collective political existence. It is at this level that we can see the penetration of *Manusmriti*'s insidious strategy that it prohibits politics exactly at that precarious site where the structural condition for a politics of refusal or repudiation might begin to exist.

At the same time, we must wonder, what can it mean to ask the Shudra to serve without resentment in any meaningful real way while emptying out the essential substance of her ontological being and historical existence. If one ponders this problem a little then the answer is quite evident: the Shudra must *appear* to serve without resentment at each and every moment of her life insofar as she is perpetually available as the very material of serviceability for society. This is the ultimate travesty for the political and ontological hopes that arise out of a sphere of 'appearances' where forms of new acts, new thought, and new life coincide. Nothing that Hannah Arendt or Paolo Virno might argue for can recuperate any such sphere of the new for the Shudra. The aesthetic command that the Shudra is instructed to obey to serve and appear to serve without resentment is the classic command given to the theatre actor: the actor in the theatre is meant to assume the persona or the mask of the character and her emotion even while neutralising the coefficient of her own being. In that sense the theatre actor, even while portraying different characters and their different degrees of subjectivity, must localise her own being at a kind of zero degree subjectivity. This is the essential 'shudrafication' that accompanies the theatrical personification in the art of acting. Reciprocally, in varna or caste society, the Shudra becomes the zero degree subject in the social hierarchy who, at the same time, serves the subjective capitalisation of society or the capitalisation of subjectivities in society.

Of course, we have already inserted an anachronistic language of capitalist analysis into a pre-capitalist social form. But in the following section, this is what we would like to argue: the analytic of shudrafication illustrates the desertification of labour as subject in contemporary capitalism. To that extent, the political form of the proletariat as the limit point of historical negativity in early forms of capitalist alienation become inaccessible to later day experiences of work. These experiences do not conform to the structure of alienated subjectivity in so far as alienation is a subjective correlate of an objective measure of exploitation. The classic Marxian theory of alienation is premised on a humanist ontology that more or less is consistent with scientific and historical forms of species-being and social being. It is with the *commanded* ontology of a capitalism of services that we are confronted with a peculiar admixture of the human being considered as a generic serviceable material, the collective space of human existence considered as a continuous circulation of power, value and enjoyment—with a total foreclosure of the possibility of another thought for the constitution of generic humanity. In what is to follow, we will argue that only the forcing of another thought can make it possible for us to imagine a political future rather than place our political hopes in an essential ontological thought already, if accidentally, planted by the history of capitalism in its own rich and mangled soil.

A Concluding Note on the Global Shudra Who 'Serves without Resentment'

An instance: In the global airline industry, including in developing countries, over the last 30 years of the so-called neo-liberal face of modern capitalism, the figure of the air-hostess is significantly ambiguous. First of all, the very term 'hostess' both evokes the obligation of hospitality and its feminine subjective association. This is certainly not specific to the recent 'neo-liberal' form since from the very beginning of air transportation of passengers the burden of 'taking care' of the travellers as well as the upkeep of the plane has been as if a natural responsibility of women. The traditional patriarchate smoothly moulded itself to the technological leap of being able to do the impossible, that is to fly in the air like a bird, and to resocialise this very technical marvel to a more or less familiar world of servitude.

But if we pay close attention to both the figuration and functioning of the present-day air-hostess, the part already contained in the hospitable persona of the 'hostess' is now articulated with a new and more inscrutable function. Let us call this the function of 'security'. Even while the feminine obligations of hospitality in the world of industry (not limited to the hospitality industry) extends even to male employees (whether the male steward on a commercial flight or the feminised Public Relations persona of employees in the manufacturing sector as well as State services such as the police), the more contemporary modality of the 'hospitalitisation' is that the otherwise feminised employee, whether a man or a woman, must perpetually be vigilant with regard to the possible infiltration of the radical anti-hospitable figure of our times—that is, the 'terrorist'. Within the empirical instance of airline work, the danger of the hijacker was always present, to which the airline staff, led by the air hostesses, would have to be alert. But the securitarian modality is not merely prompted by the physical or commercial interest of the plane's safety; it is a modality of a state function directly embodied by a private employee of a commercial firm, in this case the air hostess, while appearing pleasantly hospitable to every passenger, she studies each one of them with an eye to their conduct. The subjectivity that supports this double function is necessarily ambiguous. While the air hostess performs her professional duty to make every passenger feel both good and safe, in the larger configuration of our political and economic world today, the making of others feel good is a subjective, corporatist performance while to make them feel safe is a relatively objective, statist one. So the archaic shudra command of serving without resentment at a zero degree localisation of one's subjectivity now possesses an even more insidious *total* structure in which both the specific shudra function of the labourer who serves and the global shudrafied prescription of the servant who guards our lives in their very material survivability are combined. The threshold of this zero degree neutrality already subjecting the individual unit of labouring activity to a total command of service now becomes the horizon of a neutral political control that is meant to be incarnated in the figure of the new global shudra who is as much servant as guardian clearly the name of this neutral figure of control is the State. Between the obligation to provide hospitality to the consumer and the injunction to espy potential hostility among those very consumers (not simply in the anecdotal sense of looking out for the potential hijacker among the consumers of airlines services but to be able to seize the essential anti-social, anti-state agent of terror among the socialised and statist figure of the consumer), the ambivalence if not oxymoron contained in the linguistic origin of the word 'hospitality' is mobilised. The global Shudra is now the purveyor of both the hospitality and the hostility that are contained in the greek *hostis* from which the word 'hospitality' is derived.

Another Instance: While in the received connotation of performance particularly in theatre, we find a whole range of creative variations and improvisations that can only be summarised as a kind of repertoire of possibilities that performance generates. Theatre as such is also nothing if not a repetitive structure of appearances and presentations combining and recombining a set of finite theatrical elements. This chronicle of combinations make the stuff of an empirical history of theatre as an art. Evidently, when performance is stressed as a pure potentiality of improvisation and variation then it seeks to go beyond the restrictive structure or combinatory of theatre. This is a flickering movement of desire and history that also manifests itself in a flickering oscillation between new and different names—theatre, performance art, theatre-as-performance instead of theatre-as-representation, performance-as-ritual instead of performance-in-the-theatre, etc. But the more specific problem of extending the provenance of performance to something like the sphere of general intellectuality or generic human intelligence seems to make theatre only a historical and empirical part of this intellectuality. The autonomy of performance as intelligence makes theatre only a heteronomous instantiation of the law of Intellect-as-Performance. Virno's hypothesis was based on this larger affirmation as a political potentiality of common human emancipation from the capitalist appropriation of this very common or generic human potentiality in a dizzying historico-ontological circle. The limited sphere of an 'art' of the theatre seems only a somewhat outdated professional subjection of the neutral shudra-actor to the heteronomous Law of Text and Author. When performance comes into its own, this heteronomy is apparently freed towards a space of pure creativity or play that is nothing but the endless performativity of the General Intellect.

Localising this instance being discussed even further in 2020-21 when this essay is being written, we notice a very interesting cultural as well as economic problem in the wake of the Coronavirus pandemic gripping the world since at least March 2020. This problem is one of being unable to perform any kind of live theatre in front of a physical audience to the point that this disability results in great existential desolation and financial distress for the artiste. One of the ways in which this specific crisis has been met is by way of creating an alternative technological forum for theatre in such a way that it also gains some commercial viability in the times of physical absence and social distancing. Again this effort results in the popularisation of a name which already existed among the different genres of performance: digital performance or digital theatre. What is interesting is that one of the technological strategies to render this digital popularisation commercially viable is to convert the material of performance with digital means into the algorithm of a 'game'. Without entering into any empirical verification of how successful this strategy is in commercial terms, the strategic end itself is to be able to measure and monetise these new exigent digital performances within the calculability of a game.

There are two dimensions that can be analysed out of this recent development. One is that from a somewhat earlier stage of relativising the so-called art of theatre to only one of several anthropological variants of generic human performativity, we now encounter this very art in all its historical richness and its contemporary pathos of absence in the form of a repeatable and calculable structure that underlies the algorithm of a game being played on the computer. So the point being delivered by the present experience is not at all the ontological or cultural relativisation of theatre but the technical subservience of art to calculation. While the heterodox researches about cultural and anthropological performances that were conducted in the late twentieth century sought to produce a kind of horizontal liberation of multiple human activities as all equally vital and significant as 'performances', the present crisis actually forces onto us a renewed vertical subjection of all such activities to the regime of algorithms as well as monetisation.

The second dimension is a little more speculative but worth considering: it is exactly when the world wants to secure itself with more and more digital and artificial means of reproducing its material existence, that it enters into preemptive or immunitary constructions to be forged out of the elements of this very materiality. The most striking horizon for this kind of preemption is Artificial Intelligence. Here again, we encounter the paradox that any model of Artificial Intelligence, while based on acute observation of real human conduct in history, must reduce that very conduct to a repeatable structure of predictability and calculability. In this exact sense the performance of Artificial Intelligence must, in whatever speculative term, be the performance of a generalised serviceability: all the needs of the world must already be subject to a 'system of needs' (in Marx's words), and this system must itself be subjected to a more and more calculable and algorithmic expression. So we experience the shattering paradox that when Intelligence is ontologically conceived of as a creative and generic amateurism traversed by endless improvisation and invention, it becomes the very material basis for a highly technical set of machines that circumscribe intelligent conduct to a repeatable structure, attune collective activity to a system of needs—and 'serve without resentment' precisely because they are indeed true localisations of a zero degree subjectivity, that is, they are machines.

This speculative but not ungrounded image of the global Shudra who 'serves without resentment' which recalls Alexa, the hostess in the machine, ever available to serve our system of needs—is the void point of politics. Unlike Paolo Virno and Antonio Negri, it is not possible for us to transmute the experience of both capitalist intensification and crisis into a kind of leap of faith or revelation of ontological or political possibilities. It seems to us that this very void point that capitalism pushes us towards, which is the void of thought at the very conjuncture of hyper-performativity or hyper-productivity, must become the real challenge of politics as thought. This must first mean the renewal of Marx's own revolutionary lessons in negativity that marked the emergence of the name 'proletariat' at the limit point of industrial exploitation and class struggle in the nineteenth century. In our own times the void point that we have indicated is not without an analogous negative intensity. However, the difference is that for Marx this negativity was the originary force that led him to a certain gamble or wager on that very force as the springboard of a future organisation of society as well as to draw out a schema of that future society in terms of a transitional socialist state and the end of the state form itself; for us, in contrast, the experience of negativity is the double experience of both a vehement return to the state form within the general diminishing of state presence in neo-liberal capitalism and the affirmation of the end of state here and now.

In the pandemic times, the real political casualty of the retreat of globalisation is the imagination of an alter globalisation that so energised social and political militants in the recent past. The weakness of this type of militancy was always its empirical dependence on a globalised world to countermand it. But with capitalism the experience of a certain cyclical retreat and return is to be expected even while the intrinsic global virtuality of capital that Marx analysed pioneeringly remains in force. So the return of the state form in the current crisis is itself a contradictory empirical phenomenon because the state today apparently guards or secures the very autonomy of individual and all human enterprise. Evidently when global economic networks are dislodged, locally autonomous communitarian forces are released precisely to be consolidated and guarded by the Nation State. Thus, in a seesaw of forces, the local Shudra returns as a securitarian figure who still 'serves without resentment' at the local level during our pandemic crisis even while the empirical global Shudra in the transnational service industry is without employment and in distress. The embodiments of the local Shudras who 'serve without resentment' and in the vicinity of disease and death are health workers to begin with, followed by such figures of state as the police. The ideology of essential services, which is a shudra ideology, permeates the State's space today all over the world exactly when globalisation is seen to be in retreat. An alter global 'multitude' who cover the earth with their creative ontological performativity cannot be the horizon of any auto-organised resistance to this return of the State in its ideological as well as coercive forms. In fact, in the present historical conjuncture, it is structurally impossible to conceive of the end of the State insofar as the empirical crisis demands the presence of the State at every moment to compensate for and supplement its destructive handiwork, and according to us, this very structural impossibility must become the new trigger—not for a rejuvenated political organisation but for the minimal thought of a politics of organisation in response to this very impossibility.

An example: At the height of the pandemic with the US ravaged by infection, illness and death and the structural possibility of crowds gathering in public spaces nothing less than a scandal—the scandal encouraged by the then-president Donald Trump—with the custodial killing of George Flyod and the Black Lives Matter upsurge, there grew a popular demand to defund the police force. In a certain instinctual sense at a collective level, this demand was a demand for the end of the State here and now but it was also a demand for the end of the society of services where the police are subjectivised as a corps of securitarian service providers who must localise themselves at a zero degree subjectivity. While serving the cause of security without resentment in the most violent engagement with the world embroiling them in the most inescapable emotions including revenge and resentment at being thrown into the cauldron of sociopathy, the police are instructed to be the impassible subjective fortresses through which no individual affect must pass and all police performance must be standard, operational and procedural, that is rigorously ritual. The demand for an end to the police as an institution supported by public funds was also a demand to breach this wall of both State Sovereignty (in general) and Essential Service (in this specific time of crisis). In our view, this demand to breach State and Society was an impossible demand, and for that reason absolutely real. It was structurally impossible but intellectually real. The political dimension of this minimal upsurge of a real and impossible demand was that it was born not from a structural logic of nascent and surplus ontological potentiality in a historical situation but from something which was an inconsistent part of that situation: George Floyd's killing, though part of the long-term racial history of the society, actually interrupted the consistency of American reality as overwhelmed by the COVID-19 epidemic.

The Black Lives Matter movement did not primarily intend to transgress the structural imperative of this overwhelming reality: the imperative not to assemble in public places. But in confronting a contingent experience of structural silence coming from another inconsistent racial zone of an avowedly consistent democratic society at that time, the movement became actively indifferent to these imperatives issued by the State, and by and large agreed to by most part of society including those who participated in the movement. Thus, in response to the inconsistent exigency of the situation, the people inconsistently assembled in apparent violation of the imperative of distancing (to which most of them would probably agree in principle within the pure consistency of the epidemic situation) during the Black Lives Matter movement. Thus politics emerges as the minimal but contingent thought of an impossible but real desire not merely against the dominant tendency of a situation but in active and creative indifference to it. In this sense, politics is not an autonomous creation beyond the constraints of history but a heteronomous movement in thought and practice without giving up on a certain new found indifference to the fundamental laws of the situation. An unforeseen, impossible, and real enjoyment born of this very indifference shows that *some* politics is beginning to exist.

Works Cited

Álvaro García Linera. "The State in Times of Coronavirus: The pendulum of the "Illusory Community." *Crisis and Critique*, Volume 7, Issue 3, 24-11-2020. https://www.crisiscritique.org/uploads/24-11-2020/alvaro-garci-a-linera.pdf. Accessed 2 Feb. 2021.

Ambedkar, B.R. *Annihilation of Caste, BAWS 1.* Ed.Vasant Moon. Bombay: Education Department, Government of Maharashtra, 1979.

Badiou, Alain. *What is Philosophy? A Lecture by Alain Badiou 2010.* Ed. Cvjeticanin Srdjan New York: Atropos Press, 2015.

Doniger, Wendy. *The Laws of Manu.* London: Penguin, 2000.

Deleuze, Gilles. "Postscript on the Societies of Control." *October*, vol. 59, 1992, pp. 3–7. JSTOR, www.jstor.org/stable/778828. Accessed 2 Feb. 2021.

Hénaff, Marcel. *The Price of Truth: Gift, Money and Philosophy.* Trans. Jean-Louis Morhange. Stanford, California: Stanford University Press, 2010.

Marx, Karl & Fredrich Engels. *The German Ideology including Theses on Feuerbach and Introduction to the Critique of Political Economy.* New York: Prometheus Books, 1998.

———. *Grundrisse: Foundations of the Critique of Political Economy.* Trans. Martin Nicolous. New York: Penguin, 1993.

Negri, Antonio. *Marx beyond Marx: Lessons on the 'Grundrisse'.* Trans. H. Cleaver, M. Ryan and M. Viano. Ed. J. Fleming. New York: Autonomedia, 1991.

Ranciere, Jacques. "Time is nothing other than intervention—Jacques Rancière on Alain Badiou's *Being and Event*". Verso. https://www.versobooks.com/blogs/2579-time-is-nothing-other-than-intervention-jacques-ranciere-on-alain-badiou-s-being-and-event, 2016. Accessed 2 Feb. 2021.

Supiot, Alan, *Homo Juridicus: On the Anthropological Function of the Law.* Trans. Saskia Brown. London, New York: Verso, 2007.

Virno, Paolo, "Virtuosity and Revolution: The Political Theory of Exodus." P. Virno and M. Hardt ed. *Radical Thought in Italy: A Potential Politics.* University Of Minnesota Press, London: 2006.

11

Caste and/in Literary Imagination

A Critique of Brahmanical Aestheticism

Anandita Pan

The concept of 'aesthetics' is highly valued and at the same time debated. It was with the ancient Sanskrit literary theories that, in Indian literary tradition, aestheticism as an inherent value of art and literature, expressed through various media such as *rasa, aucitya,* and *dhvani,* came to be established. For ages poets, dramatists and artists have minutely followed the rules of how to express different emotions, how to describe different body languages, etc. With the rise of Dalit and tribal literature, however, the supremacy of Sanskrit aesthetics as the sole arbiter of aestheticism was challenged. What Dalit and tribal aesthetics have brought forth is a critique of standards proposed by Sanskrit aesthetics. What characterises aestheticism in life or a work of art? Who determines the level of aesthetic value? Why are certain aesthetic qualities valued over others? These questions constitute the core of new aesthetic sensibilities constituted through emerging literary spheres such as Dalit literature.

The evolution of Dalit aesthetics has to be understood parallel to that of Dalit literature. Identifying the social as intrinsically linked with the aesthetic in Dalit literature, Sharankumar Limbale in his iconic book, *Towards an Aesthetic of Dalit Literature,* rebukes upper-caste critics for declaring Dalit writing as not aesthetic according to standard values. Commenting on what constitutes 'Dalit literature', Limbale writes, 'Dalit writers believe that Dalit literature is a movement. They see their literature as a vehicle for their pain, sorrow, questions and problems. But when readers read the works of Dalit writers exclusively as 'literature', the common ground between the writer and the reader is disturbed' (105). Dalit literature disturbs the 'pleasure' value of canonical literature by bringing in 'disturbing' images and language. Hence, the common understanding of 'literary aestheticism' as referring to 'beauty' and 'artistry' is violated by Dalit literature.

But what is Dalit aesthetics? According to Limbale, Dalit literature's engagement with material, lived experience poses a challenge to the canonical notion of 'aesthetics'. He writes, 'What is the place of '*satyam*' in the lives of the Dalit and the Adivasi? Is that truth about which such pride is expressed, and which is considered triumphant, really the truth?' (20). Defining Dalit literature as social literature expressing the truth about lived reality, Limbale denounces the aesthetics of *rasa* wherein 'rather than being concerned with the [actual] form of an object, the concept of beauty tends to revolve around the feelings of pleasure and empathy aroused by viewing the object' (114). Dalit aesthetics, therefore, becomes a way to critique not only the aestheticism of art and literature as prescribed in Sanskrit theories but also brahmanism and how the upper castes exercise a monopoly over knowledge and art and make it their prerogative to be the only people speaking and practicing art.

This article establishes the concept of aestheticism arising from Sanskrit literary traditions as necessarily brahmanical. Replacing 'aesthetics' with 'brahmanical aesthetics', revitalises our perspective and re-aligns it with the framework of caste. In this article, I explore the theorisation of Dalit aesthetics in the following areas: the development of 'Dalit *chetna*' (also known as 'Dalit consciousness'); the value of experiential realism; and the role of language in marking agential assertion. This article, however, is not limited only to exploring the content of Dalit aesthetics; it also grapples with the idea of identity versus positionality, the question of 'who represents whom', that looms large over Dalit literary and political articulations.

Dalit *Chetna*, Realism, and New Realism

Central to the notion of Dalit aesthetics is the idea of Dalit consciousness which encompasses the literary production of the community as well. Omprakash Valmiki theorises Dalit consciousness, or 'Dalit *chetna*', as an enabling position. In *Dalit Sahitya ka Saundarya Sastra* (Aesthetics of Dalit Literature), Valmiki links the emergence of Dalit chetna to the term, 'Dalit', which encompasses the spirit of activism and identity. In Valmiki's words, the term 'Dalit' is inspirational because 'for the first time, Dalits have chosen the term. So far they lived an imposed identity' (10). He further adds that a Dalit consciousness is not merely about describing the pain, sorrow, anguish, and exploitation. *Chetna,* or consciousness has a direct relation with 'perspective' which breaks the stereotypes related to the cultural, historical and social roles of Dalits.[1] 'Dalit', then, is theorised as an agential category capable of voicing opposition and struggle.

But what are some of the components of Dalit aesthetics? Could it be truly measured in terms of beauty? Limbale in *Towards an Aesthetics of Dalit Literature* critiques the triadic concept of *satyam* (the true), *shivam* (the sacred), and *sundaram* (the beautiful), which have remained a benchmark to assess the aesthetic value of literature in the Indian literary sphere, and underscores the brahmanical nature of it. These concepts construct a system of knowledge that is rooted in brahmanism and promote sankritisation. In this process, not only are the lives and languages of Dalit people marked as unworthy of use, they are marked as invalid. Herein the notion of experiential realism gains prominence.

Kancha Ilaiah (1996) opines that the personal experience of the marginalised is important to understand the different social contexts the powerful and powerless live in. The Dalit experience helps provide an alternate perspective of the caste system, showing that the beautiful village portrayed by upper-caste Hindu poets is not where the Dalits live. A Dalit village is muckstrewn where 'the stench [is] so overpowering that one would choke within a minute' (Valmiki 1). According to Dalit writers, this alternate perspective is made possible only because the 'day-to-day experiences of the Dalit-Bahujan castes… is the only possible and indeed the most authentic way in which the deconstruction and reconstruction of history can take place' (Ilaiah xii). The construction and agential dalithood is attained by the deconstruction of the victimised Dalits.

Pointing to the subversive capacity of Dalit literature, Raj Gauthaman highlights the use of language. He argues that it is a conscious attempt to disrupt brahmanical proprieties and to 'expose and discredit the existing language, its grammar, its refinements, and its falsifying order as symbols of dominance' (263–71). The poems by Namdeo Dhasal take a mutinous stance by using slang and colloquial language. In 'Hunger' he writes:

> Hunger
> Which came first, seed or tree?
> Hunger you make things too difficult
> Hunger just tell us what breed this monkey is
> And if you can't
> Then we will screw
> Seventeen generations of you
> Hunger, you and your mother

This articulation is very different from the romanticised portrayal of pain by non-Dalit writers. Dhasal's writing hits us. It hits the hegemonic assumptions that one's caste, acquired through birth, is an unchangeable factor. What the poem shows is that caste in fact is a dynamic social construct, created and historically perpetuated, by the dominant castes to serve their purpose. He challenges the literary criteria as well as the system of caste. Rather than portraying Dalits as mute victims, silently bearing pain, he shows active resistance that arises from political consciousness. And this resistance is not an act of individual revenge. It is a collective challenge towards the very structures (not individuals) that dictate the inequalities in our society.

According to Laura Brueck, Dalit literature's purpose in using realism 'is to get their readership to acknowledge the ethical conflict at the heart of [the stories] and then to recognize it reflected in the world around them and ultimately transform it into a new reality of a just society' (99). Manohar Mouli Biswas theorises this interventionist epistemology as 'new realism'. In his postulation, the 'realistic' representations of life in Dalit writings are not mere replications of events; 'when we challenge the reality, we come to understand the truth behind it and the hidden meaning of its existence' (48).

Gendering Language

At this juncture, it is also important to recognise the contribution made by Dalit women writers in shaping a feminist sensitivity in Dalit aesthetics. In his article 'Dalit Women Talk Differently', Gopal Guru argues that Dalit women need to speak 'differently' because they face exclusion not only in the political field but also in the cultural field. He writes: 'Dalit male writers do not take serious note of the literary output of Dalit women and tend to be dismissive of it' (2549). Enumerating three reasons for this attitude, Guru says: '(1) It is not only caste and class identity but also one's gender positioning that decides the validity of an event; (2) Dalit men are reproducing the same mechanisms against their women which their high caste adversaries had used to dominate them; (3) the experience of Dalit women shows that local resistance within the Dalits is important' (2549). Two points that emerge from his opinion are that 'differences' exist not only among 'Indian' women but also within the Dalit community based on gender, and that writing becomes a way for Dalit women to articulate their struggles and resistances.

A major component of Dalit women's writings is of their lived experiences impacted by the dual regimes of caste and gender, which is reflected in writing that voices their oppression and resistance. Incorporating songs, folk tales, superstitions, and stories that have been continued through generations, Dalit women's narratives become a tapestry of events portraying a collective of women who make fun of the people in power who oppress them. Their use of everyday language becomes instrumental in this purpose. Issues of violence (in the form of public and domestic rape), sexuality, identity, marriage, religion and education have been reiterated in Dalit women's writings from the very beginning. While in Dalit male writing, such usage is directed towards the upper caste men who have kept them in slavery and ignorance, Dalit women often use it against their own husbands in order to save themselves from being beaten up. The narrator in *Sangati* recounts an incident she witnessed between Pakkiaraj and his wife Raakkamma. 'Pakkiaraj was abusing her in a vile and vulgar way, and was just about to hit her. And Raakkamma was giving it back to him, word for word. Even before his hand could fall on her, she screamed and shrieked, 'Ayyayyo, he's killing me. Vile man, you'll die, you'll be carried out as a corpse, you low-life, you bastard, you this you that…' (Bama 61). Raakkamma even lifts her sari in public and talks in abusive terms to escape from her husband's torture.

What makes *Sangati* all the more interesting is that it does not stop at narrating only the pain of Dalit women—oppressed, ruled, and crushed by state, religion, and caste—but goes one step further and shows how Dalit women courageously fight to break the shackles of authority and dare 'to make fun of the class in power that oppressed them' (vii). These women do not remain suppressed within a claustrophobic atmosphere, spending their time in the dark, but give voice to their suffering, share it with other Dalit women, and challenge patriarchy (both brahmanical and Dalit) with force. This does not mean that the women use physical violence to stop the men from torturing them. In fact, as the female characters repeatedly agree, a woman cannot counter a man physically. Instead, what they opt for is a unique shield—using vulgar language and publicly shaming the man. Language, therefore, serves as a means to deride Dalit masculinity and highlight the specificity of Dalit women's oppression. According to Bama, such language often originates from a frustrating lack of pleasurable experiences. Lakshmi Holmstrom, in the introduction to *Sangati*, comments that the 'other aspect of this language of women is its vigour, and its closeness to proverbs, folk songs, and folk lore' (Bama xx). Though deprived of any space in the popular historiography, these women retain their oral traditions by passing on the stories and songs to young girls. As such, language becomes a vessel to carry a feminist legacy and build a collective.

Who Speaks for Whom?

This oppositional consciousness has been visible in Dalit writers' posing a challenge to dominant representations of Dalits by non-Dalit writers. In discussing Premchand's celebrated short story, 'Kafan', which highlights the woeful life of Dalits, challenges have been posed for its unrealistic representation of lower-caste people as idle and heartless and the common conflation of caste with class (Brueck). On a similar note, Sarat Chandra Chattopadhyay's short story, 'Abhagi' has been criticised for representing Dalits solely as victims and for assuming that brahmanical practices of widowhood and sati are common for all castes.[2] To redress this lacuna, Dalit writers have argued that Dalit literature *by* Dalit people constitutes that true spirit of dalitness because they are borne out of the direct, lived experience. Limbale and Valmiki believe that it should be by Dalits for Dalits.

While this identity-based collective has opened new possibilities for agential assertion and alternate perspectives to flourish, one cannot ignore the potential trap of ontological ghettoisation. To truly explore the potential of the category 'Dalit', it is necessary to take it beyond identity and re-realise it as an achieved awareness. In this context, the methodological approach of the feminist 'standpoint theory' may prove suitable.

According to the standpoint theory, the viewpoint of the dominant groups fails to interrogate their advantageous situation systematically and critically, which leaves their social situation scientifically and epistemologically incapable of generating knowledge. Being in the lowest rung of the society, the oppressed group knows how power functions through those who dominate and among/upon those who are dominated. Through this knowledge, every dominated group can turn an oppressive feature of the group's condition into a source of critical insight. Thus, standpoint theory shows that a disadvantage can be turned into an epistemological, scientific, and political advantage. But this process includes active participation in the cause of the oppressed, to raise a voice for the collective in order to gain emancipation through struggle. This is the reason why standpoint is not an ascribed position. It is an achievement. The empowerment of the oppressed requires a distinctive kind of knowledge that can emerge only through political processes. Moreover, the feminist standpoint theory also proposes a re-visioning of the position of the researcher which helps to avoid the narrow alley of direct experience based on 'authenticity' and narrow identity politics. Standpoint is, therefore, an affiliative politics where not only women belonging to a particular group speak for themselves but people from all categories 'learn' about the women's position and contribute to the construction of a systematic alternative to the dominant worldview from the standpoint of women. The standpoint focuses on the object groups' experience to unfold the relation between power and knowledge, as well as to revise the position of the researcher/subject.

If we replicate this model onto the methodological approach in Dalit aesthetics, we can de-limit its scope from just identity and expand it to a critical understanding of the contours of caste as it impacts Dalits and non-Dalits differently. Such theorisation would reveal how Dalit aesthetic and literary traditions intervene in dominant brahmanical epistemologies by proving Dalit experience as a source of valid knowledge and thereby redefine the socio-cultural and the academic definitions of what counts as 'knowledge'. The Dalit standpoint thus unfolds the power politics operational in structures of caste and literature. In both cases, the systemic brahmanical control determines who can have control over caste and literary expression and what is worthy of articulation. To reiterate Marathi critic Arjun Dangle's view, 'Dalit is not a caste but a realization.'

Notes

1. Eleanor Zelliot emphasises on Dalit as a collective which allows 'pride, self-respect and a vision of the future'.
2. Biswas mentions that the idea of widowhood, an essentially upper-caste practice, is imposed on the titular character of this story. In the story, Abhagi, being abandoned by her husband, falls in utter wretchedness and wishes to die. Biswas says that in Dalit communities this is not the case.

Works Cited

Bama. *Sangati: Events*. Trans. Lakshmi Holmström. New Delhi: Oxford University Press. 2005. Print.

Biswas, M. M. *An Interpretation of Dalit Literature, Aesthetic, Theory and Movement: Through the Lens of Ambedkarism.* Trans. J. Gupta. Chaturtha Dunia. 2017. Print.

Brueck, Laura. "Dalit Chetna in Dalit Literary Criticism." Seminar 558. 2006. Print.

———. *Writing Resistance: The Rhetorical Imagination of Hindi Dalit Literature*. Columbia University Press. 2014. Print

Dhasal, Namdeo. "Hunger". *Marathi Dalit Poetry in Translation*. Accessed 9 July 2014. http://marathidalitpoetry.blogspot.com/2014/07/hungernamdeo-dhasal.html.

Gauthaman, Raj. "Dalit Protest Culture: The First Stage". *The Oxford India Anthology of Tamil Dalit Writing* edited by Ravikumar, D. and Azhagarasan, R., Trans. Theodore Bhaskaran. New Delhi: Oxford University Press. 2012. Print.

Guru, Gopal. "Dalit Women Talk Differently." *Economic and Political Weekly* 30.41/42: 2548–2550. 1995. Print.

Harding, Sandra. *The Feminist Standpoint Theory Reader: Intellectual and Political Controversies*. Routledge. 2014. Print.

Ilaiah, Kancha. *Why I am not a Hindu: A Sudra Critique of Hindtva Philosophy, Culture, and Political Economy.* Bhatkal and Sen. 1996. Print.

Jaggar, A. "Socialist feminism and the standpoint of women." *Political Thought,* edited by Michael Rosen & Jonathan Wolff. Oxford University Press. 1999. Print.

Limbale, Sharankumar. *Towards and Aesthetic of Dalit Literature: History, Controversies and Considerations.* Trans. Alok Mukherjee. New Delhi: Orient Blackswan. 2004. Print.

Valmiki, Omprakash. *Dalit Sahitya ka Saundarya Sastra.* Radhakrishna Prakashan. 2001. Print.

Zelliot, Eleanor. "The Roots of Dalit Consciousness." *Seminar* 471: 28–32. 1998. Print.

12

Aesthetics and Methodology in English Studies

A Fragmented History

Punnya Rajendran

In spite of its frequent use in the humanities and social sciences in the recent past, the term *aesthetics* does require a reintroduction ever so often in newer and emerging contexts. In particular, it is challenging to redefine the term within the dysmorphic disciplinary scope of English Studies (which today encompasses cultural critique as much as it does readings of literary texts, both comparative and otherwise). The status of aesthetics within philosophy, on the other hand, is far more well-defined and grounded in the very history of the discipline: the term aesthetics is most commonly traced back to Plato and Aristotle, Kant and Hegel, Nietzsche, Schiller and Schopenhauer, Heidegger and also Deleuze and Guattari among others. In the case of English Studies, however, we can't use the term aesthetics without encountering different and arguably more complex issues of definitions, scope, and methodology.

The history of literary criticism as well as the overlapping field of art history and art theory, our enduring interest in narrative techniques for their own sake over and above the intellectual denunciations effected by the cultural turn, the insular sub-category of scholarship called narratology which often brushes shoulders with cognitivism and psychology, and last but not the least, the fundamental nature of questions that continue to be asked in English classrooms to this day—'What does the poet mean' or 'What is the theme of the novel?' or 'What are your reactions to this image?'—all of the above indicate that English Studies (that is, the erstwhile English Language and Literature) has always had its own intimate, increasingly confused, and repeatedly disrupted relationship with the idea of aesthetics.

It might even be argued that our relationship to aesthetics can be defined in conjunction with, but also, over and above our interest in semiotics, discourse analysis, and deconstructive readings. The relationship between aesthetics and critique is a tricky one. As Rita Felski rightly points out, 'the negative has become inescapably, overbearingly normative' (3) in literary studies on account of the exclusivity of the hermeneutics of suspicion as the only means of engaging with a text. However, as Sedgwick warns us in her landmark essay that distinguishes between 'paranoid' and 'recuperative' reading, our desire to convert the text into a site of positive knowledge should not become 'sappy, aestheticizing, defensive, anti-intellectual, or reactionary' (278). This methodological balance between positive textual analysis and reactionary political praxis is the real challenge underlying the renewed use of the term aesthetics today.

This situation is further complicated when we try to prefix the adjective 'Indian' to aesthetics. The term is often loosely attached to ancient Sanskrit treatises on art. That nomenclature more or less stands to good reason, for treatises on art anywhere in the ancient world emerged only from those cultural networks directly endowed with royal patronage and imaginative prosperity—primed, in other words, for a liberal/disinterested pursuit of the arts. Today, any scholar of the postcolonial condition knows to avoid the discursive trap of this category called Indian aesthetics, the ease it might offer in terms of publishing and academic legibility notwithstanding.

Spivak's ironic and almost tongue-in-cheek response to this matter appears in her essay titled 'Aesthetic Judgement of Disgrace' which appears alongside other essays that display a range of thinking about aesthetics in the Indian context. At least four of the essays in that book (*The Bloomsbury Research Handbook of Indian Aesthetics and the Philosophy of Art*) engage with *rasa* theory in particular and Sanskrit poetics in general; all of which are placed rather unsurprisingly at the very beginning of the book. In her essay which appears at the very end of the volume, Spivak suggests a revamping of the very idea of Indian aesthetics. While the editor of the volume had chosen her chapter 'as an example of Indian philosophizing on aesthetics', Spivak wishes that the reader would make an imaginative leap when she says the following: '[i]n order to locate the "Indianness"—spiritual or not—of the argument of this chapter, the reader will have to focus on my attention to Rabindranath Tagore's robust use of "*apoman*," as it helps understand J. M. Coetzee's word "Disgrace" and on my attention to class apartheid on education in India' (391). She then proceeds to quote from Kant and Levinas before embarking on her text readings.

After outlining her own reading of Tagore's poem about Kabir in which she 'coasts through Tagore's India, Coetzee's South Africa, and the space of a tiny group of *adivasis*' (note that the third space of the *adivasis* does not coincide with Tagore's India), Spivak denies the 'Indian' in the title of the book. The comparative linguistic moves made in order to substantiate her argument about the centrality of an aesthetics of disgrace to the job of the postcolonial literary critic—such as comparing *apoman* with 'disgrace' and elsewhere 'fiction' with *maya* as well as by comparing Coetzee's Lucy to Shakespeare's Cordelia to Tagore's Kabir—coalesce towards the end of the essay into an observation about the status of public school education in rural India. She goes on to describe how an aesthetics of disgrace may equip us to critically redescribe the apparently 'disgraceful' Indian phenomenon of one-on-one private tuitions characterised by sub-par pedagogical practices such as passive rote learning.

The shift in the essay from an emphasis on the artwork (Coetzee's novel, Tagore's poem, Shakespeare's play) to an emphasis on a critical exploration of *feeling* (disgrace)—rather than of metaphors and tropes and themes and plot structures—is noteworthy here, as also is the harmonious welding of aesthetics and political praxis. Thus, it appears as though the idea of 'Indianness'—in whatever happily fragmented and mutually incompatible postcolonial conglomerate is morally and politically justifiable and responsible today—can indeed be combined with aesthetics, albeit in an unexpected and non-traditional manner. What is being displaced here is not 'Indianness' as much as any and all pre-established ideas regarding what *ought to be* the subject-matter of such a study as well as its objectives and methods.

Rather than univocally repudiate classical poetics (Sanskritic, Persian, and Tamil traditions of poetics, for example) we ought to employ a radical methodological revision by means of unapologetic intertextual readings and dismantle the hierarchical relationship that is always formed between classical poetics and everything else. Under this latter category—everything else—we clump together graciously a string of adjectival clauses: Dalit aesthetics, feminist aesthetics, environmental aesthetics, folk aesthetics, and so on. This implicit hierarchy in the name of exhaustive representation is not so much an individual's error of judgement as it is symptomatic of the ideological essence of aesthetics as a concept. Aesthetics has always been characterised by a compulsive historiographic tendency which likes to see vertical stories of artistic accomplishment everywhere. This problem bubbles to the surface each time a new book is published in India about aesthetics.

The Tussle Between Beauty and Praxis

In the light of the impressive amount of scholarship that has come out in the last three decades to recapture the word aesthetics in fascinating ways, we notice that the terms aesthetics and affect are often used interchangeably in the humanities and to a lesser extent in the social sciences. It might even appear as though the term affect is poised to displace aesthetics in use. The relationship between the two is not immediately obvious from the sheer patterns of their use in scholarly papers and books.

From the vantage point of a larger history of ideas, as neatly demarcated to us in textbook accounts, aesthetics and affect can be distinguished from each other. A chronological demarcation between the two seems self-evident. Aesthetics denotes a pre-critical tradition of thought which is essentially in praise of the artwork and is evaluative and normative in nature. It is then completely sidestepped as irrelevant by the linguistic turn and the rise of deconstructive analysis as well as the transformation of the discipline itself into the alternative pedagogical aspirations of Cultural Studies. Despite being used interchangeably with aesthetics, affect has interestingly circumvented the trap of this ideologically suspect lineage. Today, it is most commonly seen as emerging from the philosophy of that very niche trio—Spinoza-Bergson-Deleuze. It has established itself in the contemporary scene by showcasing a versatile ability to generate useful arguments about digitality and biopolitics and the anthropocene, as well as about caste, gender, and political praxis. By contrast, aesthetics still carries on its chest the scarlet letter of tradition and order. At its best, aesthetics might cater to the current political need for an identitarian poetics to supplement an identitarian politics by tapping into its residual ethnographic value. David Shulman's writing on the aesthetics of the Theyyam performance or the still-ongoing excitement in New Delhi art circles about Gond art ever since the publication of *Bhimayana* are as good examples as any in this regard.[1]

It is, therefore, a necessary task to disambiguate the two terms aesthetics and affect as much as possible. To begin with, the term aesthetics may be broadly understood under two categories. In the first and the most commonly anthologised one, aesthetics is strictly a philosophical concern. Western philosophers have always been interested in the artwork as an object and as an effect to the extent that it sheds light on the transcendental processes of being and knowing. Within Western philosophy, aesthetics is understood as yet another category of philosophical thinking (alongside metaphysics, epistemology, and ethics, and sometimes in conjunction with ethics).

In this systematic body of writing by philosophers, we can spot the twin concerns of form and effect—what are the formal properties of an artwork and relatedly, how and why and to what end does the artwork have the effect it has on people? Is it of any epistemic value, is it non-cognitive or does it constitute a third kind of non-cognitive knowledge? Is aesthetic experience of an ethical nature? Is it indispensable to being-in-the-world? While this particular trajectory need not be our central concern at the moment, below is listed a very brief selection of references to Western philosophical writing on aesthetics in order to illustrate and sample the centrality of *kalon* or the beautiful, and we shall see how many of these theories remain with us today when we reanimate aesthetics as a methodology with the support of affect theory.

Plato and Aristotle understood aesthetics using categories such as mimesis and catharsis and were concerned with judging its moral use-value in society. While they both seem to rely very heavily on the artwork (poetry and drama respectively), it is evident that the aesthetic effect exceeds the mere material coordinates of the artwork.

The word *katharsis* was used long before Aristotle employed it in his *Poetics* and it used to also denote 'cleaning' in the very medical sense of a laxative for purgation and also in a more open-ended sense as a clarification. Beauty must, in other words, serve some moral purpose. Similarly, in his theory of *disinterestedness* as the distinguishing feature of the aesthetic experience, Immanuel Kant too moves away from the artwork itself. Comparing aesthetic judgement with cognitive judgment, Kant argues that the former is non-conceptual but necessary, it is universal but unprovable, it is both subjective and commonly experienced; it exudes—to refer to the most common distillation of the idea—a purposiveness without purpose. Unlike Reason and Morality, the transcendental coordinates of aesthetic judgment seem decidedly murky.

By contrast, Hegel does not carve out an autonomous status for the aesthetic experience outside of conceptual thought. By announcing that 'the form of art has ceased to be the supreme need of the spirit' (103), Hegel means that while the sensorial realm of art used to contribute effectively to the progressive movement of human history towards a full recovery of self-knowledge through conceptual thought, art seems to have hit a dead-end during his own time and seems to have exhausted its capacities to supplement cognition: that old perfect coincidence of message and medium in art is lost forever.

The basis of Nietzsche's famous distinction between the Apollonian and Dionysian aspects of the aesthetic experience in *The Birth of Tragedy* is, roughly put, an art-as-lie theory, whereby he suggests that art makes the Truth about life 'bearable' by presenting it as a series of 'beautiful' lies; ironically, it is a necessary lie to the extent that art-as-falsehood loses all its negative connotations and becomes existentially justified. In art, says Nietzsche, 'the lie is sanctified and the will to deception has a good conscience' (153).

Heidegger accounts for the beauty/truth of Van Gogh's *A Pair of Shoes* by describing how the painting of the shoes alone (rather than the actual shoes themselves) calls into being the world of the peasant woman who wears them. Something about the equipmentality of the shoes in the peasant's everyday life (rather than its mere shape and color and texture) is allowed unique expression in the painting. According to Heidegger, there is a very fine balance between artwork that allows a world to unconceal itself and an artwork which simply offers empty pleasure.

Thus, in philosophy, the relationship between the artwork and the experiencing subject has been treated from an ontological, epistemological, and ethical perspective. In fact, Arthur Danto sums it up very well when he points out that 'from the perspective of philosophy art is a danger and aesthetics the agency for dealing with it' (13). The inalienable idea of beauty for its own sake is clearly central to the 'danger' referred to by Danto here and this bare fact has, amazingly, survived to our contemporary times. What else is Spivak trying to do by developing an aesthetics of disgrace using literary texts other than forcefully deploying beauty (formal composition) to serve a social purpose?

Today, we are equipped to enter into fruitful intellectual debate as to what constitutes and normatively constructs all notions of beauty, but at the same time, we also continue to respond spontaneously to the world based on an index of attractiveness which extends from the beautiful, the sublime, and the tranquil to the ugly, the disgusting, and the shocking. Be it the shock of watching the live news coverage of the 9/11 or the photographs of communal vandalism on the front page of a newspaper, the limpid dullness into which free entertainment on high speed Internet pushes an entire generation, or the undirected irritation that results from uninspiring and hectic work schedules—we gravitate towards what soothes and titillates the senses and withdraw from what is disturbing or boring.

These responses, very much rooted in the body and in the senses, indicate what we feel or like to feel and they take place in contradiction to what we know about the world. Therefore, they often frustrate our efforts to maintain a rational and cognitive relationship to the world. As such, intellectual possibilities remain to be tapped from this basic human capacity which may perhaps exceed and supplement the existing paradigm of cultural critique in academia.

Breaking Down the Ancient/Modern Hierarchy

Certain moments in the earlier history of English Literature overlap with the use of aesthetics in academic scholarship such as when I.A. Richards theorises on *tone* (versus *feeling*), William Empson theorises about *mood*, and Gerald Genette identifies aesthetic predicates. Similarly, we may also look back and identify literary sub-genres such as the sentimental novel and Gothic romances as categories of apprehension which are simultaneously rooted in the sensual immediacy of the text as well as emphasising an analytical distance from the text. Within this modality of appreciation marked by a formalist drive ('What really *is* art?'), we may also tentatively place all the classical (that is belonging to the ancient period) texts of art criticism. It would include ancient Chinese, Persian and Sanskrit treatises among others. The entirety of such texts (made available by the meticulous work of historians and archived against the ravages of time—and, in the case of some countries, poor public resources to maintain them) reminds us of the fundamentally comparative nature of aesthetics as a body of knowledge that reflects the socio-political order and varying structures of thinking and feeling that distinguishes the world-views of societies in the past—an approach exemplified by scholars such as Sheldon Pollock as well as David Damrosch. To look back and 'see' the aesthetics of ancient Japan and India and China, to qualify the writings on *rasa* by Abhinavagupta (950–1016CE) as a text on aesthetics, it appears necessary to distinguish a more 'ancient' version of aesthetics as functionally different from the predominantly European and modern notion of aesthetics.

The latter is modern in the broad sense that until the dawn of the modern period and until the rise of the modern self-reflexive individualistic subject, any subjective human experience remotely resembling the aesthetic comportment towards the world was to be found within the affective realm of religion. Understanding modernity, in a Weberian sense, as a steady process of rationalisation (which displaces religion in favour of scientific process, replaces feeling with rational thought, replaces lived places with impersonal spatial coordinates), the affective modality that once belonged to religion finds a new home in the autonomous realm of aesthetics. The aura of the artwork described by Benjamin is simply a melancholic substitute for what used to be the aura of the divine.

Thus, modernity ensured that art is no longer a part of lived existence (such as a stone carving on a temple wall or the stained glass windows and murals of a Renaissance church) and becomes instead an autonomous object outside of everyday life which is identified as 'art' and hangs from a museum wall to elicit a very specific kind of subjective and studied response from the viewer. This is what provokes J.M. Bernstein to say that aesthetics—both as an idea and as an experience—was invented by modern man to give expression to a directionless melancholy of the Self, to give expression to a historical sense of loss.

So, on the one hand, both the theory of *rasa* from ancient India and Bakhtin's theory of the dialogic imagination in the novel are united by an essentialising quality, by a philosophical rigour with which one attempts to define the artwork. Bakhtin's dialogic perusal of parody can, indeed, be compared and contrasted with the *hasya rasa.* In fact, Bakhtin himself traces heteroglossia back to the Dionysian carnivals of an older social order. However, at the same time, it is also very clear that the two types of scholarship do not have common points of origin, do not share the same kind of mutually constitutive relationship with their corresponding social milieu, and do not seek to accomplish the same pedagogical ends. To that extent, scholarly attempts to make comparisons (between, for example, Hegel and Abhinavgupta) might run the risk of remaining just that—a comparison, and nothing else.

As soon as we consider the following description by Pollock of what constitutes a 'semblance of *rasa'* (i.e. improper *rasa*), we see that the congenital difference between modern aesthetics and ancient aesthetics is so striking that one wonders whether the predicate *aesthetics* can be applied to both bodies of knowledge.

> Desire directed towards an inappropriate object (the wife of one's teacher, a goddess, a queen) or that is not reciprocated; desire on the part of a woman for more than one lover, "a father's grief for a son who is querulous and wicked, or grief on the part of an ascetic who has given up all attachments; spiritual disenchantment with life on the part of an untouchable"; "martial determination on the part of a lowborn man," "laughter directed at one's father" (Pollock 29)

Living today as we are in the flat geography of postmodernity and in a world that refuses to light up ethically until and unless we employ the most rigorous practices of intertextuality, it is high time to forego the standard chronological classification of aesthetics into ancient, medieval and contemporary. It is also high time to discontinue the habit of comparing the classical texts of one culture exclusively with the classical texts of another culture (such as comparing classical Tamil poetics exclusively with classical Sanskrit poetics). It also looks increasingly superfluous to direct studies in this field towards a documentation of differences, that is to emphasise how ancient Indian art treatises differ from Western conceptions of art and to consider such comparisons as an end in itself. All the above reservations refer, of course, to the field of literary studies alone. Instead, we must take apart classical texts *in* the contemporary, in conjunction with the partial theoretical parallels found in Western aesthetics, to find some moral use-value for them within our requirements of political praxis and to locate them as firmly as possible in the contemporary.

Interdisciplinary Forays in Aesthetics

Is it possible to separate the artwork from aesthetic theory? Can we generate contemporary theories of what constitutes tragedy without continued reference to the tragedies of Aeschylus? What would be the contemporary relevance of *rasa* theory without an accompanying interest in the plays of Kalidasa? On a similar vein, we may also wonder how to retain an interest in the *caesura* in prosody without an accompanying interest in the Elizabethan verses which best exemplify the *caesura* in poetry, or an interest in the dialogic imagination which is not necessarily accompanied by an exemplifying interest in Pushkin. Recent scholarship that uses the term 'aesthetics' does display precisely such a useful and interesting dissociation of method. The paradigm of critique rightly demands that any consideration of aesthetics today must subvert our conception of the artwork as a discrete, autonomous object in the world. Such a move can proceed in two directions; it can either disseminate the prevailing idea of aesthetics into a series of erasures and constructions or, it can resuscitate aesthetics with fresh methodological possibilities that deviate from its historical lineage.

A contemporary scholar of aesthetics might hark back, ironically, to the sense of *aucitya* or 'propriety' (as Pollock rightly notes, social propriety and aesthetic propriety mirror each other into a fascinating tautological bind in *rasa* theory) while reading Terry Eagleton's analysis of 'good manners' in *The Ideology of the Aesthetic.* In it, Eagleton argues that 'manners for the Eighteenth Century, signify that meticulous disciplining of the body which converts morality to style [...]. In these regulated forms of civilised conduct, a pervasive aestheticising of social practices gets underway: moral imperatives [...] infiltrate the very textures of lived experience, as tact or know-how, intuitive good sense or inbred decorum' (Eagleton 41). Compare the above description of 'inbred decorum' and 'meticulous disciplining of the body' in the following lines which describe the aesthetic (and thereby, implicitly, social) components of the erotic *rasa*:

> the "foundational factors" must be a young highborn heterosexual couple; the "stimulant factors" gardens, breezes, sandalwood cream, and so on; the "transitory emotions" anxiety, fatigue, disquiet, and the like; the physical "reactions" and "psychophysical responses" sidelong glances, fainting, horripilation, and the rest that betoken the presence of the emotions" (Pollock 25).

The possibility that our insights into the sense of *aucitya* underlying *rasa* theory can, thus, extend (beyond empirical historical studies, ethnographic analyses, and the insulated concerns of a nationalistic project) to embrace the contemporary by brushing *aucitya* against British 'good manners' (some of which was transferred onto the colonised as well) and the use of 'unutterable' abusive expletives and scatological references in Tamil *karisial* folk tales, exemplify the fresher avenues that we must today seek to explore under the flag of aesthetics.

Any one from the above list of formal erotic responses offered by Pollock—anxiety, fatigue, disquiet—may find new methodological expression today. In the growing field of disability aesthetics, we find one such example of the contemporary life of aesthetics when Ato Quayson in *Aesthetic Nervousness* describes the anxiety of the able-bodied reader who encounters disability within the text. Quayson identifies how corporeal normativity structures the smooth propriety we find in interactions between able-bodied persons, which is disrupted by sensations of anxiety, dissonance, and disorder when one struggles to 'normally' apprehend a disabled person in the world.

According to Quayson, the structural devices of the literary text betray themselves by the form of a dissonance in the reading experience on account of the disabled character. Aesthetic nervousness is, thus, a disruption of the normative aesthetics upon which the text is structured. The centrality of the artwork in Quayson's study (which includes a comparative study of the disabled characters of Toni Morrison and Samuel Beckett) is noteworthy because he also argues that the affective mechanism of dissonance, nervousness, and anxiety within literary texts is coextensive with the affects that disrupt social propriety in the real-world interaction between able-bodied and disabled persons.

Thus, we find that in many monographs which subvert the idea of aesthetics, the artwork continues to hold a very crucial position as the repository of knowledge about emotions and feelings, their ontological status as well as their social construction. This has resulted in a resuscitation of the literary text (the artwork in general), the ideological underpinnings of which are not only exposed by means of a hermeneutics of suspicion but also prized as a unique modality of human expression. Therefore, while some scholars are today concerned with how to usefully map the emotional components of a text to produce a universal sensorial compendium of sorts (for example, see Stephen Ahern's edited volume *A Feel for the Text*), others like Rita Felski are more interested in mapping the reader's emotional connection to the text (see *Uses of Literature* which theorises 'shock', 'disgust', and 'wonder' in literary production as extra-semantic components of the text).

A significant contrast may be drawn here with Gopal Guru's subsuming of aesthetics under the broader concern of political phenomenology. In 'Aesthetic of Touch and the Skin', he maps the complex social aesthetics of the leather cricket ball (as seen in the aesthete's appreciation of a cricket match) by pointing out the following paradox.

> It is only the object-like ball abstracted from the raw hide and toil of the leather worker that forms the basis of the aesthetic judgement [for the touchable]. [. . . .] The upper castes are prepared to elevate the dead skin or leather to the highest level of aesthetic appreciation while they are found to be completely reluctant to extend their association to the live skin of the leather worker (Guru 299).

A reference is also made to how upper caste politicians referred to a Dalit politician named Achutananand as '*Jutananand*' (literally, leather shoe), in which expression 'leather' as a sophisticated consumer good once again transubstantiates into the reviled human skin.

It is noteworthy that in Guru's essay, while he does not shy away from the ideological substratum underlying such social aesthetics (which, in this case, clearly extends to the aesthetics of taste underlying the beef ban and its implication on food cultures in India as well), he does agree partially with Felski's recuperative attitude towards literature by arguing in favour of engineering a new aesthetics: a forced or forceful aesthetics. A Dalit aesthetics, according to Gopal Guru, will strive towards 'resignifying the skin' (304), not only by renouncing aesthetics altogether at times but also by using literature to transform existing aesthetic habits. The need of the hour is 'an aesthetic modification of Dalit reality' (304).

Sharankumar Limbale, on the other hand, puts forward a more radical proposition when he argues that it is inappropriate to expect pleasure or beauty in Dalit literature and that Dalit literature 'should be analyzed from a sociological perspective on social values than on beauty'. Further, he insists that 'an exclusively aesthetic consideration of Dalit literature will disregard the Dalit writers' fundamental role [as social critics]' (Limbale 19).

We may take this ethically charged moment of contention in literary history as belonging not only to the Indian context but as being coextensive with a larger question of resolving aesthetics with subject-matter of an abject or liminal kind—in relation to, say, the Holocaust, writings from war-torn countries, and from other marginalised communities across the world. We may also place this debate about Dalit aesthetics in contention with discussions about beauty dating back to Kant and even further back to Plato. For example, how do the literary methods of representing collective social violence force us to interrogate and expand Kant's idea of the sublime? The category of the sublime has already been animated in the context of digital culture, war reportage, and drone photography. Similarly, from the references to untouchability and caste hierarchy in the above quoted passage on the 'semblance of *rasa*', we find an opportunity to expand the ideological underpinnings of the philosophical concept of beauty in the arts.

In her essay, Spivak tries to undertake such destabilising aesthetic comparisons by referring to fiction and *maya* as interchangeable terms.

Within the nebulous schemata of Sanksritised Hindu cosmology, the term *maya* can be distinguished from the more philosophical and erudite concepts in the scriptures since it occupies a considerable role in the popular imagination of the layperson. In opposition to philosophical terms which are confined to 'high' texts such as the Upanishads and the Vedas, terms such as *maya* (as well as *yogam, vidhi,* and *mukti*) are used and understood in common everyday speech by millions of people in the subcontinent and have their own lived social aesthetics in contemporary times as well. This is apart from the ossified textual and philosophical meaning we may draw from the use of these terms in Hindu texts.

A lyrical theory of *maya* appears in *Jnanappana,* a devotional song written in the sixteenth century by Malayalam poet Poonthanam. Addressed to a regional deity in Guruvayoor, the poem is an example of the imageries and modes of address that mark the *bhakti rasa.* However, while most devotional songs (both in Malayalam and in most other languages) limit themselves to terms of adoration, praise, and spiritual joy, the *Jnanappana* stands out by also reflecting an intricate metaphysical theory, including references to quintessentially Sanskritic ideas of the *varna* system, weaving these normative references to caste into the very fabric of the *bhakti.*

We can contrast this devotional poem with the devotional poem titled *Daiva Dasakam* composed by Sree Narayana Guru in 1914. The lines of the *Jnanappana* exclaim that there is no reason to be perturbed by anything at all since all is *maya* in the world (that is make-believe or illusion or play). There seems to be no escape from *maya*; the only solution is an ironic and ambivalent involvement without involvement in the matters of the world (a formulation that strangely echoes with Kant's purposiveness-without-purpose theory). On the other hand, the devotee in Narayana Guru's devotional poem praises the Almighty as the One who is *maya,* the maker of *maya,* and also the one who removes *maya* and delivers humankind from that illusion.

Arguably a 'secular prayer', it was recommended by the Kerala state government in 2009 that *Daiva Dasakam* should become the national prayer of India. While the idea of a 'national prayer' opens up several questions by itself, we may note here the interest taken by the state in reinventing an official version of *bhakti,* a term that is inextricably linked to the term *bakht* which is currently used to characterise a range of right-wing Hindu-supremacist political identities. As a politico-aesthetic idea, we find reverberations of it in many other political events including the more recent controversy revolving around popular *bhakti* in the entry of women into the shrine at Sabarimala ('Ready to Wait' is a modern digital *bhakti* coinage). Social aesthetics, which is interchangeable with political phenomenology for Guru, is thus an exciting term for us to shape and define today through a wide range of studies.

Recuperating the Art Object

Recent discussions in literary academic circles regarding the need to coin the phrase 'refugee poetics' (a poetics of forced displacement) point towards the particularly affirmative direction in which the reinvented field of aesthetics and affect theory seems to be headed. In this case, we find that the artwork has returned to the scene as an old-fashioned discrete museum object in the world. It is often claimed by art practitioners today that a lot of the conceptual progress and clarity needed in the backdrop of war and conflict can be engineered by a robust international community of artists. Graffiti emerges, in this context, as perhaps the artwork par excellence in today's world. Refugee art is also, sometimes, aimed at reconciliation and at the reconstruction of national psyches after events of genocidal magnitude—such as the efflorescence of museums and art practices in the Balkans designed, paradoxically, to heal through memory, to forgive without forgetting. When compared to some of the South Asian countries where the memories and documentation related to past riots and massacres are often erased without a trace and replaced with a stunning official silence, the Balkan states offer a stark contrast especially in the way they have artistically reconstructed entire cities to remember the violence forever; these art practices that involve memorialising the war exist even in the face of denials that the massacres ever took place.

Underlying the conception of a refugee poetics is the radical and provocative belief that the sensorial dimensions of the artwork (be it syntax, rhythm, intonation, color, or shock and wonder and pity and sympathy) can restructure the social process in a positive way by inaugurating fresh ways of thinking about and being in the world. This hope is, indeed, reminiscent of Adorno's *Aesthetic Theory* in which he argues in favour of the possibility of an emancipatory artwork. Similar ideas stemming from various theoretical positions have always continued to exist. For example, note Frederic Jameson's writings about the 'euphoric' quality of postmodern artworks in *Postmodernism,* his speculations about turning nostalgia from a reactionary to a liberating emotion in *Marxism and Form,* and his hypothesis about the 'waning of affect' may be interpreted as writings in the field of aesthetics and affect theory. Jameson also displays a similar optimism and affirmative spirit in 'Cognitive Mapping' in which he argues that, regardless of the postmodern thrall in which everything is inescapably wrapped, certain literary genres are aesthetically promising *because* they are politically necessary. Politically necessary aesthetic forms, according to Jameson, are those which are suspended between discrete units of phenomenological experience and a social totality on the other hand. Certain aesthetic forms today rise to the occasion by struggling to straddle these two poles of social theory (the truth of individual lived experience and the truth of social totality).

In this affirmative sense, the manner in which environmental aesthetics problematises the field is worth noting here. Several scholars use human reaction to nature as a counterpoint to the aesthetic response to the artwork, thereby expanding the scope of aesthetics beyond the artificial confines of the man-made artwork. However, what is of specific interest to us is a different direction in which environmental aesthetics can proceed as evidenced in Timothy Morton's *Ecology Without Nature.* Advocating a re-imagination of the entity called 'environment' within environmentalism by actively deconstructing our narratives about Nature, Morton draws attention to the ways in which literature conjures up images of Nature, most of which are severely ideologically compromised; the institutionalising of this aesthetic habit is located by Morton in the Romantic period.

While art conveys a sense of space and place by means of what he calls 'an ambient poetics', Morton argues that an environmental aesthetics should aim to transform our existing images of 'nature' and replace them with alternative images that can circumvent the ideological trappings of the word 'nature'. This replacing of one view of the world with another one capable of rectifying the political dysfunction of the former is precisely what Morton means by the word aesthetics in the subtitle of his book. This does not necessarily mean arguing in favour of some literary representations of nature over some others. Morton is not simply talking here about the becoming-critical of art. He is arguing in favour of an aesthetic fluctuation in our cultural structures of feeling which is necessary to change the political and existential status quo.

In this regard, the debate between Deleuze and Ranciere regarding the real-world function of the artwork is one to which scholars keep returning time and again. While Ranciere expounds the many ways in which artwork successfully provokes an ethical engagement with traumatic subject-matter (see *The Emancipated Spectator*), he is emphatic in his dismissal of the artwork's capacity to effect any real-world change. Deleuze, on the other hand, as we can see in his analysis of 'Bartleby the Scrivener' (an oft-quoted example in literary studies), is convinced of the capacity of the artwork to inaugurate new affects and percepts that are much needed for political change in the real world.

Thus, if the 'control society' is based on a new postmodern landscape of affects different from that of panoptical structures, change can be effected only by intervening in this new sensorial dimension. The following passage from Mark Fischer illustrates this complex web of affect:

> The consequence of being hooked into the entertainment matrix is twitchy, agitated interpassivity, an inability to concentrate or focus. Students' incapacity to connect current lack of focus with future failure, their inability to synthesize time into any coherent narrative, is symptomatic of more than mere demotivation. [....] If the figure of discipline was the worker-prisoner, the figure of control is the debtor-addict (Fischer 35).

So, we see that this is the nature of the global affective web from which the artwork strives to carve out an autonomous realm today. The mechanisms of affect are important to the extent that they are always caught in a battle with rationality and cognition (think about the consumption of fake news online long after everyone is made aware of the existence of fake news, or the insatiable desire to visually consume images of violence even as we denounce violence verbally). The artwork is not only deconstructed in this light but also given a newer recuperative role at the same time.

Today, most studies under the flag of aesthetics, if they wish to be in conjunction with political critique, borrow their methodology from affect theory. Likewise, most books and treatises which are related to or which expand the tenets of affect theory cannot help but offer the artwork (be it cinema, the novel, or photography) a place of importance within the analytical framework. This new position of the artwork, or the literary/audiovisual text, within English Studies is clearly the result of a revision of its status post critique.

* * *

Deleuze's use of the terms affects and precepts played no small role in opening the doors for a post-critical vocabulary of feelings and emotions and sensations, with or without an accompanying interest in the artwork (see *Essays Critical and Clinical*). His writings on Melville and Kafka, in particular, allow us to draw a distinction between identifiable feelings (sadness, rage, jealousy) and unidentifiable and emergent quasi-forces. Both categories of feelings or sensations may be found within literary studies. The references to pity and sympathy in Aristotle's *Poetics,* Rita Felski's references to shock and wonder in *Uses of Literature,* Spivak's aesthetics of disgrace, and the Dalit deconstruction of untouchability as an aesthetics of disgust, all exemplify the former. Likewise, both Martha Nussbaum in 'Emotions as Judgements of Value and Importance' and Judith Butler in 'Violence, Mourning, Politics' refer to the emotion of grief in this identifiable pre-existing sense, although they employ two different methodologies and display divergent philosophical inclinations in understanding and theorising 'grief' as an emotion.

The second category is quite an inventive one. Distinguishing affect from emotion, several scholars of the postmodern condition have attempted to map the affective landscape of late capitalism (which includes people's instinctive and mass responses to digital media, consumerism, war, etc.) by coining terms that might capture certain soporific states of disbelief, moral numbness, distractedness, and undirected performance anxiety.

Unlike the more grandiloquent emotions which have been systematised by classical mythology, these micro-emotions or affects are without direction, without intentionality, without object. In her book *Ugly Feelings,* for example, Sianne Ngai declares that her focus will be 'on irritation *instead* of anger, envy *rather than* jealousy, and "stuplimity" *as opposed to* the transcendent feeling of the sublime' (Ngai 11). She also further demarcates her line of inquiry by arguing in favour of a 'noncathartic aesthetic' and an interest in 'art that produces and foregrounds a failure of emotional release (another form of suspended "action") and does so as a kind of politics' (9). Ngai's invention of the word 'stuplimity' is an indication of the need for expanding the terminology of feelings.

Meanwhile, certain familiar words are also taken up and infused with the emergent quality of affect. For example, consider Sara Ahmed's queering of the idea of 'happiness' in 'Happy Objects' when she identifies the commonplace sentence 'I just want you to be happy' as a speech-act using which the family identifies itself as a 'happy unit' and negates an individual who is a part of it. Describing what she calls 'the psychic drama of the queer child' confronting a group of skeptical family members, she points out that 'in some parental responses to the child coming out, this unhappiness is not so much expressed as being unhappy about the child being queer, but about *being unhappy about the child being unhappy*. Queer fiction is full of such moments' (42).

Similarly, Brian Massumi recharges the commonplace word 'threat' with an affective quotient when he describes threat as 'affectively self-causing' (54). Using the U.S. invasion of Iraq in the name of a threat posed by Iraq, Massumi describes its affective dimensions thus: '[i]f we feel a threat, there was a threat' and later he adds 'then there always will have been a threat. Threat is once and for all, in the nonlinear time of its own causing' (54). Thus, a defamiliarising of the term threat takes place in this analysis by which we see the affective underbelly of threat as a state of mind with political ramifications.

Under this distinction between affect and emotion, literary texts and artwork may also be divided into two types; those that exemplify identifiable emotions and those texts that engender unprecedented and emergent states of visceral feeling, texts that effect a fluctuation in the sensorial realm. The emergence of new literary forms and genres such as graphic novels have been studied within this framework. Psychoanalytical studies done on the effect of cinema as a medium also come to mind. As mentioned earlier, artwork from conflict zones and from marginalised communities straddling the experiential gulf between the self and the other are also studied for their capacity to engender newfound affective modes of being.

* * *

The term 'Indian aesthetics' is less relevant than ever to English studies but both 'Indian' and 'aesthetics' separately are matters of great consequence and possibility today. As indicated by the above meandering effects to humbly map what has been a fragmented history of aesthetics and affect in the recent past and in the present, we are now poised to work with an idea of aesthetics which needn't be determined as either Indian or Western, an aesthetics unattached to object and without predicates and adjectives. The use of aesthetics indicates a methodology that draws its contemporary relevance from its ability to be disinterested in questions of essence and to form asynchronous critical associations about the human condition vis-a-vis a vocabulary of affects, feelings, and emotions. And in that sense, there can be no doubt that this is a revival of something that feels universalist in nature.

Notes

1. It is noteworthy that the aesthetics of Gond art (as we find the same type of images on cotton, ceramic, and jute) becomes the affect of Gond art, as soon as we consider the complex meeting point between the Gond artists, the Navayana publication house, and the metropolitan and global audience towards whom *Bhimayana* (which plays hard and fast with the Western idea of comics) is eventually marketed. When we put this publishing and reception history together with the recent charge-sheets filed against Dalit activists based on the sudden and unexpected criminalizing of certain public ideas of Dalitness, we realise that the coupling of the word 'Dalit' (in 2018, India's Ministry of Information and Broadcasting recommended against using it in public discourse) and the term 'Gond art' results in an expansion of the very idea of aesthetics. It no longer denotes an insulated space for art appreciation. Gond art can no longer remain, for the metropole, as a visual signifier that beatifies

a ceramic coffee cup or a jute cloth bag. At the same time, for the Gond artists too, their age-old technique is not longer solely rooted in the aesthetics of wall and floor decorations during the festive season in villages. Aesthetics, as we can see here, is neither evaluative nor normative, but is now generative of something new which did not exist before.

Works Cited

Adorno, Theodor. *Aesthetic Theory.* London: Continuum International Publishing Group—academi, 2004. Print.

Ahern, Stephen. *Affect Theory and Literary Critical Practice. A Feel for the Text.* Cham: Springer International Publishing, 2019. Print.

Ahmed, Sara. "Happy Objects." In Gregg, Melissa, and Gregory J. Seigworth. *The Affect Theory Reader*, 2010. Print.

Gregg, Melissa, and Gregory J. Seigworth. *The Affect Theory Reader,* 2010. Print.

Bernstein, J M. *The Fate of Art: Aesthetic Alienation from Kant to Derrida and Adorno.* Cambridge: Polity Press, 1993. Print.

Judith Butler Ph.D. (2003) *Violence, Mourning, Politics, Studies in Gender and Sexuality,* 4:1, 9-37, DOI: 10.1080/15240650409349213.

Cohen, Ted. "Why Beauty is a Symbol of Morality." in *Essays in Kant's Aesthetics.* Eds. Ted Cohen & Paul Guyer. Chicago: The University of Chicago Press, 1982, pp. 221-236.

Danto, Arthur C. "The Philosophical Disenfranchisement of Art." *Grand Street,* vol. 4, no. 3, 1985, pp. 171–189. JSTOR, www.jstor.org/stable/25006747. Accessed 8 Feb. 2021.

Deleuze, Gilles. "Bartleby; or, The Formula." *Essays Critical and Clinical.* Minneapolis: University of Minnesota Press, 1997. Print.

Eagleton, Terry. *The Ideology of the Aesthetic.* Malden: Blackwell Publishing, 2014. Print.

Empson, William. *Seven Types of Ambiguity.* New York: New Direction Publ, 1980. Print.

Felski, Rita. *Uses of Literature.* Blackwell Publishing Ltd, 2008. Print.

Fisher, Mark. *Capitalist Realism: Is There No Alternative?* Winchester, UK: Zero Books, 2010. Print.

Genette, Gérard. *The Work of Art: Immanence and Transcendence.* Ithaca: Cornell University Press, 1997. Print.

Guru, Gopal. "Aesthetic of Touch and the Skin." *The Bloomsbury Research Handbook of Indian Aesthetics and the Philosophy of Art.* Ed. Arindam Chakrabarti, 2018. Print.

Hegel, G.W.F. 1975. *Aesthetics: Lectures on Fine Art.* 2 vols. Translated by T.M. Knox. Oxford: Oxford University Press.

Heidegger, Martin; trans. David Farrell Krell (2008). "The Origin of the Work of Art". Martin Heidegger: *The Basic Writings.* New York: Harper Collins.

Jameson, Fredric. *Marxism and Form: 20th-century Dialectical Theories of Literature,* 2016. Internet resource.

Jameson, Fredric, Michael Hardt, and Kathi Weeks. "Cognitive Mapping." *The Jameson Reader.* Oxford: Blackwell, 2004. Print.

Kant, Immanuel. *Critique of Judgement,* trans. J.H. Bernard. New York: Hafner Press, MacMillan Publishing Co., Inc., 1951.

Limbale, Sharankumar. *Towards an Aesthetic of Dalit Literature: History, Controversies and Considerations.* Trans. Alok Mukherjee. Hyderabad: Orient Longman, 2004. Print.

Massumi, Brian. "The Political Ontology of Threat." *The Affect Theory Reader.* Eds. Gregg, Melissa and Gregory J. Seigworth. Durham, NC: Duke University Press, 2010. Print.

Moriarty, K.J., and A M. Dawson. "Use and Abuse of Cathartics." *Handbook of Experimental Pharmacology* (1984): 509–533. Web.

Morton, Timothy. *Ecology Without Nature: Rethinking Environmental Aesthetics.* Cambridge, Mass: Harvard University Press, 2009. Print.

Ngai, Sianne. *Ugly Feelings.* Cambridge: Harvard University Press, 2009. Internet resource.

Nietzsche, Friedrich, and Walter A. Kaufmann. *On the Genealogy of Morals.* New York: Vintage Books, 2011. Print.

Nussbaum, Martha C. "Emotions as Judgments of Values". *Relativism, Suffering and Beyond: Essays In Memory of Bimal K. Matilal.* Eds. Mohanty, J.N. and P. Billimoria. Oxford: Oxford University Press, 1997. Print.

Nussbaum, Martha C. *Philosophical Interventions: Reviews, 1986-2011.* Oxford: Oxford University Press, 2015. Computer file.

Pollock, Sheldon. *Reader on Rasa: Classical Indian Aesthetics.* New York: Columbia University Press, 2016. Print.

Quayson, Ato. *Aesthetic Nervousness: Disability and the Crisis of Representation.* New York: Columbia University Press, 2007. Print.

Ranciere, Jacques. *Emancipated Spectator.* Trans. Gregory Elliot Verso, 2009, rprt. 2020. Print.

Richards, I A. *Practical Criticism.* Routledge & K. Paul, 1964. Print.

Sedgwick, Eve K. "Introduction." *Novel Gazing: Queer Readings in Fiction.* Durham: Duke University Press, 1997. Print.

Spivak, Gayathri Chakravorty. "Aesthetic Judgement of Disgrace." *The Bloomsbury Research Handbook of Indian Aesthetics and the Philosophy of Art.* Ed. Arindam Chakrabarti, 2018. Print.

About the Contributors

Milind Brahme teaches at the Department of Humanities and Social Sciences at IIT Madras. His areas of teaching and research interest are German language and literature, literary theory, pedagogy and education.

Yigal Bronner is Professor with the Department of Asian Studies at the Hebrew University of Jerusalem. His research interests include Sanskrit poetry, poetic theory and South Asian intellectual history. He is the author of *Extreme Poetry: The South Asian Movement of Simultaneous Narration* (2010), has edited several volumes including *A Lasting Vision: Dandin's Mirror in the World of Asian Letters* (2023). Among his co-authored volumes is *Innovations and Turning Points: Toward a History of Kāvya Literature* (with David Shulman and Gary Tubb, 2014).

Mini Chandran is Professor with the Department of Humanities and Social Sciences at IIT, Kanpur. Her research areas include Indian literature and aesthetics, translation studies, and literary censorship. Her recent works include *The Writer, the Reader and the State: Literary Censorship in India* (2017) and *Textual Travels: Theory and Practice of Translation in India* (2015). Chandran is also a prolific translator of Malayalam and English. Her translations from Malayalam include Joseph Mundassery's *Kozhinja Ilakal* (*Autumnal Memories*), and from English *Ormakkurippukal* (Capt. Lakshmi Sahgal's biography *A Revolutionary Life*).

Partha Chatterjee is a political theorist, anthropologist and historian of South Asia. He is currently Honorary Professor at the Centre for Studies in Social Sciences, Kolkata, where he was Director from 1997 to 2007. He has been Professor of Anthropology at Columbia University since 1997. The founding editor of *Subaltern Studies,* he has published more than thirty books and edited volumes in English and Bengali including *I Am the People: Reflections on Popular Sovereignty Today* (2019), *The Black*

Hole of Empire: History of a Global Practice of Power (2012) and *The Politics of the Governed* (2004).

Soumyabrata Choudhury is Associate Professor at the School of Arts and Aesthetics, Jawaharlal Nehru University. His list of publications include *Theatre, Number, Event*; *Ambedkar and Other Immortals* and *Now It's Come To Distances: Notes on Coronavirus and Shaheen Bagh, Association and Isolation*. He has also written on ancient Greek liturgy, Nietzsche, Schiller and Hegel.

Jenson Joseph is Assistant Professor at Dhirubhai Ambani Institute of Information and Communication Technology, Gujarat. He was post-doctoral fellow in Humanities and Social Sciences at IIT-Bombay and Alexander von Humboldt visiting research fellow at the Institute for Asian and African Studies, Humboldt University of Berlin (2020-22). He has been published in several journals including *South Asian Popular Cultures, Studies in South Asian Film and Media,* and *BioScope: South Asian Screen Studies.*

Anandita Pan is Assistant Professor in the Department of Liberal Arts, IIT Hyderabad. Her areas of research are Feminist theory, Dalit feminism, Dalit studies and the partition of Bengal. She has published in several journals including *Economic and Political Weekly, South Asian Review, Indian Journal of Gender Studies,* and *Contemporary Voice of Dalit*. Her book, *Mapping Dalit Feminism* (2020) explores how different forms of discrimination combine and overlap, challenging the apparent homogeneity of the categories, 'woman' and 'Dalit'.

Sheldon I. Pollock is the Arvind Raghunathan Professor of South Asian Studies at Columbia University. A preeminent scholar of Sanskrit, the intellectual and literary history of India, and comparative intellectual history, his publications include *The Language of the Gods in the World of Men: Sanskrit, Culture, and Power in Premodern India* (2006). Among his recent edited volumes are *A Reader on Rasa: Classical Indian Aesthetics* (2016), the first in a series of historical sourcebooks on classical Indian thought, and *Literary Cultures in History: Reconstructions from South Asia (2003).*

Punnya Rajendran teaches at the Department of English Studies, Central University of Tamil Nadu. Her research interests include aesthetics and affect theory, trauma studies, 'melancholia' in literary and cultural representations as well as colonial medical history. She has published on Deleuzian literary aesthetics in relation to gender and caste. Her current research project uses the framework of affect to address concerns of critical pedagogy in departments of English in Indian college classrooms.

E.V. Ramakrishnan is an Honorary Professor at the Department of English and Comparative Literature at Central University of Kerala. A bilingual literary critic, Indian English poet, and translator who works between Malayalam and English, he has published widely in both languages. His books in Malayalam include *Aksharavum Aadhunikatayum* (1992) which won the Kerala Sahitya Akademi Award for literary criticism in 1995 and *Malayala Novelinte Deshakalangal* (2017). His critical works in English include *Making It New: Modernism in Malayalam, Locating Indian Literature* (2013), *Indigenous Imaginaries* (2017) and *Mikhail Bakhtin: A Critical Introduction* (2023). He has published four volumes of poetry in English and his several edited volumes include *Literary Criticism in India: Texts, Trends and Trajectories* (2021) and *The Tree of Tongues:An Anthology of modern Indian poetry*.

K. Satchidanandan is an Indian poet, playwright, editor and critic, writing in Malayalam and English. A pioneer of modern poetry in Malayalam, he is the former editor of the *Indian Literature* journal and the former secretary of the Sahitya Akademi. He is also an advocate for secular anti-caste views, supports causes like the environment, human rights and free software and is a well-known speaker on contemporary issues. Satchidanandan has 60 books in Malayalam, including 21 poetry collections and an equal number of translations of poetry, as well as plays, essays and travelogues and four critical works in English. He is the winner of 35 awards, prizes and honours, including four from the Kerala Sahitya Akademi, three National Awards, and the Dante Medal from Italy.

V.S. Sreenath is Assistant Professor in the Department of Humanities and Social Sciences, IIT Madras. His research interests include literary theory, comparative aesthetics and colonial modernity. He has co-authored *An Introduction to Indian Aesthetics: History, Theory and Theoreticians* (2021) along with Prof. Mini Chandran and has been published widely in the *Journal of Indian Philosophy*, *South Asian Review*, and *Indian Literature* among other journals.

Swathi Sudhakaran is with NPTEL, IIT Madras as a project officer. Her areas of research include literary and performance studies, with a focus on questions of aesthetics.